SLAVERY, SECESSION, AND SOUTHERN HISTORY

Edited by

Robert Louis Paquette
and
Louis A. Ferleger

University Press of Virginia
Charlottesville and London

The University Press of Virginia

© 2000 by the Rector and Visitors of the University of Virginia

All rights reserved

Printed in the United States of America

First published in 2000

☉ The paper used in this publication meets the minimum requirements
of the American National Standard for Information Sciences—Permanence
of Paper for Printed Library Materials, ANSI Z39.48-1984.

Frontispiece: detail of *Burial of Latané,* engraving by A. G. Campbell, after the painting by
William D. Washington. (Courtesy of the Virginia Historical Society, Richmond)

Library of Congress Cataloging-in-Publication Data

Slavery, secession, and southern history / edited by Robert Louis Paquette
and Louis A. Ferleger.

    p.   cm.

Includes bibliographical references and index.

ISBN 0-8139-1951-7 (alk. paper) — ISBN 0-8139-1952-5 (pbk. : alk. paper)
1. Slavery—Southern States—History. 2. Southern States—History—
1775–1865. 3. Southern States—Social conditions—19th century.
4. Secession—Southern States. I. Paquette, Robert L., 1951– II. Ferleger, Lou.
E441.S646 2000
975'.00496—dc21

                                                99-045449

For Gene,

The historian's one task is to tell the thing as it happened. This he cannot do, if he is Artaxerxes's physician, trembling before him, or hoping to get a purple cloak, a golden chain, a horse of the Nisaean breed, in payment for his laudations. A fair historian, a Xenophon, a Thucydides, will not accept that position. He may nurse some private dislikes, but he will attach far more importance to the public good, and set the truth high above his hate; he may have his favourites, but he will not spare their errors. For history, I say again, has this and this only for its own; if a man will start upon it, he must sacrifice to no God but Truth; he must neglect all else; his sole rule and unerring guide is this—to think not of those who are listening to him now, but of the yet unborn who shall seek his converse.

Lucian, *The Way to Write History*

Contents

Preface

Few historians during the last half century have done more to shape scholarship on slavery, the course of the South to secession, and southern history than Eugene D. Genovese. On these subjects alone he has authored and coauthored, edited and coedited, scores of essays and more than a dozen books, including *Roll, Jordan, Roll: The World the Slaves Made* (1974), arguably the most penetrating analysis ever written on slavery in the antebellum South. In recent years Genovese has refocused his attention on the masters, and with his wife and coauthor Elizabeth Fox-Genovese, also a recognized authority on southern history, he is nearing completion of what promises to be a monumental work on the mind of the Old South's ruling class of slaveholders.

In this volume nine colleagues (Fogel, Engerman, Davis, Coclanis, Wilson, Glymph, Faust, Ferleger, and Steckel) and three former students (Paquette, Ambrose, and Malvasi) explore those areas of scholarship in which Genovese has exerted his greatest influence. For many years Robert William Fogel and Stanley L. Engerman taught with Genovese at the University of Rochester. Their prizewinning book *Time on the Cross: The Economics of American Negro Slavery* appeared in print the same year as *Roll, Jordan, Roll*, and indeed, both books earned for their respective authors a share of the prestigious Bancroft Prize in American history in 1974. They have enjoyed a lengthy friendship with Genovese that has generated stimulating exchanges on the nature of slavery in the United States and of the larger transatlantic economic system in which the Old South's peculiar institution was embedded. Although over the years Genovese has conceded ground to Fogel and Engerman on the economics of slavery, they point out how from the time of his first book, *The Political Economy of Slavery* (1965), his evolving interpretation of the impact of slavery on the southern economy has forced historians and economists alike to draw significant distinctions between economic growth and economic development. Today no serious student of the antebellum South denies that slavery, in a strict accounting sense, returned on average a handsome return to masters on investments. But scholars continue to debate the long-term economic impact of slavery: whether the antebellum South could have sustained its high rate of economic growth and slavery's influence on immigration, industrialization, urbanization, attitudes toward work, the generation of internal markets, and the development of human capital.

The debate on whether the slaveholders of the Old South were, at core, capitalists also continues even though Genovese agrees with Fogel and Engerman that southern slaveholders exhibited a considerable degree of profit consciousness and market responsiveness. Acceptance of the ingenuity of southern slaveholders, the flexibility of slavery, and the skills and versatility of slave labor has profound implications for interpreting the Civil War, especially its repressibility or irrepressibility. Genovese has consistently argued for southern distinctiveness, forcefully posing the question of why, if antebellum slaveholders were essentially capitalists, they refused to veer off the road to secession to embrace one or another plan of gradual, compensated emancipation. In *The Southern Tradition* (1994) Genovese has asserted that "the principal tradition of the South—the mainstream of its cultural development—has been quintessentially conservative." In delineating the antebellum basis of that tradition, he sees southern slaveholders as a kind of unique hybrid, modern and forward-looking yet also resistant to innovation, in but not of an expanding global market driven by burgeoning free-labor systems.

Unlike some southern conservatives, Genovese has always insisted on placing slavery at the center of antebellum southern history. For him paternalism in the Old South defined a historically specific relation of domination shaped by the slaves as well as the masters. Fogel and Engerman recount Genovese's insights into the psychology of slavery, the experiences of slaves, their family life, and their responses to enslavement. They regard his assessment of African-American Christianity to be peerless. Genovese has argued for the evolution of a semiautonomous slave culture in the antebellum South. Whites and blacks shared much, but they also lived apart. Slaveholders talked about their family, black and white, yet how much they truly understood about the minds and hearts of their slaves remains a perennial question for historians.

Genovese's achievement in reconstructing the world of slaves owed a good deal to his remarkable agility in crossing disciplinary boundaries and in applying a comparative method. Like the Old South's leading intellectuals, Genovese understood that before the advent of capitalist social relations, dependent labor, in one or several forms, had provided the surplus product necessary for the social division of labor in all of the world's great civilizations. Thus, he frequently juxtaposed the experiences of slaves in the Old South with, for example, those of Roman slaves, Russian serfs, and Latin American peasants. Genovese has played no small role in encouraging the boom in slavery studies during the last quarter century, during which time the literature has mushroomed to cover analyses big and small from almost every conceivable perspective, which overlap with every humanistic and social scientific discipline. Slavery has served as a cutting-edge tool to examine large questions within disciplines and as a creative way to reexamine transcendent questions about the human condition itself.

No more qualified person exists to address the problem of slavery from a global perspective than David Brion Davis, the greatest living authority on the history of slavery. His essay, which begins Part I, reconsiders those features that have made this ubiquitous institution similar to other kinds of dependent statuses yet also significantly different from them. The condition of slaves varied considerably from place to place, yet even the most privileged slaves proved vulnerable to degradation, dishonorment, and dehumanization. After observing how in the real world slaves were crucially defined by their work, Davis explicates the meaning of their repeated comparisons with beasts and of bestial metaphors that served in both Western and non-Western societies to progressively dehumanize slaves. Owners of slaves, like owners of cattle, tried to domesticate their property and to develop a logic of enslavement appropriate to the slaves' allegedly bestial nature. Yet wherever slavery existed, a crucial contradiction emerged from the masters' attempt to reduce to bestiality those who were, despite their enslavement, irreducibly human and who persistently engaged in a struggle to redeem themselves from social death.

Robert Paquette follows Davis with a comparative analysis of the slave driver, one of the more controversial types of privileged slaves in the Americas. Enslaved agricultural foremen managed the cultivation of commercial crops on plantations throughout the Americas and, indeed, outnumbered white overseers by far. Yet, as Paquette argues, generations of writers on slavery, historians as well as novelists, have tended either to ignore the driver or to portray him as the depraved henchman of the master. He has not found in the voluminous fiction on slavery written before the ending of slavery anywhere in the Americas one representation of the driver as a rebel. Drawing on Genovese's groundbreaking interpretation of the driver in *Roll, Jordan, Roll*, Paquette explains, in contravention of the driver's stereotyped image, his emergence at the front of many of the most important acts of collective slave resistance in the history of the Americas. The slaves, Paquette contends, had more to do in elevating this privileged slave to his ambivalent middling position than most writers have realized. Nor does the relative dearth of slave drivers among runaways contradict their conspicuous leadership of slave rebellions.

During the late eighteenth and early nineteenth centuries, slave drivers came to wield conspicuous authority on the rice plantations of the Carolina and Georgia low country over slaves who were usually organized by task rather than in gangs. Specialists, including Genovese, have frequently commented on how important the task system was to the evolution of the master-slave relation in the low country, although they disagree sharply about the origin and nature of the system. Peter Coclanis sees the task system neither as static nor as some distinctive alternative to the gang system. He does not find climatic, technological, Afrocentric, or certain neoclassical economic interpretations of the origins of the task system satisfactory and instead argues for the interpretive value of an agency model drawn from recent advances in economic theory that deal with the problem of imperfect information. Agency theory allows Coclanis to explain the origin of the task system in a way that includes elements of previous interpretations and to acknowledge both the power of the masters in making ultimate decisions and the role of the slaves in setting the specific terms of the task system.

Throughout his scholarly career and regardless of shifts in his own political thinking, Genovese has demonstrated an exemplary sensitivity to black accomplishment under slavery in the United States that never lapsed into romanticism. Nor has he underestimated the competency of the masters and the sophistication of southern intellectuals. In fact, Genovese has stressed to a broad audience not only that the Old South had an intelligentsia worthy of the name but that in many fields—history, political economy, theology—it equaled or bettered its antebellum northern counterpart. Among southern intellectuals John Calhoun strides like a colossus, and in Part II, on secession, Clyde N. Wilson, distinguished editor of more than twenty volumes of Calhoun's writings, offers a searching treatment of Calhoun's understudied thinking on economics. Calhoun, as Wilson points out, had more to say about economics than about any other searing issue of the Jacksonian period, including slavery. Calhoun's economic proposals won him significant political support, in the North as well as the South. Leading historians of the Jacksonian period such as Arthur Schlesinger Jr. and Robert Remini have either overlooked Calhoun's economics or reduced his views to caricature. Wilson

shows how Calhoun, as a modern slaveholder and free trader, sought to promote the material progress of freeholders while maintaining the South's
organic system of social relations. Northern allies saw merit in Calhoun's
concern about the redistributionist and atomizing tendencies inherent in
allegedly nationalist economic programs. To Wilson, Calhoun's economic
thinking reflected "brilliant insight and high statesmanship," but in under-
girding an older vision of republicanism that placed faith in the independent
freeholder, Calhoun challenged another far more statist vision for the republic that would ultimately triumph during the Civil War.

For his essay Douglas Ambrose has chosen to compare two other antebellum southern intellectuals: James Henley Thornwell, the so-called Calhoun
of the Church and the Old South's most notable Presbyterian theologian, and
Henry Hughes, one of the more imaginative and eccentric of the Old South's
proslavery defenders. Ambrose's analysis provides a needed corrective to
those who have seen the South's antebellum intelligentsia as uniformly anti-
centralist and antistatist. Although Thornwell and Hughes arrived at their
statist positions by different paths—Thornwell through Old School Presbyterianism and Hughes through the "science" of sociology—Ambrose argues
that both advocated the exercise of state power to limit individual masters. By
proposing that the law be used to correct abuses, especially those associated
with irresponsible masters, Thornwell and Hughes demonstrated their desire
to strengthen the South's unfree labor system and hierarchical society in their
struggle against the values and political power of the North's free-labor
society.

Drew Faust has also taken antebellum southern intellectuals very seriously,
probing their words and deeds in a succession of acclaimed books that have
delineated southern social patterns and structures of power in the antebellum period and during the Civil War. In "Moment of Truth," a title drawn
from a chapter in *Roll, Jordan, Roll,* Faust uses the figure of Catherine Edmonston, mistress of a large antebellum cotton plantation in North Carolina,
as a window into the mind of the master class and the world the slaveholders
made. Edmonston, no closet abolitionist, applauded secession, believing that
slavery was ordained by God and that her own dependence within the southern hierarchy conformed to a divinely sanctioned natural order. Yet, as Faust
observes, the hardships brought by the Civil War challenged Edmonston's
privileged and often naive assumptions about her slaves, the South, men and
women, and the order of things. Faust suggests that the tensions and desires
within Edmonston reveal weaknesses within her class that ultimately helped
to undo the Confederacy.

Mary Chesnut, the Old South's most celebrated female diarist, also found the Civil War to be a revolutionary experience. Her famous diaries, rewritten in the 1880s with publication in mind, reveal, in Thavolia Glymph's words, "a narrative of war and a narrative at war with the reality of life after the Confederacy." Glymph carefully documents textual changes from the 1860s to the 1880s in how Chesnut portrays African-American women. Pejorative words and passages, including bestial metaphors, surface in the 1880s version that do not exist in the original diaries. The Moment of Truth, Glymph contends, had led to leveling between white and black women against which Chesnut spitefully reacted with reworked, hardened prose. To reclaim the purity and status of herself and other white women in the aftermath of emancipation, Chesnut engaged in another Civil War, targeting black women with contempt and debasement while muting previous criticism of white women. For Glymph, Chesnut's literary imaginings and reimaginings speak to the revolutionary impact of the Civil War on gender and race relations.

Eugene Genovese has credited novelists like William Faulkner with having a firmer grasp of the distinctiveness of southern life than many historians have had, and Louis A. Ferleger and Richard H. Steckel recognize the enduring power of Faulkner's fictional images over students of southern history. Yet in Part III Ferleger and Steckel take issue with the relentless depiction by Faulkner and other writers of white southerners as undersized and unhealthy physical specimens. Like Paquette in his essay on the slave driver, Ferleger and Steckel show how mutually reinforcing streams of history and literature can fashion mighty stereotypes, which recent advances in quantitative methods in the social sciences can effectively challenge. Economists and other social scientists have labored for decades to develop satisfactory measures of a population's relative physical and material well-being. Ferleger and Steckel borrow from the new science of auxology (the study of human growth) and from regional income data to conclude that "the typical southerner from the eighteenth to the twentieth century bettered the national average in health and nutrition." In the end Faulkner is diminished, for the available data on height from the time of the French and Indian War to World War II show southerners to be taller on average than northerners.

Genovese has long argued for secession as a revolutionary experience and for the Civil War as a death struggle between distinctive civilizations with not merely competing but fundamentally irreconcilable worldviews. The Old South stood in defense of ritual, tradition, order, authority, hierarchy, particularism, and an organic society of mutually interrelated and interdependent, albeit unequal, parts. The antebellum North, dynamic and aggrandizing, contraposed a progressive egalitarian faith whose central tendency was toward atomizing individualism. The North's triumph in the Civil War attended by the abolition of slavery transformed social relations in the South, but as Genovese has also stressed, the essentials of the Old South's worldview lived on in subsequent generations of southern thinkers. Mark Malvasi weighs the burden of antebellum southern history on Allen Tate, one of the most brilliant members of the so-called Fugitive school of southern intellectuals headquartered at Vanderbilt University in the 1920s and 1930s. Malvasi concentrates on Tate's only novel, *The Fathers* (1938), and discerns in the central struggle between Major Buchan, patriarch of an old Virginian family, and George Posey, an impulsive and self-centered outsider, lineaments of the civilizational conflict Genovese outlined in *The World the Slaveholders Made* (1969). For Tate, southerners had failed long before Lee tendered his sword to Grant by not living up to their professed values. *The Fathers*, according to Malvasi, is Tate's "most complex and complete judgment of the antebellum South." It is also a brilliant meditation on the direction of Western civilization and on the impoverishment by modernity of humanity's spiritual life.

During his career as a professional historian, Eugene Genovese inspired many, learned from others, admitted mistakes, remained steadfast on principle, and moved on when the evidence could no longer support a previous position. These essays taken together refine, extend, and even challenge Genovese's work while making their own distinctive contribution to the study of slavery, secession, and southern history. With the challenges, he should be especially pleased. Those few who survived the demands of his graduate classroom and passed their exams under his supervision can recall one of his favorite dictums: "A friend who is no critic is no friend at all."

The editors wish to thank Wayne Hatmaker, who generously relinquished his free time usually spent rooting for the hapless Boston Red Sox to research and prepare Appendix B, the bibliography of writings by Eugene D. Genovese. It includes such discoveries as several early items written by him under the pseudonym Vittorio della Chiesa. David Brion Davis's essay "The Problem of Slavery" originally appeared, in slightly different form, in *A Historical Guide to World Slavery*, edited by Seymour Drescher and Stanley L. Engerman (New York: Oxford University Press, 1998), and as "At the Heart of Slavery" in the 17 October 1996 issue of the *New York Review of Books*. As revised by the author, it is reprinted here by permission of the editors and Oxford University Press.

Happily, Sally Carman and Carole Freeman proved sufficiently progressive to handle the technological problems of an anthology created in the computer era, despite Paquette's incessant demands. Bobby Fong, Dean of the Faculty at Hamilton College and a man of true Christian charity, paid for Sally's overtime.

Lewis Bateman, with his unqualified admiration for Eugene Genovese, provided most helpful advice in the preparation and organization of this volume. Nancy C. Essig, Director and Editor-in-Chief of the University Press of Virginia, and Dick Holway, Social Sciences Editor, responded to this volume with an enthusiasm and professionalism that can only be described as exemplary. We not only thank them but look forward to working with them on future projects.

Abbreviations

Fox-Genovese	Elizabeth Fox-Genovese, *Within the Plantation Household: Black and White Women in the Old South* (Chapel Hill, N.C., 1988)
Genovese, *Roll*	Eugene D. Genovese, *Roll, Jordan, Roll: The World the Slaves Made* (New York, 1974)
HSP	Historical Society of Pennsylvania, Philadelphia
NOPL	New Orleans Public Library
SCDAH	South Carolina Department of Archives and History, Columbia
SCHS	South Carolina Historical Society, Charleston
SCL	South Caroliniana Library, University of South Carolina, Columbia
SHC	Southern Historical Collection, University of North Carolina, Chapel Hill
Stampp	Kenneth M. Stampp, *The Peculiar Institution: Slavery in the Ante-Bellum South* (New York, 1956)
WMQ	*William and Mary Quarterly*

SLAVERY,
SECESSION,
AND SOUTHERN
HISTORY

Introduction

Changing Views of Slavery in the United States South: The Role of Eugene D. Genovese

ROBERT WILLIAM FOGEL AND STANLEY L. ENGERMAN

FEW HISTORICAL TOPICS in recent memory have generated more vibrant research and controversy and have produced more dramatic shifts in interpretation than has the study of antebellum slavery in the southern United States. The reinterpretation of slavery reflects the use of new and different sources of data and of new understandings of human belief and behavior. Reinterpretation has also been influenced by politics, both those of individual scholars and national political currents. Slavery studies, of course, hardly stand alone in experiencing such changes, but the centrality of slavery to American history, as well as to contemporary political debates, can explain the unusual attention it has attracted.

The negative effects that slavery had upon the slaves and the need to view them solely as victims were major themes of many abolitionists and of subsequent historians who often described slaves as destroyed individuals without a developed culture. Similar conclusions about the slaves emanated from proslavery advocates and latter-day racists, but here the absence of a culture was attributed to those racial factors that presumably earlier had made slavery necessary and were seen as the cause and not the outcome of enslavement. With several important exceptions and numerous variations, the slave as a cultureless victim remained a predominant view among scholars through the end of World War II. Except for a few anthropologists and historians, little attention was given to slave accomplishments and their actual patterns of living. The belief in the omnioppressiveness of slavery and of the masters was widely held, at least in the United States. Yet over the next several decades the interpretations of slavery and the slave experience shifted in much of the scholarship, from regarding slaves mainly as victims to seeing slaves as actors able to forge, under constraints, their own lives and culture. Whereas earlier attention was given primarily to masters, now more attention was given to slaves, with interpretations often appearing to depict the slaves as confronting only a limited degree of direct influence by masters. These historical reinterpretations were based upon the work of numerous scholars and became the dominant view of American slavery after the 1960s and 1970s.

During this period several major reinterpretations of American slavery, slave life, and slave culture emerged.[1] Some of these changing views resulted from the new reliance placed on the Work Projects Administration (WPA) narratives of former slaves, as well as much more intensive use of plantation documents and records of southern planters. Others were based primarily on a different way of looking at slavery, such as the groundbreaking examination by Alfred H. Conrad and John R. Meyer of available data relating to investments in slaves and the new views of slave culture coming from the detailed analysis of various forms of folklore and related sources. Thus, relative to the previous scholarly consensus, the 1970s saw the emergence of new views concerning both slaves and planters, as well as of the South's economy and society.

Eugene Genovese has made significant contributions to many different aspects of the history of antebellum southern society. Unlike most scholars dealing with slavery, he has written history both from the top down and from the bottom up. His first book, *The Political Economy of Slavery* (1965), used a Marxist analysis of class relations and class power to provide a major reassessment of the southern master class. He stressed, as had Marx and the Marxists, the backwardness and premodern (and, at times, antimodern) character of the southern labor system. The closing chapter, however, shifted rather dramatically from a focus on economics to one on culture and ideology in explaining the onset of the Civil War. There he argued that rather different economic scenarios for the South were consistent with the onset of the sectional crisis and that to attribute disunion to questions such as the possible profitability of antebellum slavery was to narrow the big issues unduly. This shift to culture and ideology has characterized much of his subsequent work on the planters.

Genovese's departure from narrowly defined economic issues did clarify understanding of the nature of antebellum sectional differences and, indeed, is historically consistent with the emergence in the 1830s of the economic debate about slavery as a central part of class relations and political warfare. By taking southern white culture and ideology more seriously than many previous scholars had, Genovese has been able to provide a better understanding of the events of the antebellum period as perceived by those alive at the time.

This approach has been expanded into a description of the intellectual life of the white South including the role of religion and religious beliefs, a theme that has also been central to his interpretation of the slave's culture. In both cases, white and black, his willingness to take religious belief seriously, whatever Marx may have said about it, has become central to the understanding of the South.

Starting with a 1970 essay published in the *New York Review of Books,* Genovese shifted concentration to the slaves. This work was a variant of history "from the bottom up," then fashionable in England with the work of E. P. Thompson on the British working class. His work on slave culture and the slave's belief and behavior has been influential in shaping interpretations of slavery in the United States and also has been extended to slavery elsewhere. Even if the specifics of his interpretation are not accepted, the model of slave-master interaction remains a central part of the current approach to slavery. Some earlier focus on the slaves in the 1920s and 1930s by black historians such as Carter Woodson and Charles Wesley had not entered the scholarly mainstream, leaving the theme to be developed by Genovese and others after World War II.[2]

Genovese was not, of course, the only major influence in the post–Ulrich Phillips reinterpretation of slavery and slave life. Nor did all the scholarship point in the same direction. The cumulative impact of new information and new interpretations has meant, however, that slavery and its consequences recently have come to be seen in a different light. The earliest influential onslaught on the received views was probably Kenneth Stampp's *The Peculiar Institution* (1956). By an extensive reexamination of planter letters, plantation documents, and court materials, Stampp was able to reverse much of Phillips's views on planter behavior and the treatment of slaves. An influential essay by Stanley Elkins, which drew on existing literature to ask questions about the effects of slavery on the slave psyche and slave culture, followed in 1959. In a different vein a 1958 article by the two economists Alfred H. Conrad and John R. Meyer systematically examined the question of the profitability of slavery to antebellum southern planters and briefly discussed related economics issues such as "slave-breeding," southern economic growth, and the coming of the Civil War.

These works each triggered significant and extensive scholarly debates on issues of fact, interpretation, and morality, and together they set the stage for subsequent scholarship on slavery. Within the next two decades, major works on slavery, such as Genovese's *The Political Economy of Slavery* and *Roll, Jor-*

dan, Roll (1974), as well as John Blassingame's *The Slave Community* (1972) and Herbert Gutman's *The Black Family in Slavery and Freedom* (1976), served to influence other writings on slave life and culture, while a debate triggered by our *Time on the Cross* (1974) served to present much new material on the economic and demographic aspects of the antebellum South. Many useful works were published on the slave trade, slavery in the colonial era, antislavery thought and politics, and the period after slavery, in addition to these central works on antebellum slavery. Within the 1970s slavery and antislavery, not just in the United States but everywhere else, seemed to be a dominant subject of historical study, and in some ways scholars are continuing to digest the enormous amount of information that these studies generated.

Genovese's writings on slavery cover nearly forty years and deal with many aspects of the southern slave system. His articles and books (the earlier works written individually and the later ones jointly written with Elizabeth Fox-Genovese) have had a great influence on the study of southern history and slavery, and several of his views have provided the central arguments for many recent studies of slavery. His first book, as befitted a then Marxist, was a study of the political economy of slavery, although he used the same title as that of the antebellum proslavery work of the Virginian Edmund Ruffin. The various chapters in Genovese's book have earned rather mixed grades in the world of scholarly debate. Some of the specific arguments about the weakness of the economic performance of the South and on the unprofitability of slavery have not fared well in their boldest forms, as Genovese himself has suggested in clarifying remarks contained in later writings.

Yet Genovese's use of the distinction between economic development and economic growth has led to considerable research and discussion of an economic and a cliometric nature. His main argument has been for the limited prospects for a southern economy dependent on production in agriculture, no matter how expansive, because it had a limited ability to adapt to those modern manufacturing methods that alone could generate continued growth. Whether the failure to diversify was due to underdeveloped human capital, entrepreneurial failures, lack of consumer demand, inappropriate banking policies, or mainly a misguided restriction to agriculture to buttress slavery, research on southern manufacturing has led to a better understanding of the southern slave economy, as well as a more detailed context within which to examine the southern economic decline in the aftermath of the Civil War. What Genovese as well as economic historians such as William Parker and Gavin Wright have indicated is that an economic analysis of the South need not necessarily provide an overall favorable verdict as to its economic performance, even when it points to such relatively clear-cut phenomena as the profitability of slave ownership and the impressive growth in southern regional output.

The basic argument, however, of a capitalist northern versus a noncapitalist southern economy has persisted in Genovese's subsequent writings, including those coauthored with Fox-Genovese. This contention, even with some modifications based on the new details on the performance of the southern economy, continues to have great appeal to those scholars trying to explain North-South differences before the Civil War, whether or not they accept Genovese's full set of economic and underlying cultural categories making for the differences.

Genovese's discussion of sectional differences raises interesting issues. Some scholars have argued that the southern economy was "embedded in a world market," although with a large subsistence sector and with only a limited "penetration of market relations." This position seemingly places the locus of the precapitalist South in the behavior of planters and the nonslaveholders of the South, as well as of the slaves, as none are considered to be responsive to the economic signals of the market. Moreover, Genovese and Fox-Genovese state that "in essential respects the slaveholders of the Old South had much more in common with northern Americans of all classes than they did with, say Russian boyars or Prussian Junkers," thus narrowing somewhat the range of differences in behavior to be expected, particularly within the economic sphere. They also claim that "in historical analysis, ostensibly marginal differences count for everything." And, compared to the North, the South was "just different enough" in terms of some "special features of material, ideological and psychological development" to bring on a civil war.[3]

Genovese's major work, one of great and continuing influence, is *Roll, Jordan, Roll: The World the Slaves Made.* It deals primarily with slave life, even though most other issues of United States antebellum slavery are covered in order to provide the full context for examining and understanding slave belief and behavior. It deals sensitively with several basic difficulties in writing about slavery, in particular the need to provide a setting in which the behaviors of masters and slaves achieve some degree of psychological consistency. (We could, for example, pose the following question about other recent works on slaves and on masters: Could the patterns of behavior recently described for slaves have emerged from the harsh treatment accorded by the masters Stanley Elkins describes?) This constraint of behavioral consistency has posed serious intellectual problems and has led to some moral criticisms of Genovese's work as being too kind to masters. It is important here to distinguish between what is ideologically desired today (as well as what may have seemed politically most useful) and what seems to be empirically the most accurate historical presentation of the relationship between masters and slaves at the time.

A description of harsh masters may have met the moral demands of the abolitionist critique, but too much control and harshness might have led, as in Elkins's argument, to psychologically affected or, at the extreme, psychologically destroyed slaves, with limited ability to function independently or to develop their own culture. Too kind or, according to some definitions (although not Genovese's), paternalistic masters will offend the belief in what the powers of slave ownership could have meant, but a pattern of master behavior that seeks to maintain enough control so as not to disrupt the existence of the system but does not necessarily attempt to control every facet of slave life, does suggest an environment where slave beliefs and culture could exist and perhaps even flourish. This view suggests that even if there had been some psychological damage resulting from the slave condition, such destruction was limited. Whether masters did not care what slaves did as long as it did not threaten the system, or if they tried to impose behavior identical to or different from their own remains difficult to answer.

Some writers now present a view, perhaps best described as "slaves without masters." Such a claim presents what today may be regarded as a morally acceptable view of slave life, but without confronting the implications such slave behavior poses for understanding the masters. This avoidance of confrontation, however, is clearly not the way that Genovese shapes his argument. For him there is no easy, one-sided resolution of the issue. His sense of complexity makes for a richer, more coherent view of the institution, even while opening him to attack for what he has not said.

In addition to his general arguments concerning slave culture and master-slave interaction, Genovese has raised a number of specific issues regarding the slave experience. He argues that slaves in the Old South resembled peasants in their work ethic more than they did factory workers. He points out that slave work was done irregularly in spurts (daily as well as seasonal), a pattern found in agricultural production in almost all places, given the key role of climate and seasonality in setting production schedules and work needs. Whether a rapid transition to nonagricultural work attitudes was possible for slaves or ex-slaves remains, however, an open question, as does Genovese's conjecture that this system "ill-prepared black people to compete in the economic world into which they would be catapulted by emancipation."[4]

Genovese also has argued that the slaves were able to negotiate with masters, who were compelled to accept their ability to bargain and negotiate for better conditions within the system, but this accommodation did not imply that slaves accepted the system. Revolt in the United States, given the population ratios and the geographic terrain, would have been nearly suicidal. Genovese argues that it is not appropriate to always expect armed revolt by slaves given these factors. Indeed, such uprisings did not often occur in other slave societies or, for that matter, in most free societies. A more long-term form of resistance, well described by Genovese, is evident in the slave's survival as a human being, with a chosen culture, doing what can best be done under adverse conditions, with a culture developed under major constraints merging African and European cultures. The fact that slaves could rise in occupational status within the system and thereby gain more favorable rewards does not necessarily imply that they would have desired this or accepted it as the preferred outcome under other conditions, if different opportunities had been available (as they were during the Civil War). In the United States and elsewhere in the Americas, for example, elite slaves such as drivers were frequently leaders of protests and revolts.[5]

Genovese's analysis of slave resistance has sought to describe the complex ideological components, to examine how they differed in various parts of the Americas, and to analyze how they varied in most places over time with the rising share of American-born slaves and the declining number of new arrivals from Africa. He explores the context of collective slave resistance and the question of whether slave rebels were forward-looking or backward-looking in what they hoped to accomplish should they achieve independence. Genovese concludes that a transition in the aims of slave revolt did occur at the end of the eighteenth century, giving rise to a more revolutionary basis than previously thought.

Genovese's arguments regarding the goals and values of masters have been widely debated. Although certainly profit conscious and market responsive, slaveholders in their personal relations with their slaves developed a pattern of behavior that Genovese describes as paternalistic. These relations meant slaves imposed corresponding constraints on masters. Nevertheless, the power of the owners and of the white society ultimately set bounds on the situation, because whatever happened was influenced, controlled, and sanctioned by the power of the master.

Finally, and perhaps of greatest significance, has been Genovese's major contribution to the examination of the role of religion in slave society. Religion, he argued, "developed into the organizing center of their resistance within accommodation" and was "the slaves' most formidable weapon for resisting slavery's moral and psychological aggression."[6] Afro-Christianity developed and spread from early in the settlement period, leading to deeply held religious beliefs that were carried forward after emancipation. They reflected in part the way by which whites and owners tried to influence the slaves, but also the manner in which the slaves were able to shape things themselves. Genovese argues that the slaves' religion "exhibited greater continuity with African ideas than has generally been appreciated," but that it also "reflected a different reality in a vastly different land and in the end emerged as something new."[7] Religious beliefs shaped all aspects of the slave's life and were one important form of resistance developed under enslavement.

This considerable body of work by Genovese and others on American slavery has, of course, not solved all the problems of historical interpretation and, indeed, has often led to significant difficulties in bringing together the materials and their interpretation. It is clear, however, that many of these problems of interpretation are not unique to the study of slavery. Rather they are general problems encountered in presenting the history of any group and are particularly acute for a minority group attempting to recover its past. They are especially complex in cases where ambiguity exists as to whether the purpose at hand is to get the historical past correct or to provide a more favorable understanding of the past for the present generation (if there is any perceived conflict between the two). Thus studies of ethnic and gender histories deal with many of the same difficulties that were first confronted in the writing of the history of slavery.

Historians of slaves and slavery often distinguish between treating the slaves as victims or as actors. Given the skewed power relations, there can be a focus on the absolute (legal) power of the master to control and to oppress slaves and the very limited opportunities for individual behavior and community development on the part of the slaves. Such a concentration on the master's power and legal ability to victimize the slaves makes it extremely difficult to describe satisfactorily the ability of slaves to believe and act somewhat independently within the system. It is as if allowing slaves to be actors somehow implies that the masters were less powerful and the system was less evil than would otherwise be the case.

This basic distinction between victims and actors has important implications for the study of a number of cultural issues regarding slavery. The question of how patterns of culture develop and are transferred across time and place, an issue obviously central to the study of other immigrant groups as well, requires a sense of both the impact of the migration process and the relative degree of openness of the system after arrival. The extent to which earlier beliefs may be most critical in shaping the cultural patterns in the Americas and the degree to which there was some assimilation, whether coerced or chosen, to the dominant groups should not be considered independently of the nature of the slave system. These possibilities raise questions about the nature of cultural differences among slaves in different parts of the United States, as well as between slaves in the United States and slaves elsewhere in the Americas.

Also of importance when describing the mechanism of cultural transference is the examination of the nature of the culture that is transferred. Various approaches to American slavery suggest that this new slave culture could be influenced by the cultures of the master class, the oppressed class (whether carried over with only limited changes from Africa or out of new patterns emerging after arrival), or some other groups in society having contacts with the slaves, such as lower-class whites. The processes of transference that have been described include culture transferred directly by planters' actions, by the slaves' observation of what those around them are doing, or by mimicking either the planters or some other group; each of these would imply different forms of behavior and of control on the parts of both slaves and masters. And if one asks what specific patterns the masters would hope to achieve, beyond the ability to control the slaves and make money off of them, still further complications arise. In regard to some characteristics, for example, it has been claimed that the masters wished the slaves to mimic their behavior; this was true perhaps in some respects, but it is doubtful that the masters wanted their slaves to mimic their work ethic or behavior (certainly not if earlier arguments about planters are to be accepted).

A central debate regarding American slavery, which reached its intellectual peak in the 1940s argument between E. Franklin Frazier and Melville J. Herskovits, concerns the significance of African aspects to American slave culture. Subsequent examinations of slavery in the United States and elsewhere in the Americas have compared numbers of slave imports, slave population shares, and the sizes of units on which slaves lived to discover the relative numbers of native-born to African-born in the population and the extent frequent black-white contacts could be expected. These demographic factors indicate that African patterns generally were able to persist longer and more completely outside of the United States, particularly in Brazil and the Caribbean. The United States, it appears, had an unusually mobile slave pop-

ulation, particularly with the southward and westward movement of the cotton plantation system starting in the early nineteenth century. As Allan Kulikoff has demonstrated, little seems clear about the nature and effects of
interregional mobility, with its family breakups, on the emerging patterns of
slave belief and behavior or about how the culture of the early seaboard
South (which had a higher percentage of African-born) was transmitted to
the newer areas.[8]

Peter Kolchin has raised the question of the extent to which a large-scale
slave community can be said to have existed in the United States, given the
relatively small size of slave plantations in the South compared to the size of
the sugar plantations in the West Indies and Brazil and serf villages in Russia.[9]
The effect of the size and the geographic dispersion of plantations, the degree
of slave mobility across units, and the frequency of contacts among slaves on
different units, all would influence the process of diffusion of cultural patterns. Thus arguments suggesting an extensive pattern of cultural dispersion
would imply that there was flexibility in allowing contacts and movements
across plantations. Such flexibility is also indicated by, for example, the apparent frequency of cross-plantation marriages among slaves, particularly in
the older areas of the South.

A significant and long-standing problem concerns the ability of scholars
to make generalizations about the slave experience and to indicate the relative
importance of specific environmental factors. Southern slavery differed over
time, and it varied in different parts of the South in regard to crops produced,
locational patterns of plantations, size of units, and demographic composi-
tion (age, sex, place of birth of slaves), each of which might be expected to
influence the specific nature of the process of cultural adjustment. The acknowledged variations in slave culture in the different parts of the South
stemmed either from patterns held before the slaves arrived or else from what
happened to them after they arrived in the South. Exploring these variations
requires some understanding of the basis of the master-slave interaction,
both what was legally specified and what actually happened.

Another aspect of the recent study of African-American history is the
more explicit linking of slavery with the postslavery era to see what behavior
emerged then and to understand what this would imply for the slave era. Did
the rather sudden change in legal status have a dramatic effect on individual
and group behavior, or would we expect more continuity in beliefs regarding
family, work, land ownership, and education? The determination of what
happened in the postbellum period and, as important, the linking of the

postbellum period to specific patterns under slavery have not yet attracted as much attention as has the study of slavery, but more research no doubt will be done on the postemancipation years.

The recent literature describing slaves as actors tends to emphasize positive aspects of slave behavior or at least to suggest a more nuanced portrayal of slave characteristics than had earlier writings, so as to indicate that slaves were not reduced as a people to ciphers by the system and that some independence of choice and belief was—somehow—attained. Yet to be an actor in this sense of creatively responding to circumstances need not preclude some of what might be regarded as negative aspects, if the conditions are so difficult and the power is so unbalanced. To describe the slaves as actors need not deny the sometimes destructive tendencies of the slave experience, but it does raise the question of why masters permitted this to happen—what constraints influenced planter behavior, and why was it impossible for planters to fully exercise the powers that the laws seemed to permit?

Once this wide range of differences in slave behavior is acknowledged, the questions arise, familiar to all historians, of how generalizations can be validly made and what the relative numbers following different patterns of behavior are. Should the writer present the material as if only the central pattern of behavior existed, allowing perhaps for a limited number of deviations to be explained? Scholars now show a greater willingness to accept the possibility of nonuniformity of behavior by masters and by slaves, as well as variability in individual behavior reflecting different economic, demographic, and other conditions. Generalizations may be useful for moral arguments, however, and that is why historical generalization often seems to be preferred in the discussion of slavery.

Another change in the interpretation of slavery, examining slavery as a controlled labor institution, has emerged from studies dealing with other labor institutions, breaking down the once-sharp gap between slave and free labor. A basic view has emerged of the common processes among laboring powers in different institutions, contained in the interaction of mutual interests, with bargaining and accommodations within what was permitted legally. Laws can establish the bounds of behavior, but actual behavior may either exceed these legal limits or not approach them at all. Slavery was, in some senses, one variant of the general issue of labor organization and human interaction, no matter what legal arrangements existed. Although slavery does differ from free labor in certain important aspects, it is difficult, some argue, to make sharp distinctions between free-labor capitalism and slave labor, because elements of harshness and mildness, of paternalism and profit seeking, exist in both, even if to differing degrees. In the cases of both free labor and slave labor a concern with the very short-run returns will lead to actions different from those to be expected of businessmen or planters concerned with a long-run solution. The length of the planning horizon will affect both businessmen and planters: What a capitalistic planter will do differs if he wants short-term profits or if he is willing to allow for a long-term perspective.

Indeed, Genovese does suggest that there need not be any difference in behavior (in contrast with belief) between a paternalistic master and one who aimed for plantation profitability, despite the differences in motivation. It may have been that sheer ruthlessness would not have paid for the planters in the long run over which slavery existed. This focus on a long-run perspective underlies Genovese's critique of Elkins's concentration camp analogy, pointing to the differences between the slave plantation, where production was shaped for over a long time period, and the concentration camp, which operated to kill people quickly, with only infrequent concern with production.

In large measure the basic outcome of Genovese's work on slavery in the past quarter century has been to change a historical interpretation. The slave system, with its stress on the difficulties and presumed inflexibility of slave labor, is now seen as much more flexible than it had been previously thought. Cruelty there often was, and greater cruelty was always possible; but the nature of personal interaction, economic incentives, and other motives placed some constraints on the behavior of masters, and the result, although not intended, provided opportunities for the development of a rich and sustainable slave culture. In this reinterpretation the writings of Eugene Genovese have played a major and most influential role because of the extent of his research as well as the depth of his insight into human relations.

Notes

We wish to thank Larry E. Hudson Jr., David Brion Davis, and the editors for comments on an earlier draft.

1. Any attempt to give references to demonstrate a direct influence of Genovese on specific authors raises the possibility of either omitting some authors or including some who would argue that there was no such influence. Recent works on slavery that are particularly useful as guides to the historiography of United States slavery are John B. Boles, *Black Southerners, 1619–1869* (Lexington, Ky., 1983); Peter Kolchin, *American Slavery, 1619–1877* (New York, 1993); Peter J. Parish, *Slavery: History and Historians* (New York, 1989); Donald

R. Wright, *African Americans in the Colonial Era: From African Origins through the American Revolution* (Arlington Heights, Ill., 1990); *African Americans in the Early Republic, 1789–1831* (Arlington Heights, Ill., 1993). See also Randall Miller and John David Smith, eds., *Dictionary of Afro-American Slavery* (New York, 1988). And, for detailed bibliographic listings, see Joseph C. Miller, *Slavery and Slaving in World History: A Bibliography,* 2 vols. (Armonk, N.Y., 1999); John David Smith, *Black Slavery in the Americas: An Interdisciplinary Bibliography, 1865–1980* (Westport, Conn., 1982). In addition, several of the issues discussed are examined in more detail in Robert William Fogel, *Without Consent or Contract: The Rise and Fall of American Slavery* (New York, 1989), and the accompanying volumes published in 1992.

2. Jacqueline Goggin, *Carter G. Woodson: A Life in Black History* (Baton Rouge, La., 1993).

3. Elizabeth Fox-Genovese and Eugene D. Genovese, *Fruits of Merchant Capital: Slavery and Bourgeois Property in the Rise and Expansion of Capitalism,* (New York, 1983), 17.

4. Genovese, *Roll,* 292.

5. See chap. 2 below.

6. Genovese, *Roll,* 651.

7. Ibid., 162.

8. Allan Kulikoff, "Uprooted Peoples: Black Migrants in the Age of the American Revolution," in Ira Berlin and Ronald Hoffman, eds., *Slavery and Freedom in the Age of the American Revolution,* (Charlottesville, Va., 1983), 143–71.

9. Peter Kolchin, *Unfree Labor: American Slavery and Russian Serfdom* (Cambridge, Mass., 1987), pt. 2.

PART I

SLAVERY

1

The Problem of Slavery

DAVID BRION DAVIS

As EVEN ARISTOTLE ACKNOWLEDGED, the idea or concept of chattel slavery must be distinguished from historical varieties of servitude and dependence. More than thirteen hundred years before Aristotle, the Hammurabi Code—and presumably even earlier systems of law—defined a concept of chattel slavery that served as a way of classifying the lowliest and most dependent workers in society. The salient features of this legal and philosophical status, such as salability and inheritability of ownership, would reappear through the ages in scores of cultures. Yet in the ancient Near East, as in Asia, Europe, Africa, and the preconquest Americas, various forms of slavery and servitude almost certainly emerged long before they were systematized by laws or legal codes. But such laws and codes encouraged the wielders of power to make the actual condition of servitude conform as much as possible to the ideal model of hereditary dishonor and powerlessness—much as wielders of power promoted the opposite ideal model of hereditary kingship. Still, as historians have carefully examined specific slave systems, they have often expressed surprise over the privileges and even freedom enjoyed by certain individual slaves.

In ancient Babylonia and Rome, as in the medieval Islamic world and sub-Saharan Africa, chosen slaves served as soldiers, business agents, and high administrators. In seventeenth-century Virginia a black slave named Francis Payne harvested enough tobacco to buy his owner two white indentured servants and then purchase freedom for himself, his wife, and his children. Payne later married a white woman and sued a white planter. In the interior of Britain's Cape Colony in southwestern Africa, black slave herdsmen in the 1820s were allowed to tend herds of livestock in regions so remote that they would travel many weeks without supervision or even sighting a white figure of authority. In the 1850s an American slave named Simon Gray served as the captain of a flatboat on the Mississippi River, supervising and paying wages to a crew that included white men. Entrusted with large sums of money for business purposes, Gray carried firearms, drew a regular salary, rented a house where his family lived in privacy, and took a vacation to Hot Springs, Arkansas, when his health declined. Some decades earlier a South Carolina slave named April Ellison won his freedom after learning how to build and repair cotton gins. After changing his first name to William, buying the freedom of his wife and daughter, and winning a legal suit against a white man who had failed to pay a debt, Ellison became a wealthy planter and owner of sixty-three slaves, a statistic which placed him by 1860 among the upper 3 percent of the slaveholders in South Carolina.

Such exceptional examples point to the often forgotten fact that regardless of law or theory, a slave's actual status or condition could historically vary along a broad spectrum of rights, powers, and protections that would include, as suggested by Sir Moses Finley, claims to property or power over things; power over one's own or others' labor and movement; power to punish or be exempt from punishment; privileges or liabilities within the judicial process; rights and privileges associated with the family; privileges of social mobility; and privileges and duties in religious, political, and military spheres.[1]

Although most slaves in human history no doubt gravitated toward the bottom of such a scale, the spectrum of slave conditions clearly overlaps a larger spectrum that includes all varieties of oppression and powerlessness. Thus some forms of contract labor, though technically free, would score lower on the larger spectrum than many systems of conventional bondage. For example, Chinese "coolies" who were transported in the mid-nineteenth century across the Pacific to the coast of Peru died in appalling numbers from the lethal effects of mining and shoveling seabird excrement for the world's fertilizer market.

The same point applies to much convict labor, which as "involuntary servitude" is specifically legitimated by the Thirteenth Amendment of the United States Constitution as an exception to its national abolition of slavery. If the twentieth century witnessed the slow eradication of most chattel slavery in Africa, Asia, and the Mideast, it also set wholly new records for cruelty and atrocity as tens of millions of men, women, and children were subjected to state servitude by Nazi Germany, Communist Russia, Communist China, and smaller totalitarian nations. Even in the southern United States, innocent African Americans were forced to labor in chain gangs and endure other forms of penal servitude that approximated the Soviet and Chinese gulags. In contrast to traditional chattel slaves, who usually represented a valuable investment, these political or ethnic prisoners were by definition expendable. As late as the 1990s testimony from former political prisoners in China has proved once again how torture, constant surveillance, and a near starvation diet can transform human behavior. Students of slavery should at least be aware that strong-minded men and women admit that in the Chinese camps they fawningly kissed up to guards, stole food from one another, informed on friends, and finally became convinced that it was their own fault that they were dying from starvation.[2]

The difficulties of appraising or ranking slave systems have been underscored by Orlando Patterson's great comparative study *Slavery and Social Death*.[3] In some primitive societies, such as the Tupinambá of Brazil, slaves were spared from heavy labor but were destined to be eaten, like sacrificial animals, following a ceremonial killing. Some societies that achieved high rates of manumission by allowing slaves to purchase their freedom were extraordinarily brutal and oppressive in other ways, such as sanctioning torture and mass executions. Impressive-sounding laws to protect slaves were seldom enforced. As Jean Bodin pointed out in the sixteenth century, only an absolutist state could override the antithetical or competitive authority of slaveholders. Yet this principle of slaveholder autonomy could also mean that slaveholders might strongly encourage slave marriages and slave families, as in the nineteenth-century United States South, even though such marriages had no legal standing.

Although Orlando Patterson has been especially interested in premodern slavery and in the social and psychological functions of "natal alienation" and "generalized dishonor," we should remember that the central quality of most forms of slavery has been defined by the nature of the work performed — whether, for example, the slave was cutting sugarcane or sweating in the boiler room of a sugar mill in the tropical West Indies; or serving as a sex object in a Persian harem; or wearing fine linens and driving rich white people in a coach in Virginia; or performing as an acrobat, a dancer, soldier, doctor, or bureaucrat in Rome.

But when we think of highly privileged slaves — the wealthy farm agent in Babylon, the Greek poet or teacher in Rome, the black silversmith, musician, or boat captain in the American South — we must also remember another crucial point. Being slaves, they could at any moment be stripped of their privileges and property. They could be quickly sold, whipped, or sometimes

even killed at the whim of an owner. All slave systems shared this radical uncertainty and unpredictability. Even the Mamluk army officer or powerful eu-
nuch who issued orders in the emperor's name could not summon the aid of
a supportive family, clan, or lineage. Whatever rights or privileges a slave
might have gained could be taken away in a flash, leaving an isolated man or
woman as naked as a beast at an auction. This vulnerability, this sense of
being removed from the increments and coherence of historical time, may be
the essence of dehumanization.

Though historians have long recognized dehumanization as a central
aspect of slavery, they have failed to explore the bestializing aspects of dehumanization, despite the significant clue Aristotle provided when he called
the ox "the poor man's slave." Drawing on the historically ubiquitous comparisons of slaves with domestic animals, Karl Jacoby has argued convinc-
ingly that the domestication of sheep, goats, pigs, cattle, horses, and other
animals during the Neolithic Revolution served as a model for enslaving
humans.[4] Whether used for food, clothing, transport, or heavy labor, these
social animals underwent an evolutionary process of neoteny, or progressive
juvenilization. That is, they became more submissive than their wild counterparts, less fearful of strangers, and less aggressive (signified morphologically
by a shortening of the jawbone and a decrease in the size of the teeth). Far
from being fortuitous, these changes in anatomy and behavior were closely
geared to human needs, especially in farming.

To control such beasts, humans devised collars, chains, prods, whips, and
branding irons. They also castrated males and subjected animals to selective
breeding. More positive incentives arose from a kind of paternalism in which
human beings replaced the dominant male animal that had exercised some
control over the social group. As Jacoby astutely observes, the same means of
control were applied to human captives once the harvests of grain and flocks
of animals accumulated by agricultural societies had revolutionized the objectives of warfare. A well-planned raid to steal the wealth a community had
saved from a year of labor might also involve some indiscriminate raping and
the kidnapping of a few dozen workers.

No doubt the archetypal slave, as Gerda Lerner has maintained, was a
woman.[5] And in patriarchal societies women were treated like domesticated
or petlike animals in order to ensure their dependency and appearance of inferiority. Women not only worked in the fields but reproduced, augmenting
the size and wealth of tribes and lineages. In the Hebrew Bible, as in Homer
and other early sources, male captives were typically killed on the spot; otherwise they might have escaped or risen in revolt. Women, one gathers, were

customarily raped and then enslaved as concubines. But with the rise of great urban and agricultural states, the need for servants and labor for public works coincided with improved techniques for controlling male prisoners, whose inability to understand their captors' language might have made them seem more like animals than men. As the laws governing chattel property evolved in the earliest civilizations, it was almost universally agreed that a slave, like an animal, could be bought, sold, traded, leased, mortgaged, bequested, presented as a gift, pledged for a debt, included in a dowry, or seized in a bankruptcy. These vulnerabilities applied even to the most privileged slaves in Babylonia and other ancient civilizations; for the Western world they were eventually codified in Roman law. Despite the many attempts to equate human captives with domestic animals—the first African slaves shipped to Lisbon in the mid-1400s were stripped naked and marketed and priced exactly like livestock—slaves fortunately have never been held long enough in distinctive, endogamous groups to undergo evolutionary neoteny. Looking back at history from the perspective of modern science, we can be confident that no group of slaves remained genetically distinct over the immense period of time required for significant hereditary change. Yet neoteny was clearly the goal of many slaveholders despite their lack of any scientific understanding of how domestication had changed the nature and behavior of tame animals.

In ancient Mesopotamia slaves were not only named and branded as if they were domestic animals but were actually priced according to their equivalent in cows, horses, pigs, and chickens. And as Orlando Patterson has pointed out, the key to the "Sambo" stereotype of the typical slave, "an ideological imperative of all systems of slavery," is the total absence of "any hint of 'manhood.'" Patterson quotes the description by the historian Stanley Elkins: "Sambo, the typical plantation slave, was docile but irresponsible, loyal but lazy, humble but chronically given to lying and stealing; his behavior was full of infantile silliness and his talk inflated with childish exaggeration. His relationship with his master was one of utter dependence and childlike attachment: it was indeed this childlike quality that was the very key to his being."[6]

What needs to be added is that this stereotype describes precisely what a human male slave would be like if slaves had been subjected to neoteny, the same process that domesticated tame animals. While ancient Greeks identified similar slavelike traits with "barbarians," and the stereotype was much later associated with so-called Slavs—the source for the word for slaves in Western European languages—it was only in the fifteenth century, when slavery increasingly became linked with various peoples from sub-Saharan

Africa, that the slave stereotype began to acquire racist connotations.[7] As slavery in the Western world became more and more limited to black Africans, this arbitrarily defined "race" took on all the qualities, in the eyes of white people, of the infantilized and animalized slave.

Since humans have always had a remarkable ability to imagine abstract states of perfection, they also succeeded at an early stage in imagining a perfect form of subordination. Plato compared the slave to the human body, the master to the body's rational soul. Slaves incarnated the irrationality and chaos of the material universe, as distinct from the masterlike Demiurge. There was thus a cosmic justification behind Aristotle's dictum that "from the hour of their birth, some men are marked out for subjection, others for rule." Aristotle's ideal of the natural slave, which would help shape virtually all subsequent proslavery thought, also in effect pictured what a human being would be like if "tamed" and disciplined by neoteny.

Aristotle began by stressing the parallel between slaves and domesticated beasts:

> Tame animals are naturally better than wild animals, yet for all tame animals there is an advantage in being under human control, as this secures their survival. And as regards the relationship between male and female, the former is naturally superior, the latter inferior, the male rules and the female is subject. By analogy, the same must necessarily apply to mankind as a whole. Therefore all men who differ from one another by as much as the soul differs from the body or a man from a wild beast (and that is the state of those who work by using their bodies, and for whom that is the best they can do)—these people are slaves by nature, and it is better for them to be subject to this kind of control, as it is better for the other creatures I have mentioned.

Aristotle then proceeds to distinguish the natural slave as having a different body and soul:

> For a man who is able to belong to another person is by nature a slave (for that is why he belongs to someone else), as is a man who participates in reason only so far as to realise that it exists, but not so far as to have it himself—other animals do not recognize reason, but follow their passions. The way we use slaves isn't very different; assistance regarding the necessities of life is provided by both groups, by slaves and by domestic animals. Nature must therefore have intended to make the bodies of free men and of slaves different also; slaves' bodies strong for the services they have to do, those of free men upright and not much use for that kind of work, but instead useful for community life.

Aristotle did recognize that on occasion "slaves can have the bodies of free men, free men only the souls and not the bodies of free men." Even more troubling was the fact that some people "of the most respected family" sometimes became slaves "simply because they happened to be captured and sold." Yet such instances of injustice could not weaken Aristotle's concluding conviction that "it is clear that there are certain people who are free and certain people who are slaves by nature, and it is both to their advantage, and just, for them to be slaves."[8]

This tactic of animalization may well be universal in human life. Oppression, degradation, and insult are reinforced every day by calling people dogs, pigs, apes, and sons-of-bitches, terms that instantly divide people and enhance the nonanimal superiority of the animalizer. Enslavement is simply the most extreme and institutionalized manifestation of this design. And as Aristotle noted, the slave was not totally dehumanized or seen as only an animal or nothing but an animal. Unlike an animal, Aristotle said, the slave could recognize or apprehend reason even if he could not possess reason at the core of his being. In order to bestialize or animalize other humans, we must first learn to animalize animals and then, for at least a few moments, ourselves.

When I think of myself wholly in terms of my eating, sleeping, urinating and defecating, cutting toenails (claws), scratching an itch, aging and dying, there can be no question that I am a finite mammal. But when I solipsistically regard my own consciousness as the central repository for all the directly known information about human history, this planet, and the cosmos, I can only wonder why this particular moment I am the felt and observable me and can easily fantasize that I must have been chosen in some way to live at this particular moment in history. As Dr. Edward Tyson put it in 1699: "*Man* is part a *Brute,* part an *Angel;* and is that *Link* in the Creation, that joyns them both together." Or Edward Young, an eighteenth-century religious poet who was much favored by the British abolitionists: "*Helpless* Immortal! Insect *infinite!* / A worm! a God! I tremble at myself, / And in myself am lost! At home a stranger."[9]

Defining ourselves as rational animals, *Homo sapiens,* we continue to marvel over our amazing capacity for self-transcendence and rational analysis—for viewing ourselves from a vantage point outside the self, for analyzing our own introspection, and for imagining what it would be like to be someone else, even a slave or an animal. In an anthropomorphic mood we empathize with animals and endow them with self-awareness and altruistic motives. But then, following the seventeenth-century French philosopher Descartes, we can look on animals as mere mechanisms, networks of nerves and tissues driven by hormones and instincts—a deterministic model we can even apply to ourselves when we wish to escape responsibility or guilt.

Animalization, whether applied to animals, other humans, or ourselves, involves an exaggeration of all the so-called animal traits that humans share, fear, and sometimes romanticize, while denying the rational and spiritual capacities that have given mankind a sense of pride, of being made in the image of God, of being only a little lower than the angels. According to the philosopher Nietzsche, "Man didn't even want to be an animal."

Because we are animals and not omniscient gods, we will never know what goes on subjectively inside the brains of supposedly lower animals. Still, domestication did require the creation of close bonds between humans and animals. And for millennia men and women have loved all kinds of pets, have treated animals as companions, and have even worshiped animals as deities. Though slaves were denied such godhood, they could sometimes be loved or become trusted companions. And the view that slaves were essentially children was often a variant on the animal metaphor. Like children, animals are petted, cuddled, and nurtured or made to perform tricks as well as labor. Indeed in many cultures small children were referred to and treated as if they were animals: little deer, little bear or wolf, little lion; and in antiquity untold thousands of babies and children were sold into slavery or abandoned so that others would bring them up as slaves. However loved or cherished a slave might be, animalization implied the excision or removal of some inner human quality that helped to protect an adult man or woman from being treated as a mere object—as opposed to a moral center of consciousness.

Various Greek philosophers, especially the Cynics and Stoics, saw a fundamental contradiction in trying to reduce any human being to such a petlike or animal status. "It would be absurd," Diogenes of Sinope reportedly said, when his own slave had run away, "if Manes [the slave] can live without Diogenes, but Diogenes cannot get on without Manes." When pirates captured Diogenes and took him to a slave market in Crete, he pointed to a spectator wearing rich purple robes and said, "Sell me to *this* man; he needs a master." Externally, according to the Stoics, the servant might be the instrument of his master's will, but internally, in his own self-consciousness, he remained a free soul.

In other words, the master's identity depended on having a slave who recognized him as master, and this in turn required an independent consciousness. Contrary to Aristotle and in contrast to the relationship between a man and pet dog, the roles of master and slave could be reversed: Diogenes could become the slave, and Manes, who even as a slave might have had a freer soul and been less enslaved to his passions, could become the master.[10]

This is the basic "problem of slavery," which arises from the irreducible humanness of the slave. Although slaves were supposed to be treated in many respects like dogs, horses, or oxen, as reflected in all the laws that defined slaves as chattel, the same laws had to recognize that throughout history slaves have run away, outwitted their masters, rebelled, murdered, raped, stolen, divulged plots for insurrection, and helped protect the state from external danger. No masters or lawmakers, whether in ancient Rome, medieval Tuscany, or seventeenth-century Brazil, could forget that the obsequious servant might also be a "domestic enemy" bent on theft, poisoning, or arson. Throughout history it has been said that slaves, if occasionally as loyal and faithful as good dogs, were for the most part lazy, irresponsible, cunning, rebellious, untrustworthy, and sexually promiscuous. This central contradiction was underscored in Roman law (the Code of Justinian), which ruled that slavery was the single institution contrary to the law of nature but sanctioned by the law of nations. That is to say, slavery would not be permitted in an ideal world of perfect justice but was simply a fact of life that symbolized the compromises that must be made in the sinful world of reality. This was the official view of Christian churches from the late Roman Empire to the eighteenth century.[11]

The institution of slavery, then, has always given rise to conflict, fear, and accommodation. The settlement of the New World magnified these liabilities, since the slaves now came from an alien and unfamiliar culture; they often outnumbered their European rulers; and many colonial settlements were vulnerable to military attack or close to wilderness areas that offered easy refuge. Accordingly, the introduction of black slavery to the Americas brought spasmodic cries of warning, anxiety, and racial repugnance. But the grandiose visions of New World wealth—once the Spanish had plundered the Aztec and Inca "Indians"—seemed always to require slave labor. Because many experiments at enslaving Native Americans failed, African slaves became an intrinsic part of the American experience.

From the Spanish and Portuguese to the English, Dutch, and French, colonizers turned to the purchase of slaves in Africa as the cheapest and most expedient labor supply to meet the immediate demands of mining and tropical agriculture. The institution of slavery in the Americas took on a variety of forms. Some were the result of cultural differences, for example, between

Catholics and English Protestants; some depended on the differences between the work performed—mining as distinguished from agricultural labor.
But Anglo-American slavery was not unique in animalizing human beings—
or in defining the bondsman as chattel property endowed with elements of
human personality. In the mid-eighteenth century, when black slaves could
be found in all regions from French Canada to Chile, there was nothing unprecedented about New World chattel slavery, even the slavery of one ethnic
group to another. What was unprecedented by the 1760s and early 1770s was
the emergence of a widespread conviction that New World slavery symbolized all the forces that threatened the true destiny of the human race.

This eruption of antislavery thought cannot be explained by economic
interest. The Atlantic slave system, far from being in decay, had never appeared so prosperous, so secure, or so full of promise. The first groups to de-
nounce the principle of slavery, and all that it implied, were the perfectionist
and millennialist Christian sects—Diggers and Ranters among them—who
challenged all traditional authorities and who sought to live their lives free
from sin. In essence, their ideal involved a form of mutual love and recognition that precluded treating men as objects or animals, even as objects with
souls. The sectarian groups that emerged in the English civil wars of the mid-
seventeenth century looked for a form of authentic service, or selflessness,
which could not be used as a lever for exploitation. Because they strove to realize a mode of interpersonal life that was the precise antithesis of chattel
slavery, they threatened the existing social order and were either annihilated
or reduced to spiritualistic withdrawal.

The notable exception was the Society of Friends, which early found a way
to compromise with the society around it and thus to survive. The Quakers
not only contained and stabilized their quest for a purified life but institutionalized methods for bearing witness to their faith. They did not, in their
religious zeal, call for the faithful to reject the conventional trappings of
church and state, as many other millennialist sects did. In other words, the
Quakers achieved a dynamic balance between the impulse to perfection and
the "reality principle." They also acquired considerable economic and political power and were the only sect to become deeply involved with the Atlantic
slave system. By the early eighteenth century there were Quaker planters in
the West Indies and Quaker slave merchants in London, Philadelphia, and
Newport, Rhode Island. Partly because of the Friends' testimony against war,
slaveholding occasioned moral tensions that were less common among other
denominations. For social critics within the sect, the wealthy masters and

slave-trading merchants presented a flagrant symbol of worldly compromise and an ideal target for attack. For a variety of reasons the Seven Years' War (1756–1763) brought a spiritual crisis for the Society of Friends, resulting in much soul-searching, attempts at self-purification, and finally commitment to withdraw entirely from slaveholding as well as slave trading.

The Quakers' growing anguish coincided with other reformist developments in Western culture, particularly the culture of British Protestantism. First, the rise of secular social philosophy, from Thomas Hobbes onward, necessitated a redefinition of the place of human bondage in the rational order of being. Yet in the language of humanist philosophy, slavery was extremely difficult to justify. Because John Locke celebrated the importance of natural liberty, he had to place slavery outside the social compact, which was designed to protect man's inalienable rights. Locke thus imagined slavery as *the state of War continued, between a lawful Conquerour, and a Captive.* Even by the 1730s such arguments were beginning to appear absurd to a generation of English and French writers who had learned from Locke and others to take an irreverent view of past authority and to subject all questions to the test of reason.

It was Montesquieu, more than any other thinker, who put the subject of black slavery on the agenda of the European Enlightenment in his *Pensées* and *L'esprit des lois.* He weighed the institution against the general laws or principles that promoted human happiness and encouraged his readers to imagine the response of a defender of slavery to a national lottery that would make nine-tenths of the population the absolute slaves of the remaining tenth.[12] By the 1760s the antislavery arguments of Montesquieu and Francis Hutcheson were being repeated, developed, and propagated by the intellectuals of the enlightened world, including such different thinkers as Burke and Diderot. John Locke, the great enemy of all absolute and arbitrary power, was the last major philosopher to seek a justification for absolute and perpetual slavery.

A second and closely related transformation was the popularization of an ethic of benevolence, personified in the "man of feeling." The insistence on man's inner goodness, identified with his power of sympathy, became part of a gradual secularizing tendency in British Protestantism. Ultimately, this liberal spirit led in two directions, each described by the titles of Adam Smith's two books: *The Theory of Moral Sentiments* and *The Wealth of Nations.* Smith's theories of sympathetic benevolence and individual enterprise both condemned slavery as an intolerable obstacle to human progress. The man of

sensibility needed to objectify his virtue by relieving the sufferings of innocent victims. The economic man required a social order that allowed and
morally vindicated the free play of individual self-interest. By definition, the
slave was both innocent and a victim, because he could not be held responsible for his own condition.

For Smith, the African's enslavement, unlike the legitimate restraints of society, seemed wholly undeserved. He represented innocent nature and hence
corresponded, psychologically, to the natural and spontaneous impulses of
the man of feeling. Accordingly, for Smith, the key to progress lay in the controlled emancipation of innocent nature as found both in the objective slave
and in the subjective affections of the reformer. The slave would be lifted to a
level of independent action and social obligation. The reformer would be assured of the beneficence of his own self-interest by merging himself in a transcendent cause. These results, at least, were the expectation of philanthropists
who increasingly, as the eighteenth century wore on, transformed the quest
for salvation from a sinful world into a mission to cleanse the world of sin.

By the eve of the American Revolution, there was a remarkable conver-
gence of cultural and intellectual developments that at once undercut traditional rationalizations for slavery and offered new modes of sensibility for
identifying with its victims. Thus the African's cultural difference acquired a
positive image at the hands of eighteenth-century primitivists and evangeli-
cal Christians, such as John Wesley, the founder of the Methodist Church,
who searched through travel accounts and descriptions of exotic lands for examples of man's inherent virtue and creativity. In some ways the "noble savage" was little more than a literary convention that conflated the Iroquois and
South Sea islander with sable Venuses and tear-bedewed daughters of "injur'd
Afric."

The convention did, however, modify Europe's arrogant ethnocentrism
and provide for at least a momentary ambivalence toward the human costs of
modern civilization. It also tended to counteract the many fears and preju-
dices that had long cut the African off from the normal mechanisms of sympathy and identification. Ultimately, literary primitivism was no match for
the pseudo-scientific racism that drew on the Enlightenment and that reduced the African to a "link" or even separate species between man and the
ape. But for many Europeans, as diverse as John Wesley and the Abbé Raynal,
the African was not a human animal but an innocent child of nature whose
enslavement in America betrayed the very notion of the New World as a land
of natural innocence and new hope for mankind. By the early 1770s such
writers, following the path of the pioneering American Quaker Anthony

Benezet, portrayed the black slave as a man of natural virtue and sensitivity who was at once oppressed by the worst vices of civilization and yet capable of receiving its greatest benefits.

This complex change in moral vision was a precondition for antislavery movements and for the eventual abolition of New World slavery from 1777, when Vermont's constitution outlawed the institution, to 1888, when, in a state of almost revolutionary turmoil, Brazil finally freed some half million remaining slaves. But the diffusion of religious and secular antislavery arguments in no way guaranteed such an outcome. If Washington, Jefferson, Madison, and other slaveholding founders could view human bondage as an embarrassing and even dangerous social evil, they also respected the rights of private property and expressed deep fear of the consequences of any general and unrestricted act of emancipation. The United States Constitution was designed to protect the rights and security of slaveholders, and between 1792 and 1845 the American political system encouraged and rewarded the expansion of slavery into nine new states.

As the American slave system became increasingly profitable, the moral doubts of the Revolutionary generation gave way in the South to strong religious, economic, and racial arguments that defended slavery as a "positive good." Historians are still sharply divided over the fundamental reasons for slave emancipation, which ultimately required an imposition of power even in the regions that were spared a Haitian Revolution or an American Civil War. Yet whatever weight one gives the contending economic and political interests that were involved in the abolition of slavery, it was the inherent contradiction of chattel slavery—the impossible effort to bestialize human beings—that eventually evoked a revolution in moral perception. What finally emerged was a recognition that slaves could become masters or masters slaves, and that human beings are therefore not required to resign themselves to the world that has always been.

Notes

1. M. I. Finley, "Between Slavery and Freedom," *Comparative Studies in Society and History* 6 (1964): 247–48.

2. Jonathan Spence, "In China's Gulag," *New York Review of Books*, Aug. 10, 1995, 15–18.

3. Orlando Patterson, *Slavery and Social Death: A Comparative Study* (Cambridge, Mass., 1982).

4. Karl Jacoby, "Slaves by Nature? Domestic Animals and Human Slaves," *Slavery and Abolition* 15 (April 1994): 89–97.

5. Gerda Lerner, *The Creation of Patriarchy* (New York, 1986), 76–100.

6. Patterson, *Slavery and Social Death*, 96. The quotation describing the Sambo stereotype comes from Stanley Elkins, *Slavery: A Problem in American Institutional and Intellectual Life* (Chicago, 1959). Without implying any biological or hereditary change, Elkins argued that slavery in the United States was so distinctively harsh that it produced a psychological transformation in slaves and created many Sambos.

7. The Slavic root for slave, *rab*, as in *rabotat*, to work, made its way into *robot* (actually the old Czech word for serf). The likening of a slave to a robot or inhuman machine parallels the comparison of the slave to an animal or a permanent child.

8. Thomas Wiedemann, *Greek and Roman Slavery* (London, 1981), 18–20. I have found Wiedemann's translation of this part of the *Politics* clearer than that of Richard McKeon and others.

9. Edward Tyson, *Orang-outang; sive Homo Sylvestris: or, The Anatomy of a Pygmie Compared with That of a Monkey, an Ape, and a Man* (London, 1699), 55; Edward Young, *The Complaint: or, Night-Thoughts on Life, Death, and Immortality* (London, 1755), 3.

10. Robert W. Harms, *River of Wealth, River of Sorrow: The Central Zaire Basin in the Era of the Slave and Ivory Trade, 1500–1891* (New Haven, 1981), describes cases in the Zaire Basin in Africa in which a slaveholder lost his wealth in gambling and then became enslaved to one of his own former slaves. This interchangeability of power and status is one of the characteristics that differentiates the oppression of human slaves from the oppression of animals. This point is overlooked in Marjorie Spiegel's fascinating and disturbing recent book, *The Dreaded Comparison: Human and Animal Slavery* (New York, 1996). While some of my own earlier work has touched on the connections between slavery, racism, and animalization, I hope to explore this theme far more systematically in *The Problem of Slavery in the Age of Emancipation: Dilemmas of Race and Nation*, forthcoming.

11. The meaning and desirability of baptizing slaves became a contentious issue at the Synod of Dort in 1618, the last international meeting of Protestant leaders and theologians from Great Britain and the Continent. While the delegates could not agree on a single policy regarding the baptism of pagans, their written opinions narrowed the gap between Christian masters and baptized slaves and either ended or limited the marketability of Christian slaves. Giovanni Deodatus, a Swiss professor of theology, even ruled that masters should "use them [baptized slaves] as hired servants clearly according to the customs of other Christians." Robert C. -H. Shell, *Children of Bondage: A Social History of the Slave Society at the Cape of Good Hope, 1652–1838* (Hanover, N.H., 1994), 332–70, shows that these principles had some limited and temporary effect at the Cape of Good Hope but were specifically counteracted by colonial legislation in North America.

12. It should be noted that defenders of slavery drew some comfort from Montesquieu's emphasis on the importance of environment and climate; he even surmised that slavery might be founded on natural reason in tropical countries, where coercion might be a needed inducement to labor.

2

The Drivers Shall Lead Them:
Image and Reality in Slave Resistance

ROBERT L. PAQUETTE

You know, whoever can make people skilled in governing men can obviously
also make them skilled masters of men; and whoever can make people skilled
masters can also make people skilled to be kings.

—Xenophon, *Oeconomicus*

All that is wanted in your plantation is full authority over your drivers. They
are good planters and only want watching to make them do, what they very
well know.

—John Couper to Pierce Butler, 15 February 1818, Wister Family Papers, Historical
Society of Pennsylvania

THE MASS ENSLAVEMENT of human beings, wherever it has occurred, has
never resulted in the creation of a mass of undifferentiated slaves. Every
slave society has produced elite or privileged slaves who have represented
their masters in positions of influence and authority. For more than four centuries, European colonists and their descendants enslaved millions of
Africans and their descendants on plantations throughout the Americas.
From the beginning some masters named one or more of their enslaved
males to serve as agricultural foreman. The stability and prosperity of
tobacco, cotton, coffee, indigo, rice, and sugar plantations, among the
most sophisticated enterprises of their day, hinged to a great extent on his
performance.

Different masters called this slave foreman by different names: *capataz* in
Puerto Rico and mainland Spanish America; *feitor* or *capataz* in Brazil; *contramayoral* in Cuba; *bomba* in the Danish Virgin Islands; *commandeur* in the
French Caribbean; *basia* or *bomba* in the Dutch Caribbean; driver, ranger, or
headman in the British Caribbean; driver and overlooker in the antebellum

United States. In many places masters assigned the duties of foreman to slaves without giving them the name. They recognized that a good driver was "a faithful slave, of good judgment and maturity," "the soul of the plantation," "the most important personage in the slave-population of an estate," "the most intelligent and trustworthy [slave] — one who could command respect from the Negroes."[1] He could be found in every state of the antebellum South, typically as a big, tall adult male in his late thirties or early forties, and in conspicuous numbers in such Black Belt regions as the Carolina low country and the lower Mississippi Valley.[2] Many great sugar plantations in the Caribbean and northeastern Brazil even boasted a hierarchy of drivers to supervise the labor of hundreds of slaves.

Everywhere in the Americas the driver had similar duties. With horn, bell, or conch shell, he summoned his fellow slaves from sleep to begin a hard day's work. He handed out tools and provisions along with the field assignments. He superintended the pace of field work and disciplined new slaves, young slaves, and African-born slaves to the peculiar rhythms of plantation life. He interceded to settle disputes between slaves. At night they returned to quarters secured by keys that frequently dangled from his hip. Masters, or their hired administrators, listened to the driver's report on what had been accomplished today and what needed to be done tomorrow. They confided in the driver and considered his advice on purchases, which included slaves, and on problems within slave families and on the shortcomings of individual workers, perhaps even of the white overseer above him. According to the superhuman standard of one French Caribbean planter, the driver "ought to possess fidelity, affection, intelligence, sobriety, discretion, justice, and severity. They should know to preserve distance and authority . . . give attention to every thing and render account of every thing to the master. Lastly, to be perfectly skilled in work of every kind."[3] Masters held the driver accountable for failures. The dirty jobs of tracking down runaway slaves or punishing rebellious slaves often fell to him. Indeed, the collective memory of every slave society in the Americas cannot easily recall the driver without also equipping him with a lash.

Commensurate with his elite status, the driver had more privileges and material comforts than his fellow slaves. He enjoyed greater freedom of movement both on and off the plantation. He lived in a larger hut or cabin, usually situated in a commanding place in the quarters. Nearby his home he tended a larger garden plot or provision ground. His wardrobe might include a distinctive hat or cap, good boots that actually fit, and a pocket watch to go into a tailored waistcoat or navy pea jacket. When masters allotted provisions to their slaves, the driver received larger portions of food, including meat, a bolt of cloth, and perhaps even a promised cash incentive for a job well done. Some drivers carried firearms on the plantation with their masters' permission and in flagrant violation of laws passed in every slave society in the Americas. More than a few of the many free-colored drivers who worked on plantations largely outside the United States had received their freedom as a reward for previous service as slave drivers.

Both history and fiction, however, have proved less generous to the driver. If noticed at all, he tends to lurk in the shadows of the plantation, a crude and elemental character, without any of the depth or ambivalence of his difficult position. Before the end of slavery in the Americas, novelists in Western Europe had produced an extensive romantic literature on the noble African, none of whom, once enslaved, ever became a driver. The remarkable Aphra Behn claimed that her influential little novel *Oroonoko* (1688) about a brave and gallant warrior prince of "Coromantien" sold into slavery in Surinam derived from her own experiences there when it was briefly under English rule. Although she never mentions slave drivers by name in her story, she alludes to their existence when Oroonoko attempts to rouse his fellow slaves into rebellion by berating them for living like dogs and not like men: "Whether they worked or not, whether they were faulty or meriting, they, promiscuously, the innocent with the guilty, suffered the infamous whip, the sordid stripes from their fellow slaves, till their blood trickled from all parts of their body."[4]

The great slave revolution in the French colony of Saint Domingue inspired the teenage Victor Hugo to write *Bug-Jargal,* first published in 1826 and one of the more widely read romantic novels of the nineteenth century, with at least four English translations alone before the United States Civil War. Bug-Jargal, an enslaved prince of Congo, powerful, humane, and honorable, possesses many of the same noble attributes as Oroonoko. Before breaking his fetters to lead one of several armies of slave rebels during the revolution, Bug-Jargal toils on a great sugar plantation in the northern plain where, in fact, the slave revolution began. None of Hugo's rebel chieftains are *commandeurs,* and only once during the entire novel does he pause to notice their existence on a plantation: "It is fair to say that these slaves, intermediary links, who would fasten in some way the chain of servitude to that of despotism and would find a malicious pleasure in overburdening others with work and vexation, combined the baseness of their condition with the insolence of their authority."[5] They did not dare, however, to whip Bug-Jargal.

In *Uncle Tom's Cabin,* another transatlantic bestseller, Harriet Beecher Stowe constructed one of the most influential and enduring fictional images of the driver by flanking Simon Legree on his Red River cotton plantation with two sadistic black henchmen named Sambo and Quimbo. These "two gigantic negroes," as Stowe imagined them, possessed "coarse, dark, heavy features; their great eyes, rolling enviously on each other; their barbarous, guttural, half-brute intonation; their dilapidated garments fluttering in the wind—were all in admirable keeping with the vile and unwholesome character of everything about the place."[6] Indeed, Stowe's exquisite imagination makes Sambo and Quimbo so vile and unwholesome that they test the redemptive power of the Christ-like Uncle Tom. He eventually dies from a savage whipping inflicted by the drivers but not before Tom's quintessential goodness leaves them guilt-stricken and finally begging for forgiveness.

William Gilmore Simms, the South's foremost antebellum novelist and one of Stowe's sharpest critics, portrayed the slave driver in two of his short stories, published together in 1845. Unlike Stowe, he sketched from firsthand knowledge of drivers derived from long residence in the South Carolina low country and from southern travel outside the state. Yet if Simms's drivers look different from Stowe's black demons, they think and behave with similar simplicity. The plot of "Caloya: or The Loves of the Driver" revolves around the misadventures of Mingo, an oversexed driver on a large Ashley River plantation in South Carolina, who has the urge to seduce a young, comely Catawba woman. Simms introduces Mingo as "a stout negro fellow, of portly figure and not uncomely countenance. He was well made and tall, and was sufficiently conscious of his personal attractions, to take all pains to exhibit them." Simms grants his slave Lothario an imposing physical presence and even concedes a certain grace and appeal to his physical movements, but Mingo rarely thinks, he emotes; he has temperament but little mind, and by alternately rutting and raging, he is driven circuitously to a rude pratfall from his master's grace. When called upon to defend himself against charges of writing immoral trash, Simms argued for slaves as worthy literary subjects for highbrows but did concede, "It is a tale of low life—very low life—that is true."[7]

A more fortunate driver called Abram superintends a slave gang on an Alabama plantation in the story of "The Snake of the Cabin." This reflexively loyal and dutiful slave, forsaking a bribe and a promise of freedom from a malevolent stranger who intends to abscond with the estate's slaves, warns his master, whom he helps to spring a trap. A struggle ensues in which the steadfast Abram, seriously wounded, kills the outsider. Simms gives Abram a less central role than Mingo but offers a more promising characterization that implies a direction different from the one Simms ultimately traveled. Abram is a "faithful negro . . . shrewd, cool, sensible—perhaps forty years of age—honest, attentive to his business, and from habit, assuming the interest which he managed to be entirely his own. His position gave him consequence, which he felt and asserted, but never abused."[8] Simms's words hint at the existence in Abram of an independent will, an expanding consciousness of self, derived from his authoritative management of the plantation. By inference, Abram has stature in the slave quarters. He mediates the relations between the master and the other slaves. He acts as a leader of his people. Yet this apparent insight remains unexplored, and at the end of the story, Abram more closely resembles Uncle Tom than Mingo.

Stowe's and Simms's characterizations of the driver might be dismissed as additional evidence of the inability of prejudiced whites to fathom the mind of oppressed blacks. But the fictional driver fares no better with Martin Delany, the leading black nationalist in the antebellum United States. Born free in Virginia, then transplanted a few years later to Pittsburgh where he spent much of his adult life, Delany began his serialized novel *Blake* in the 1850s to inspire racial pride and a Pan-Africanist vision of violent resistance to slavery. He drew on a journey to the Southwest as a young man for his story of Henrico Blacus, a free-born Cuban sold into slavery in the United States by an unscrupulous sea captain. Described as Delany saw himself as "black—a pure Negro—handsome, manly and intelligent," what Cubans would have called a free *moreno,* Blacus becomes Henry Holland, a privileged slave on a big plantation near Natchez, Mississippi.[9] When Holland's beloved wife is sold downriver and freighted to Cuba, Henry runs away, then stealthily moves about the South and afterwards to Cuba recruiting slave leaders to carry out a plan for a massive regionalized slave insurrection. Like Stowe, Delany brings his protagonist to a Red River cotton plantation. Henry learns from a slave woman that Jesse, the driver, "treat black folks like dog, he all de time beat 'em, when da no call to do it. . . . He beat us if we jist git little behind de rest in pickin'! Da wite folks make 'em bad."[10]

Her lament recalls a searing passage in an incendiary pamphlet with which Delany was most surely familiar. David Walker's *Appeal . . . to the Colored Citizens of the World* (1829) placed the driver on an abridged list of barbarities perpetrated on blacks by "the enlightened Christians of America." "They take us (being ignorant), and put us as drivers one over the other, and make us afflict each other as bad as they themselves afflict us."[11] Downtrodden people throughout history have reserved special contempt for those who betray their own kind, without necessarily forgetting who holds ultimate responsibility for their plight come Judgment Day. Black radicals like Delany and Walker hammered at the theme of black disunity because they saw it as a principal cause of black degradation. Delany seized the fictional driver to send his own people a stern warning. Not only do slave drivers fail to figure into Henry Holland's ambitious plan of insurrection anywhere in the South, but after planting a seed of revolt on the Red River plantation, he fulfills a promise to the slave woman by dispatching the traitor Jesse to the lower reaches.

In Latin America the driver, despite his ubiquitous presence on sugar plantations, appears only sporadically in the fiction written during slavery and never in a central role or as a rebel. White Cuban and Brazilian novelists, for example, preferred to focus their attention on the tragic, often blindly incestuous relations of beautiful mulatto females to score antislavery points. Cuba witnessed an extraordinary burst of literary activity in the late 1830s and early 1840s when British abolitionists, United States annexationists, Cuban anticolonialists, and slave insurgents threatened to snatch the Cuban pearl from Spain's imperial crown. Four antislavery novels were written, three of them under the auspices of Domingo Del Monte, an impressive intellectual and patron of other Cuban intellectuals.[12] For the most part these novels conformed to the Latin American *costumbrista* literary tradition in that they were intended for nationalistic purposes to describe meticulously and scrupulously Cuba's folkways and natural features. The young white patriots within the Del Monte circle also sought to awaken like-colored Cubans to the corrupting influence of slavery, to show how it reinforced colonial servility, thwarted nationalist aspirations, and threatened Africanization of Cuban culture and institutions.

In the most famous of these realistic novels, Cirilo Villaverde's *Cecilia Valdés*—sometimes referred to as Cuba's *Uncle Tom's Cabin*—drivers merit attention, albeit fleetingly. During one scene on a coffee estate west of Havana in 1830, members of two elite white families gather. A *contramayoral* reports on the estate's operation to Isabel Ilincheta, the absentee owner's virtuous and economic daughter. "Who was the *contramayoral*?" Villaverde asks. "A slave like a foremast, of the color of pitch, broad-faced, with an open expression and an intelligent gaze." He receives praise from Isabel for his "good common sense" and efficiency in carrying out his responsibilities, although he is cautioned on the overuse of the lash, for "while you have it in your hand, you'll want to use it."[13] Later, on a much larger sugar plantation owned by the father of Isabel's prospective bridegroom, two African-born drivers from the "warlike" Lucumí (Yoruba-speaking) nation respond to the command of a cruel white overseer by lashing a rebel slave to the edge of death. With the overseer within earshot, they subsequently refrain from responding to questions about slave treatment on the estate. And when one driver again inflicts punishment on a slave, its ferocity so upsets the visiting Isabel that she drops a drink on herself.

Of the members of the Del Monte circle, Anselmo Suárez y Romero had, arguably, the sharpest eye for how slavery shaped colonial Cuba's customs and institutions. In 1839, a few years after graduating from Cuba's most prestigious academy, the youthful Suárez completed a tragic love story with the ironic title of *Francisco: El ingenio; ó, Las delicias del campo* (*Francisco: The Sugar Mill, or The Delights of the Country*) while residing on a sugar plantation southeast of Havana. Although the famous Irish abolitionist R. R. Madden received a manuscript copy just before his departure from Cuba that year for use as ammunition in the worldwide antislavery crusade, the novel was never published during Suárez's lifetime, a victim in Cuba of Spanish censorship. Like Villaverde, Suárez gives a principal role to a beautiful *mulata*. Unlike him, however, Suárez has her smitten not by an upper-class white pretty boy whom she can never marry because of Cuban color prejudice—or worse, she should not marry because he is actually her half-brother—but by an "exceptional" darker-skinned, African-born slave, a coach driver of "angelic virtues" named Francisco. He contends with a sadistic planter's son who wants to possess Dorotea and, as a result, is torn from her to endure repeated beatings and lashings on a sugar estate. There he faces a slave driver every bit the thuggish equal of Stowe's Sambo and Quimbo, serving a white overseer who exudes even less charm than Simon Legree.

Twice during the story the narrator explains in virtually the same words that the slave driver holds his position precisely "because of his barbarity in cracking the lash and his inhumanity in treating the other [slaves], his brothers and comrades." This relentless human bloodhound "obeys religiously" the commands of his white superiors and excoriates Francisco nearly to his death.[14] Nothing in the scattered fictional references to the *contramayoral* betrays a sophisticated understanding, which Suárez, to judge by traces in his nonfiction, may have attained. But for the didactic purposes of his antislavery novel, he chose to use the driver to deliver a more potent moral lesson to other white Cubans about the singularity of Francisco and just how far the slave system had degraded and corrupted those black and white around him.

A handful of Afro-Cuban writers struggled to the surface during the colonial period, but not one published so much as a passage that would have qualified or challenged the conventional image of the driver in the antislavery literature. Martín Morúa Delgado, the outstanding Afro-Cuban novelist of the nineteenth century, did openly question Cirilo Villaverde's portrayals of the oppressed in *Cecilia Valdés,* assuming a critical stance analogous to Martin Delany's in his reimagining of *Uncle Tom's Cabin.* Morúa's first novel, tellingly entitled *Sofía,* sought wisdom about the psychology of the enslaved by cleverly reworking the mulatto Cecilia Valdés into the "mulatto" Sofia, who turns out not to be a mulatto at all but the abandoned child of a white prostitute "darkened" by her subsequent enslavement, not by the facts of her birth. A mulatto himself, the son of a Basque baker and a freed African mother, Morúa grew up in the port city of Matanzas, which was intimately linked to Cuba's heartland of sugar plantations. A search for the slave driver among the cast of characters in what Morúa tendered as superior literary realism turns up one brief reference, a flashback by Sofía to her enslaved childhood on a sugar plantation and to a horrible scene of torture she saw inflicted on a female slave named Filomena by "el negro contramayoral."[15]

As a stock character toting a whip or cudgel, which, like prejudice, was always of ready application, the slave driver can be found in memorable and forgettable novels written before emancipation by well-known, little-known, and anonymous authors of varying nationalities on both sides of the Atlantic. Antislavery novelists tended to emphasize the driver's brutality to his fellow slaves, his ignobility magnifying the heroic proportions of the black protagonist. Proslavery novelists, fewer in number, tended to emphasize the driver's instinctive obedience and deference to his superior. If the driver was prone to excess in keeping a well-ordered plantation, so much the better to justify the paternalistic master and allow him to prove his characteristic benignity by intervening on behalf of the other slaves. In both genres the driver emerged almost always as primitive and one-dimensional. Yet however pale the fictional characterizations, they do not suffer markedly in comparison with those presented for generations after emancipation by leading historians of slavery. They, like the novelists, either touched on the driver perfunctorily or ignored him entirely.

Gilberto Freyre, a colossus in the historiography of Brazilian slavery, said nothing about the driver in his most important books. In words that Stowe would have liked, the Cuban ethnologist Fernando Ortiz in his classic 1916 account of Cuban slavery quoted approvingly the declaration of a Cuban countess that the *contramayoral* was "a figure more terrible" than the overseer, "the most dreaded adversary, a slave like the others, and therefore hard and cruel toward his fellow slaves, especially with those from a tribe hostile to his. Then he becomes ferocious, implacable with the spirit of revenge."[16] Manuel Moreno Fraginals's prizewinning study of colonial Cuban sugar plantations, first published as one volume in 1964 and then expanded into three volumes in 1978, contains little more than a definition of the *contramayoral*. C. L. R. James's magnum opus on *The Black Jacobins* briefly mentions two drivers among the many privileged slaves who predominated within the ranks of the rebel leadership during the Saint Domingue revolution. But James preconditioned the revolution by referring to slave drivers "armed with long whips . . . giving stinging blows to all [slaves] who, worn out by fatigue, were compelled to take a rest—men or women, young or old." Drivers also belong to James's categorical listing of privileged slaves who had a "strong attachment to their masters" and were "permeated with their vices."[17]

In her landmark 1965 study of slavery in the British Leeward Islands, Elsa Goveia devoted only a few quoted lines to slave drivers, relying on one European visitor to Antigua in the late eighteenth century for their description as "mostly black or mulatto fellows of the worst dispositions." They carried whips that they used liberally "wherever they see the least relaxation from labour; nor is it a consideration with them, whether it proceeds from idleness or inability, paying at the same time, little or no regard to age or sex."[18] Orlando Patterson's lengthier description two years later in an influential book on Jamaican slavery comported with the brief assessments of other students of slavery in the British Caribbean: "It was not unusual for 'the great villain' to occupy this post. . . . These drivers often abused their authority. They had their own favorites, especially among the women; and if they bore a grudge against any of the slaves they could easily take it out on them in the field."[19]

For the majority of the twentieth century, leading African-American historians in the United States treated the driver with what looks like pained restraint or silence. Carter Woodson's first edition of *The Negro in Our History* (1922) fired a parting shot at the end of a section on plantation management that recounted the abuses of slaves by white overseers: "The situation was not any better when the slaves were placed under a Negro driver." By the fourth edition (1927), Woodson had added, "Some say it was worse."[20] In *The Gift of Black Folk* (1924), W. E. B. Du Bois left the driver out of a chapter on labor that presented a wide range of skilled jobs performed by blacks during slavery. From 1947 to 1994, through seven editions of *From Slavery to Freedom*, the standard text in African-American history, John Hope Franklin's slightly more flexible judgment on the driver has remained the same: "On some plantations a slave called the driver was selected to assist the owner or overseer in getting work out of the slaves. The other slaves frequently resented this delegation of authority to one among them, and the driver was sometimes viewed as a traitor, especially if he took his duties seriously."[21]

White southern historians like U. B. Phillips and Charles Sydnor who dominated the academy's view of slavery during the first half of the century had more to say, some of it complimentary. Ironically, the racial bias that diminished their considerable insight into the master-slave relation and into the overall operation of the slave system allowed them to accept more or less at face value the ample testimony from planters about the skills and leadership of some drivers and their centrality to the operation of some estates.[22] From the perspective of the bottom up, however, such slave "achievement" might look more like a sellout, as it probably did to Du Bois and to a postwar generation of white liberal historians.

When the desultory references to the driver in *The Peculiar Institution*, Kenneth Stampp's celebrated reversal of the essentials of the Phillips interpretation of slavery, are totaled, they emphasize the driver's identification with the master and his distance from his fellow slaves. According to Stampp, drivers could be loyal and efficient managers but also "notoriously severe taskmasters," more brutal than the masters.[23] In drawing an analogy between slavery and a Nazi concentration camp, Stanley Elkins underscored this view by calling attention to the camp type known as the Kapo, a prisoner "placed in a supervisory position over his fellow inmates who outdid the SS in sheer brutality."[24]

The driver has undergone rehabilitation during the last quarter of the century, acquiring presence, intelligence, and ambiguity, as part of a remarkable outpouring of scholarship on slavery. If not a rebel, neither was he simply a plantation Kapo like Stowe's Sambo and Quimbo, nor a black factotum like Simms's Abram. The southern historian Clement Eaton foreshadowed the major revisions to come in his second edition of *The Mind of the Old South* (1967) by including a new chapter on "The Mind of the Southern Negro" in "recognition of the rising importance of the Negro in American life and of the incompleteness of any study of the southern mind that leaves him out."[25] Eaton not only recognized that to be effective managers slave drivers had to have an active mind, but that some were among the "remarkable individuals," the "outstanding leaders in the plantation hierarchy." He rejected what he called the "abolition stereotype" of the slave driver as the planter's bestial enforcer and documented his assertion that both masters and overseers "often deferred" to the driver's experience and judgment.

A rapid succession of writings on the driver followed in the 1970s as Robert Starobin, Robert Fogel and Stanley Engerman, Eugene Genovese, Leslie Howard Owens, Randall Miller, and William Van Deburg uncovered considerable evidence that contradicted the antislavery stereotype and, in effect, deepened and extended Eaton's largely overlooked contribution.[26] If nothing else, the first estimates of the number of enslaved agricultural foremen in the Old South made them harder to ignore in any discussion of plantation life. Drivers outnumbered white overseers by far, and on "a majority" of large plantations, those with fifty or more slaves, Fogel and Engerman determined that "the top non-ownership management was black." Genovese went further: "Probably, at least two-thirds of the slaves in the South worked with a black man who had direct access to the master with no white overseer between."[27] In such numbers the driver had to move from the margin toward the center of the debates about the nature of slavery in the United States. The more difficult questions concerned his social role, status, psyche, and personality, his ability to walk tall on the conflicted middle ground between the master and the less advantaged slaves, and whether the driver could claim legitimacy as a leader in the quarters if he satisfied or surpassed the master's expectations. On this last point the high praise Fogel and Engerman accorded the driver's managerial competence in running profitable plantations could be deftly backhanded into a pointed complaint about the driver's characteristic servility and his easy accommodation to white power.

Although all of the revisionist studies of the slave driver in the 1970s took issue with the antislavery stereotype, each reached conclusions with varying shades of gray about his general character and behavior. Starobin, for example, strayed only measuredly from the antislavery stereotype, locating the driver closer to the forces of control, with masters and overseers, rarely among the "privileged bondsmen" who led their fellow slaves in developing successful strategies of survival and resistance.[28] Genovese, however, boldly argued for slave drivers as one of the key sources of slave leadership in the Old South. The image of the brutal slave driver, he maintained, had originated in the Caribbean, where it had a firmer basis in fact, and from there crossed into mainland North America with the expansion of the plantation system. For the most part slave drivers in the United States counseled accommodation, but accommodation did not preclude resistance under favorable circumstances, nor did it imply any necessary loss of moral authority among the slaves, for given the overwhelming forces arrayed against them, violent confrontation with whites amounted to gravedigging. "Most drivers strove to mediate between the Big House and the quarters to lower the level of violence, to maintain order in the most humane way available—which to be sure, was not always all that humane."[29]

In response, a skeptical John Blassingame returned to the sources for another reading. When he first published *The Slave Community* in 1972, he placed the driver by the side of the master, describing him merely in passing as "part of the coercion necessary to keep the plantation machinery humming." His reappraisal of "Status and Social Structure in the Slave Community" in 1976 agreed with the revisionists that the driver held "an ambivalent position" on the plantation but stated that he "was usually too close to the master. Like the overseer, it was a hated position . . . near the bottom of the slave hierarchy." Blassingame counted few, if any, drivers among the rebel slaves who were "accorded the highest status in the quarters." With the publication of the second edition of *The Slave Community* in 1979, Blassingame's published sympathy for the driver—and space devoted to him—had grown, but he still ranked among the least significant personages in the community of the slaves, mostly a failure in the slaves' eyes. He was "the master's man."[30] To be sure, the antislavery stereotype of the driver went too far, but according to Blassingame much in the testimony of slaves and former slaves recommended it.

For Latin America and the Caribbean, curiously enough, no comparable body of specialized work on the driver exists, and to date the antislavery stereotype remains strong in historical circles. Monica Schuler's passing observation in 1970 that "many a leader" of African ethnic slave revolts in the British and Dutch Caribbean came "from the ranks of the head drivers" went unexplored during the decade, and Schuler herself seemed surprised at the "acquiescence" of slaves in the "power vested" in drivers by their masters.[31] During the 1970s the most detailed treatment appeared as a chapter on the *commandeurs* in a massive study of slavery in the French Antilles by Gabriel Debien. Much of this chapter consists of a detailed accounting of their duties as described in plantation manuals, but Debien also focused attention on the reasons for the gradual replacement during the eighteenth century of white *commandeurs,* usually indentured servants, by first African and then creole slaves, many of the latter mulattoes. He openly wondered how masters made the choices they did, if the selection of certain African slaves to be *commandeurs,* for example, had anything to do with their previous status in Africa as village chiefs or as members of royal families or with their ability to communicate with both master and slaves by bridging languages. At one stage of the development of plantation slavery, masters seemed to prefer *commandeurs* who were not from one of the dominant African ethnic groups in the French Antilles such as the Aradas and Congos. His sources, like those used by the revisionists in the United States, revealed examples of rebellious drivers as well as loyal and brutal ones. "It was not unusual to see drivers running away," and at least several drivers headed mass desertions from estates.[32] Debien covered slave revolts and conspiracies in a separate chapter, but there drivers do not enter into the picture.

The revisionist historians in the United States also admitted that under certain conditions the driver, like any other slave, could rebel as an individual. But the seeming absence of substantial evidence of his presence at the front or in the middle of more extreme forms of collective slave resistance affected how far each historian went in recasting the image produced by lengthy, mutually reinforcing streams of history and fiction. Starobin allowed that "drivers could . . . become leaders of escape attempts and resistance movements, but most of them were trapped in their onerous role [as agents of control]." In a footnote he vaguely referred to the participation of drivers in Denmark Vesey's conspiracy yet declared that those who led movements of collective resistance "derived primarily from slave craftsmen and religious figures . . . whose position was even more independent than that of other privileged slaves" like the drivers.[33] Genovese observed that "in a few cases drivers [in the United States] led plots to murder masters or raise insurrections" but "rarely did they use their moral authority in the quarters to promote direct resistance and insurrection. The brutal and hated drivers of the Caribbean led or at least participated in insurrections much more readily." Subsequently, William Van Deburg, the author of the only monograph ever written on slave drivers, stated flatly, "There is little evidence to show that drivers [in the United States] sought to engage in conspiracies or widespread insurrectionary activity aimed at overthrowing the slave system."[34]

Although certainly infrequent, slave revolts and conspiracies break the deceptive surface calm and expose for scrutiny, probably better than any other event, the life beneath, a slave society's inner workings, illuminating what was real and what was feigned for all those willing to see. It is hard to think of a surer test of stature in the quarters than the person who comes to the head of a movement to lead it against long odds in a desperate battle with the known price of failure horrific or, alternatively, the commanding voice that persuades long-suffering souls to trade a risky effort at a dimly lit opening to freedom for a promise of patient, incremental gains.

Archives on both sides of the Atlantic continue to yield fresh information about dozens of major slave conspiracies and revolts in the Americas, and within the last ten years or so, a number of excellent books and articles have analyzed changing patterns of slave resistance in an entire country or region and from a comparative perspective. A careful reading of this and other evidence demands that the driver be given a new hearing, for the inescapable conclusion is that for at least the eighteenth and nineteenth centuries, the driver played a vital role in many, perhaps the majority, of the most significant conspiracies and revolts in the history of the Americas, including those in the United States. He led revolts of predominantly African slaves; he led revolts of predominantly creole slaves.

In a recent study Carolyn Fick searched French colonial archives for information on the popular character of the great slave revolution in Saint Domingue. Among other things, she wanted to know how different kinds of slaves from different places organized the insurrection, mobilized for battle, and then coalesced into formidable armies that eventually swept to victory in what at the time was the world's most valuable plantation colony. The insurrection began in the North Province, where the largest slaveholdings and sugar plantations were concentrated. Considerable planning went into the uprising. It "was by no means a spontaneous or unmediated event." For Fick, the leadership of the *commandeurs* stood out. Their "predisposition . . . proved central in the launching of a conspiracy," and for weeks before the 22 August 1791 uprising, they assembled secretly to advance their plans. The crucial meeting took place about a week before. Several hundred slave representatives from plantations all over the North Province met at a plantation on the fertile Plaine du Nord. "All of the delegates were upper-strata slaves . . . most of them *commandeurs*."[35]

A slave revolt in the Dutch colony of Berbice in 1763 involved thousands of slaves, lasted more than a year, and came close to creating an independent black state. Whites had to abandon Fort Nassau and for months remained holed up at a post near the mouth of the Berbice River breathlessly awaiting response to their scattershot cries for help. Akan-speaking Africans participated as both leaders and soldiers, although ethnic tensions within the rebel forces surfaced between creole and African slaves. "Governor Coffy" and "Captain Accara" were both Akan-speakers and privileged slaves, although apparently not drivers. According to one of the most detailed accounts, the rebels "set up a sort of government maintaining strict military discipline and a sharp watch." Rebel *bombas* appeared at the "head" of certain rebel forces, and one of Cuffy's chief advisers was a literate "foreman from Plantation Helvetia." In order to keep other estates from rising, whites sent at least one agent, a free mulatto, upriver "with the object of encouraging the black overseers (Bombas) and slaves there, in the name of the Governor, to further loyalty," promising freedom to the *bombas* if they kept their gangs in order.[36] Although some *bombas* refused to join the rebellion and others bided their time to observe the shifting winds, the mulatto struck no deals, for on his way upriver he was cut down by the rebels.

The first major slave revolt in the Danish Virgin Islands erupted on Saint John in November 1733, lasted well into the spring of the next year, and cost scores of white and black lives. It had a strong ethnic flavor with slaves from the so-called Mina nation predominant, and only with French support from Martinique was the movement finally stamped out. It began with a bold ruse that led to the capture of the fort that overlooked Coral Bay. In the early morning about a dozen slaves, pretending to be woodcutters, asked for admittance to supply the fort with fuel. Once in, they unloaded on the sleepy garrison with concealed cane knives. After securing the place, they fired cannon shots to signal their fellow conspirators to rise. Who led the assault? Two *bombas,* named Claes and Kanta. The last major outbreak of collective slave resistance in the Virgin Islands occurred in Saint Croix in July 1848 on the eve of legislated emancipation. Thousands of slaves from all over the island massed in front of Fort Frederiksted with the cry of freedom on their lips, and from the nervous governor they extracted the announcement they wanted. The head of this huge demonstration was "Gotlieb Bordeaux, alias General Buddoe, formerly driver on La Grange estate."[37]

The transformation of western Cuba into a plantation economy during the first half of the nineteenth century produced one of the most intense periods of collective slave resistance in the history of Latin America. East of Havana the fertile clays and rolling plains of Matanzas province boomed with coffee and sugar plantations, which consumed the lives of tens of thousands of African slaves. Here during a twenty-year period from 1825 to 1845, most of the largest slave uprisings in Cuban history occurred, and *contramayorales* figured prominently in the majority of them. The most destructive slave revolt in Cuban history erupted during the summer of 1825 in a coffee-growing district. Hundreds of slaves participated. More than twenty estates were sacked and burned; 15 whites and 43 blacks were killed; 170 slaves were wounded. The leaders of the revolt were identified as three *contramayorales,* two of whom were free persons of color.[38]

In 1844 Spanish officials in conjunction with frightened planters directed a savage repression primarily against slaves and free persons of color in response to a conspiracy uncovered in December 1843 on a sugar plantation in Matanzas province. In March and November of that same year on plantations in the same province, serious slave insurrections had broken out. Thousands of persons of color were subsequently tortured and killed during months of investigations that turned up evidence of a vast revolutionary conspiracy of people of color, rural and urban, slave and free, in Cuba's western Black Belt of sugar plantations. *Contramayorales* headed pockets of the violent unrest in 1843, and the government officials who investigated the so-called conspiracy of La Escalera saw the *contramayorales* as key players in coordinating the rising of rural slaves with that of urban coconspirators.[39]

Three large-scale slave insurrections in the British Caribbean during the nineteenth century, in Barbados (1816), Demerara (1823), and Jamaica (1831), intensified metropolitan debates about legislating a gradual end to slavery in the colonies. The revolt in Barbados embraced thousands of slaves across the island and led to the torching of about one-quarter of the island's sugar crop and the death of more than a hundred slaves. Although the slave population at this time was overwhelmingly creole, the acknowledged leader of the revolt was an African-born ranger named Bussa. He had many lieutenants. Hilary Beckles, the leading authority on the revolt, identified twenty-two of them, and of the nineteen with known occupations, all but five were drivers. Thus, he preferred to call the Barbados revolt a "slave-drivers' war."[40]

The explosion in Demerara, which involved more than ten thousand slaves, surpassed that in Barbados in size, if not in destruction. Whites blamed an agent from the London Missionary Society for stirring up trouble, and many of the leaders of the revolt had attended services at the missionary's chapel. Emilia Viotti Da Costa, in a richly contextualized analysis of the revolt, has little to say about the role of the drivers, although she noted that Richard, a runaway driver, returned to his plantation on the revolt's first day "as the leader of the most aggressive group of blacks."[41] The trial records, however, contain the extraordinary testimony of the slave Paris, eventually executed as one of the ringleaders, on how this massive uprising was led and organized. It deserves quoting at length.

> Barre the butcher carried letters from Jack to Sam, the Governor's servant in town, and to the head driver at Herstelling [plantation], who was to be the [revolt's] leader of the east side of the river; at Rome [plantation], the head driver [was the leader]; at Providence, the head driver and Mr. Blake's

cook; at Ruimveld, the head and the second drivers; at La Penitence, the head driver and the manager's cook; but the head driver at Herstelling was to be the head of the whole; on Filleen's estate, the attorney's butler; on Best, the second driver, who was also to be the leader on the west side, and to send over the whole of the Negroes from that side to take the town, which was our grand object; Colin, at Mr. Meerten's; head driver at Belle Vue; west coast, Rotterdam first and second drivers, head men of the west coast, Rotterdam first and second drivers, head men of the west coast Wakenam; Good Success, first driver; Essequibo, Annandale, first driver, who was to have passed over to Belle Plaine, with one thousand Bush negroes, and from thence to have found his way to town. Columbia, first driver and butler; Hampton Court, first driver and d[itt]o; Main Stay, first driver and head butler; Tarsus, first driver and head butler; Caledonia, first and second, drivers; Sophienberg, first driver; Hobabo Julius, Mr. Edmonstone's head driver.[42]

During the eighteenth century Jamaica experienced numerous revolts by Akan-speaking slaves, at least several of which were led by drivers. The rebellion of 1831 had few rivals in the Americas in its toll of death and destruction. It had a rural center; more than five hundred slaves either died during the conflict or were subsequently executed; perhaps as many as fifty thousand slaves were ultimately involved, and hundreds of estates were destroyed before it was extinguished. Slave drivers clearly helped to initiate the first blows in Saint James parish from where the violence spread to other western parishes. White observers commented on the salience of privileged slaves as ringleaders, especially "the head people."[43]

For reasons by now familiar to specialists, the United States and the area of mainland North America that became the United States generated slave revolts of lesser magnitude and in fewer numbers than did the Caribbean, where the balance of forces was more favorable. Without question, studies of the most famous acts of collective slave resistance, the conspiracies of Gabriel and Denmark Vesey and Nat Turner's rebellion, have strengthened the abolitionist stereotype of the slave drivers, for at best they provide, as Robert Starobin indicated, a footnote in Vesey's conspiracy and apparently were not among the leaders and soldiers of Gabriel's conspiracy and Nat Turner's rebellion.

But these three familiar cases hardly exhaust the list of slave revolts and conspiracies. The largest slave revolt in United States history erupted in lower Louisiana in 1811, a short distance upriver from New Orleans in the sugar parishes of Saint Charles and Saint John the Baptist. Eyewitnesses placed the number of rebels at between 180 to 500. These "brigands" included mulatto and black slaves, privileged slaves and field hands, native-born and African slaves. The undisputed "principal chief" of this diverse band was a mulatto slave driver named Charles Deslondes, allegedly from Saint Domingue. Another slave driver, also of mixed ancestry, served as his chief lieutenant. One African-born rebel, a Congo slave named Jupiter, who had in his possession when captured a gun, a beechwood club hardened by fire, and a bolt of linen, was interrogated about the intentions of the rebels. They were going to New Orleans, he said, "to kill whites." Asked who was going to lead him and the others, he responded, "The driver."[44]

Six years before the 1811 revolt, authorities in New Orleans detected a plot masterminded by a white Frenchman named Grand Jean to raise in rebellion people of color throughout the Mississippi Valley. A report informed the New Orleans City Council that his plan called for agents "to be sent to Natchez and other parts of the country [so that] all the Drivers of the different plantations were to be gained over."[45] The best study of slavery in colonial Louisiana has established beyond peradventure that the Pointe Coupée conspiracy of 1795, which centered in a district of tobacco and indigo plantations upriver from New Orleans, was broadly based and revolutionary in character, one of the largest acts of collective slave resistance in the history of colonial North America. The prime movers were slave drivers. As far back as 1729, the French colonists almost suffered ethnic cleansing from the lower Mississippi Valley at the hands of the Natchez Indians. Their allies included slaves recruited from French tobacco plantations with the help of slave *commandeurs*.[46]

Outside of Louisiana, slave drivers led conspiracies and revolts in several states. No historian has delved into the 1792 slave conspiracy in Virginia that preceded Gabriel's and may have exceeded his in size. One source claimed that slaves of the Eastern Shore "to the amount of about 900, assembled in different parts, armed with muskets, spears, clubs &c. and committed several outrages upon the inhabitants." The principal of these "banditti" was Celeb, a favorite slave of a Mr. Simkins who "had long lived with him in the capacity of overseer."[47] An insurrectionary plot uncovered near Savannah, Georgia, in 1806 appears to have been masterminded almost exclusively by low-country drivers. A rereading of the trial proceedings for the more famous Denmark Vesey conspiracy (1822) in conjunction with testimony from other primary sources suggests that low-country drivers around Charleston had a more important role than previously believed.[48] Evidence also exists that the Georgetown, South Carolina, conspiracy of 1829 was headed by a driver. Shortly thereafter an advocate for white overseers groused to the *Charleston Mercury* about "the complete demoralization of the negroes" in the low country. The "small planters and their property," he explained, "have fallen into the hands of black drivers, a set of men, than which there does not exist on the face of the earth any, on whom there can be placed less dependence."[49]

In support of this anonymous complainant, several recent studies of slavery in the United States have argued for an "enlarged role" for drivers in Louisiana by the beginning of Spanish rule and on low-country plantations from the time of the American Revolution to the early decades of the nineteenth century. During roughly the same period, Caribbean drivers in plantation societies with few whites and high rates of absentee masters enjoyed even greater authority, which despite spasms of bloody repression in the aftermath of slave rebellion probably continued to expand up to emancipation. After about 1830, however, the driver's role in the United States seems to have contracted, probably to expand again during the Civil War. Robert Fogel has attributed the antebellum decline in the ratio of drivers to field hands to growing white fears of abolitionist activity and slave revolt. Yet contraction, at least in some regions, led to only nominal changes, for as planter Charles Manigault of South Carolina advised his son in 1859, "It is a common thing with persons in our predicament, with a well trained and disposed gang, to get what is called a 'Key Keeper,' just to scrrene the law of having a white man on one plantation, who under written instructions will be guided by the experience of the Driver . . . as to the management of the crop."[50]

Although no great slave revolts broke out in the United States after Nat Turner's, a larger number of admittedly small-scale slave revolts and conspiracies occurred than has been commonly appreciated, and the role of enslaved foremen in some of these may yet be established.[51] In addition, slave drivers in the United States and elsewhere commanded less extreme forms of collective resistance such as protests, demonstrations, mass flights, including desertions to enemy lines during war, and work slowdowns and stoppages. Armstead Robinson, who studied the collective resistance of slaves during the United States Civil War as closely as anyone, concluded about plantation unrest that "during the war, black drivers often turned against their former masters."[52]

In light of these and many other examples that can be drawn from the history of slave rebellion in the Americas, the clichéd image of the driver as the "master's man" or as the "great villain" will not do. The point here is not to romanticize the slave driver as a perpetual rebel but to argue, given the reevaluated evidence on slave rebellion, for the vital role of the driver as an authoritative figure and community leader among slaves. A quarter century of revisionist scholarship on slavery throughout the Americas has documented the initiatives of slaves in constructing a semiautonomous world of their own, in everything from sexual practices to naming patterns. This same insight has not usually been extended to the selection of the driver. To be sure, masters elevated him into his elite position, but in many cases they did so only after the slaves themselves had advanced him as a leader. In selecting slaves who could "command respect" and motivate their fellow slaves, masters could not easily discern attributes of authority in a prospective driver without the existence first of a preestablished favorable collective judgment from the quarters. Nor could drivers, any more than their masters, rely solely on brute force to get the crop out, for brutal drivers, even more readily than brutal white overseers, could be removed by resistant slaves, who in certain cases even tried to assert the choice of foreman as a customary right.[53]

Even if a driver was imposed on the slaves, he could not easily succeed in his elite position without moving to build support from below with at least a substantial portion of his charges, with whom he was in close daily contact. Drivers won loyalty from their fellow slaves by turning a blind eye to their misdemeanors, by hunting down predatory animals that threatened the quarters, by standing up to white overseers and the dreaded patrollers, and by working and teaching. That disproportionately few runaway slaves were drivers does not deny their presence at the head of collective movements, including mass desertions, and may indicate a level of commitment on the plantation to other slaves that made them all the more attractive as community leaders during times of crisis. That drivers tended to retain a high market value well into their senior years suggests how important their agricultural skills and versatile knowledge of the productive process were in the appointments masters made. A recent study of the nineteenth-century Cuban slave market noted that whereas the average prices for prime field hands showed "year-to-year fluctuation," those for drivers had a "long-term upward trend."[54] Skills and knowledge also imparted status to the driver and his family and, when possible, were transmitted from father to son. Some masters clearly tried to keep the job of driver within the family. In the 1820s on the insular estate of Thomas Butler of South Carolina, an absentee planter, a slave named Sambo held the position of driver even though years before his father, also a driver, had led a disturbance on the estate.[55]

For gangs of predominantly African slaves, as Gabriel Debien speculated, favorable judgment might reflect previous status as warriors or royalty in

West Africa. Some African-born slaves may have even filled a position similar to the driver in their homeland.[56] Yet Debien and other scholars probably have overstated the ability of masters to use the driver and ethnic differences among slaves to divide and rule. Throughout the Americas slaving captains delivered far more homogeneous cargoes than previously believed to masters who had little control over supply. David Geggus's plantation data for Saint Domingue during the great slave revolution show that Congo and Igbo drivers were indeed conspicuous in the younger plantation zones where these African ethnicities predominated, despite negative white stereotyping that rated them considerably inferior for the job to, say, the available Fon.[57]

For largely creole slaves, favorable judgment from the quarters might mean some combination of demonstrated attributes like masculine strength, experiential knowledge, and negotiating skill. Some slaves wanted drivers who could indeed overlook, although not in the sense of the word the master intended. One wealthy Louisiana planter who lived through the slave revolt of 1811 and who knew his slaves well left for posterity this bit of wisdom: "For it is the same with the black as with the white man. Assemble together for the first time twenty or fifteen . . . men . . . and within forty-eight hours after being brought together, though strangers to each other, the great majority will place their eyes on certain men among them, for their wisdom, courage, and virtue, to whom they, unknowingly to one another, determine to look up, as leaders or chiefs, to conduct, counsel, and advise them."[58]

If the driver's predisposition proved crucial to whether slaves rebelled, his reluctance to run away or raise a revolt hardly translates into loyalty to the master. To the extent that the driver was attached to the slave community that had accepted him as a leader, he had to watch his own behavior, to appear honest and loyal to the master, when, in fact, he was neither, only careful and restrained, where any individual misstep could result in group punishment. Drivers who were able leaders of their people assessed the balance of forces against them, weighed alternatives, and projected the deadly consequences of rash acts. Like leaders everywhere, they sometimes miscalculated and led those who followed, for whatever reason, into disaster. Slave drivers certainly had their ears to the walls of the quarters, yet during the entire history of slavery in the Americas, when the number of betrayed slave plots rivaled the number of those that got off the ground, rarely did slave drivers, unlike other kinds of privileged slaves, become traitors to the cause.

When in 1831 Nat Turner and his rebel band reached the Newit Harris plantation, they found that the resident whites had already fled, but not

Aaron, the estate's driver, who stood his ground and firmly tried to halt the bloodletting. Despite death threats from Nat's followers, Aaron talked tough to them about the certainty of their defeat, for Aaron knew firsthand of the vastly superior white forces in nearby Norfolk, and with defeat, he correctly predicted that all of Southampton's slaves would suffer terrible consequences. Similarly, Solomon Northup recalled his response as a driver on a Louisiana sugar plantation when plans were being laid in 1837 by a slave named Lewis Cheney to agitate the slaves of the region: "Such an idea as insurrection . . . is not new among the enslaved population of Bayou Boeuf. More than once I have joined in serious consultation [with my fellow slaves], when the subject has been discussed, and there have been times when a word from me would have placed hundreds of my fellow-bondsmen in an attitude of defiance. Without arms or ammunition, or even with them I saw such a step would re-sult in certain defeat, disaster, and death, and always raised my voice against it."[59] This is not a voice of loyalty.

Many of the published primary sources that refer to the driver and are widely cited by historians should be handled with great care. Most of the travelers who toured the Americas and who wrote about slavery came unfa-vorably predisposed toward the driver by what they had already read in the available literature. Like television journalists who parachute into the world's trouble spots, they stayed a short time, relied on others for information, and when they deigned to venture out, they did not always understand what they saw. To an effete white outsider, a big, physical, barking driver could look in-timidating and brutal, and when he snapped the whip for all to see with what Northup himself called his "marvelous dexterity," the choreography could go undetected.

Nor did young slaves or former slaves who were children at the time of their enslavement always understand the driver's position. Forty-one vol-umes of published testimony compiled from interviews of former slaves in the United States conducted in the 1920s and 1930s by Fisk University and the Work Projects Administration contain more than two hundred references to slave agricultural foremen.[60] Slightly less than half of this number can be classified as neutral in that they speak of slave drivers or foremen but give no opinion of them. Of those that do, the negatives outweigh the positives. Some of the complaints bear an almost formulaic quality, as if the testifiers were re-peating what parents had told them, perhaps as a way to scare unruly children into discipline. Without question, the distressing image of slaves' whipping fellow slaves scarred child witnesses. But they could not be expected to distinguish punishment the driver had to inflict from punishment he only appeared to inflict or from punishment he wanted to inflict. In seeing drivers lash their fellow slaves, the young would not likely have considered the results if a white overseer had done the whipping. In societies where masters often retaliated for individual acts of resistance with socialized punishment, the driver would also have made enemies in trying to curb the headstrong from risking more than their own skin. By merely acting as an authority in the quarters, the driver would have engendered bad blood in some slaves who may have also possessed long memories.

No one can deny that some drivers scourged the weak, played favorites, and sexually abused slave women, among other crimes. But painstaking research in courthouse documents at the parish and county level in the United States and at the major repositories for colonial records in Western Europe and Latin America should serve to enhance the revised image of the driver as a frequent leader in the slave community and in slave rebellion. Brazil, in particular, remains underexplored with respect to the slave driver, although criminal records for a leading coffee region of southeastern Brazil during the mid-nineteenth century appear to show considerable conflict between white Portuguese *feitores* (overseers) and slave *capatazes*.[61]

More needs to be known about how the driver mediated relations between slaves of different statuses and origins and between rural and urban slaves, about his use of accommodation to attain the privilege, mobility, and intimacy with whites necessary to plan and raise rebellions, and about the ritualization of his status and power in the quarters. Missionaries of various faiths in the West Indies have left compelling testimony about the crucial significance of the driver's posture in their efforts at converting the mass of estate slaves. Slave drivers often wore several hats, whether as religious authorities or artisans, and few slaves had a more important role in communication, indeed, in the development of creole languages, than did the driver. No study of plantation slavery can afford to ignore how the ubiquitous driver mediated the master-slave relation, and no discussion of the impact of planter paternalism is complete without such an assessment.

One eye-opening example took place in the aftermath of John Brown's attack on Harpers Ferry, when excited whites North and South publicly buzzed about the prospects of slave rebellion in the United States. No less an exemplar of the South's master class than Edmund Ruffin decided that the urgency of the matter warranted his sending "correct information" about Brown, abolitionism, and slavery to the slaves on his Virginia plantation. One might imagine, given Ruffin's personality and his own view of the seriousness of the issues, that he would have personally summoned his slaves to gather round the veranda and forced them to submit to a gust of paternalistic admonition. Instead, Ruffin approached his slaves through his driver, Jem Sykes. Unhappily, no record of Sykes's translation to the slaves of the "correct information" has survived, but a few years later during the Civil War Sykes participated in and probably led a collective action that drove Ruffin's son-in-law from the plantation.[62]

In more than a few cases, particularly where master absenteeism was rife, drivers acquired considerable power, and white owners or administrators became utterly dependent on them, continuing to rely on them despite laws in some countries that encouraged their replacement by white overseers because of security concerns.[63] Whether in the United States or in the Caribbean, the driver led by respect as much as by fear. Although violence and attrition claimed the worst of them, the best, smartened and toughened by the adversity inherent in their middle position, cut an impressive figure. As one white descendant of a low-country rice magnate recalled about her father's driver, "Moses receiving the tablets of the law was not more impressive to me as child."[64] The history of slave resistance in the Americas indicates that large numbers of slaves may well have agreed with her.

Notes

I wish to thank the members of the St. George Tucker Society, especially Douglas Ambrose, Peter Coclanis, Stanley Engerman, Gwendolyn Midlo Hall, Rod McDonald, Leslie Rowland, and Julie Saville, for their searching criticism of the first version of this essay, which was presented at the society's 1995 annual meeting.

1. François Chevalier, ed., *Instrucciones a los hermanos jesuitas administradores de haciendas* (Mexico, 1950), 63; P. J. Laborie, *The Coffee Planter of Saint Domingo . . .* (London, 1798), 164; Thomas Roughley, *The Jamaica Planter's Guide . . .* (London, 1823), 79; Henry W. Ravenal, "Recollections of Southern Plantation Life," *Yale Review* 25 (June 1936): 760–61.

2. Robert William Fogel, *Without Consent or Contract: The Rise and Fall of American Slavery* (New York, 1989), 47.

3. Laborie, *Coffee Planter,* 164–65.

4. Aphra Behn, *Oroonoko: or, The Royal Slave. A True History* (New York, 1973), 60–61.

5. Victor Hugo, *Oeuvres completes de Victor Hugo,* 82 vols. (Paris, n.d.), 41:41. All translations are my own unless otherwise noted.

6. Harriet Beecher Stowe, *Uncle Tom's Cabin,* ed. Elizabeth Ammons (New York, 1994), 299–307, 309, 359–60.

7. William Gilmore Simms, *The Wigwam and the Cabin,* rev. ed. (New York, 1970), 363–428; "A Letter to the Editor," *The Magnolia; or Southern Monthly* 3 (Aug. 1841): 377.

8. Simms, *Wigwam and the Cabin*, 149–75, esp. 167.

9. Martin R. Delany, *Blake, or The Huts of America* (Boston, 1970), 16.

10. Ibid., 77.

11. David Walker, *Appeal, in Four Articles; Together with a Preamble, to the Coloured Citizens of the World . . .*, ed. Charles M. Wiltse (New York, 1965), 65–66.

12. See William Luis, *Literary Bondage: Slavery in Cuban Narrative* (Austin, Tex., 1990), for a general discussion of Cuban antislavery novelists.

13. Cirilo Villaverde, *Cecilia Valdés*, 2 vols. (Havana, 1984), 2:13–16, 35, 90, 95, 124.

14. Anselmo Suárez y Romero, *Francisco: El ingenio ó las delicias del campo* (Havana, 1947), esp. 61–64, 77, 82, 113.

15. Martín Morúa Delgado, *La familia Unzuazu* (Havana, 1975), 41. For biographical information, see the appendix by Nicolás Guillén, 245–65.

16. Fernando Ortiz, *Los negros esclavos*, rev. ed. (Havana, 1975), p. 208.

17. Manuel Moreno Fraginals, *El ingenio: Complejo económico social cubano del azúcar*, 3 vols. (Havana, 1978), 3:127: C. L. R. James, *The Black Jacobins: Toussaint L'Ouverture and the San Domingo Revolution*, 2d ed. (New York, 1963), 10, 19, 86, 89.

18. Elsa V. Goveia, *Slave Society in the British Leeward Islands at the End of the Eighteenth Century* (New Haven, 1965), 131.

19. Orlando Patterson, *The Sociology of Slavery: An Analysis of the Origins, Development, and Structure of Negro Slave Society in Jamaica* (1967; rept. London, 1973), 62–63.

20. W. E. B. Du Bois, *The Gift of Black Folk: The Negroes in the Making of America* (Boston, 1924); chap. 2; Carter Woodson, *The Negro in Our History*, 4th ed. (Washington, D.C., 1922), 224.

21. John Hope Franklin and Alfred A. Moss Jr., *From Slavery to Freedom: A History of African Americans*, 7th ed. (New York, 1994), 130.

22. Ulrich Bonnell Phillips, *American Negro Slavery: A Survey of the Supply, Employment, and Control of Negro Labor as Determined by the Plantation Regime* (1918; rept. Baton Rouge, La., 1966), 60–62, 272, 284, 304, 322; Phillips, *Life and Labor in the Old South* (Boston, 1929), 257, 260, 262, 290, 305, 320, 322; Charles Sackett Sydnor, *Slavery in Mississippi* (1933; rept. Gloucester, Mass., 1965), 68, 73–74.

23. Stampp, 34, 40–45, 54, 151–52, 172, 175, 335.

24. Stanley Elkins, *Slavery: A Problem in American Institutional and Intellectual Life*, 3d ed. (Chicago, 1976), 113.

25. Clement Eaton, *The Mind of the Old South*, rev. ed. (Baton Rouge, La., 1967), 175–99, esp. 183–87. See also William Kauffman Scarborough, *The Overseer: Plantation Management in the Old South* (Baton Rouge, La., 1966).

26. Robert Starobin, "Privileged Bondsmen and the Process of Accommodation: The Role of House Servants and Drivers as Seen in Their Own Letters," *Journal of Social History* 5 (Fall 1971): 46–70; Robert William Fogel and Stanley L. Engerman, *Time on the Cross: The Economics of American Negro Slavery* (Boston, 1974); Genovese, *Roll;* Leslie Howard Owens, *This Species of Property: Slave Life and Culture in the Old South* (London, 1976); Randall M. Miller, ed., *"Dear Master": Letters of a Slave Family* (Ithaca, N.Y., 1978); Miller, "The Man in the Middle: The Black Slave Driver," *American Heritage* 30 (Oct.–Nov. 1979): 40–49; William L. Van Deburg, *The Slave Drivers: Black Agricultural Labor Supervisors in the Antebellum South* (New York, 1979).

27. Fogel and Engerman, *Time on the Cross*, 212; Genovese, *Roll*, 366.

28. Starobin, "Privileged Bondsmen," 52–53.

29. Genovese, *Roll,* 378–79.

30. John Blassingame, *The Slave Community: Plantation Life in the Antebellum South* (New York, 1972), 161; Blassingame, "Status and Social Structure in the Slave Community: Evidence from New Sources," in *Perspectives and Irony in American Slavery,* ed. Harry P. Owens (Jackson, Miss., 1976), 137–52, esp. 137, 140, 151; Blassingame, *Slave Community,* 2d ed. (New York, 1979), 258–61.

31. Monica Schuler, "Ethnic Slave Rebellions in the Caribbean and the Guianas," *Journal of Social History* 4 (Summer 1970): 382.

32. Gabriel Debien, *Les esclaves aux Antilles Françaises (XVII–XVIII siècles)* (Basse-Terre, 1974), 119–33.

33. Starobin, "Privileged Bondsmen," 58.

34. Genovese, *Roll,* 387; Van Deburg, *Slave Drivers,* 165.

35. Carolyn Fick, *The Making of Haiti: The Saint Domingue Revolution from Below* (Knoxville, Tenn., 1990), 86, 91, 94.

36. J. J. Hartsinck, "The Story of the Slave Rebellion in Berbice-1762," *Journal of the British Guiana Museum and Zoo,* no. 20 (1958): 39–41, no. 21 (1959): 38–39, no. 22 (1959): 47–54.

37. Aimery P. Caron and Arnold R. Highfield, *The French in the Saint John Slave Revolt of 1733–34* (n.p., 1981), 19; Neville A. T. Hall, *Slave Society in the Danish West Indies: Saint Thomas, Saint John, and Saint Croix* (Baltimore, 1992), 74, 208–11.

38. The best study of the 1825 revolt is Israel Moliner Castañeda, "Las sublevaciones de esclavos en Matanzas," *Islas,* no. 85 (1986): 28–31.

39. Robert L. Paquette, *Sugar Is Made with Blood: The Conspiracy of La Escalera and the Conflict between Empires over Slavery in Cuba* (Middletown, Conn., 1988), 67–68, 237, 254–55.

40. Hilary Beckles, "The Slave-Drivers' War: Bussa and the 1816 Slave Rebellion," *Boletín de estudios Latinoamericanos y del Caribe* 39 (Dec. 1985): 85–109; Beckles, *Black Rebellion in Barbados: The Struggle against Slavery* (Saint Michael, Barbados, 1984), 87–120, esp. 96.

41. Emilia Viotti Da Costa, *Crowns of Glory, Tears of Blood: The Demerara Slave Rebellion of 1823* (New York, 1994), 173.

42. *Correspondence and Papers Relating to Slavery and the Abolition of the Slave Trade, 1823–24,* Irish University Press Series of British Parliamentary Papers, vol. 66 (Shannon, Ireland, 1969), 172–73.

43. B. W. Higman, *Slave Population and Economy in Jamaica, 1807–1834* (London, 1976), 227–30; Michael Mullin, *Africa in America: Slave Acculturation and Resistance in the American South and the British Caribbean, 1736–1831* (Urbana, Ill., 1992), 255–56, 375 n. 36. David Barry Gaspar's analysis of the revolutionary slave conspiracy in Antigua in 1736 provides more evidence. He has identified the occupations of nine of the ten "Main Ringleaders." Two of the nine were drivers ("The Antigua Slave Conspiracy of 1736: A Case Study of the Origins of Collective Resistance," *WMQ,* 3d ser., 35 [April 1978]:323).

44. Saint Charles Parish Original Acts, book 41, 1811, no. 2, Saint Charles Parish Court-house, Hahnville, Louisiana (microfilm in NOPL); *Moniteur de la Louisiane* (New Orleans), 17 Jan. 1811.

45. Mayor John Watkins to New Orleans City Council, 28 Sept. 1805, Messages of the Mayors, NOPL; John Watkins to Secretary Graham, 6 Sept. 1805, *The Territorial Papers of the United States,* ed. Clarence Edwin Carter, 28 vols. (Washington, D.C., 1934–69), 9:500–504.

46. Gwendolyn Midlo Hall, *Africans in Colonial Louisiana: The Development of Afro-Creole Culture in the Eighteenth Century* (Baton Rouge, La., 1992), 100–101; Daniel H. Usner Jr., *Indians, Settlers, and Slaves in a Frontier Exchange Economy: The Lower Mississippi Valley before 1783* (Chapel Hill, N.C., 1992), 66.

47. *Boston Gazette and the Country Journal*, 4 June 1792; "A Journal and Travel of James Meacham," *Historical Papers Published by the Trinity College Historical Society* (New York, 1914), 94.

48. On drivers in the Vesey conspiracy, see, e.g., pp. 15–16 of the memoirs of Samuel Wragg Ferguson of South Carolina (copy), Perkins Library, Duke University, and *The Trial Record of Denmark Vesey* (Boston, 1970), esp. 19–21. Bulkley's farm, a key rendezvous point for the rebels, "was under the charge" of Billy Bulkley, according to *An Account of the Late Intended Insurrection among a Portion of the Blacks of This City* (Charleston, S.C., 1822), 25. Billy was also a convicted conspirator. For the 1806 conspiracy in Georgia, see Robert MacKay to Eliza Anne MacKay, 29 Dec. 1806, *The Letters of Robert MacKay to His Wife . . .*, ed. Walter Charlton Hartridge (Athens, Ga., 1949), 50–51.

49. *Charleston Mercury*, 2 Oct. 1829. See also reference to the story of a slave conspiracy told by J. C. Vaughan of South Carolina to James Redpath, *The Roving Editor; or, Talks with Slaves in the Southern States* (New York, 1859), 269–73.

50. James McGowan, "Creation of a Slave Society: Louisiana Plantations in the Eighteenth Century" (Ph.D. diss., University of Rochester, 1976), 181; Philip D. Morgan, "Black Society in the Lowcountry, 1760–1810," in *Slavery and Freedom in the Age of Revolution*, ed. Ira Berlin and Ronald Hoffman (Charlottesville, Va., 1983), 118–19; Joyce E. Chaplin, "Tidal Rice Cultivation and the Problem of Slavery in South Carolina and Georgia, 1760–1815," *WMQ*, 3d ser., 49 (Jan. 1992): 55–56; Fogel, *Without Consent*, 52, 398; Charles Manigault to Louis Manigault, 3 March 1859, *Life and Labor on Argyle Island: Letters and Documents of a Savannah River Rice Plantation*, ed. James M. Clifton (Savannah, 1978), 283–84.

51. Winthrop Jordan, *Tumult and Silence at Second Creek: An Inquiry into a Civil War Slave Conspiracy* (Baton Rouge, La., 1993), has recently probed one example in Mississippi. Although evidence of the occupational status of the alleged slave conspirators is scant, at least one driver was involved, and revealingly, another was sounded out for his opinion early on and spoke caution. He did not betray the plot. Jordan does not entertain the possibility that the carriage drivers, who appear to be central to the conspiracy, also had other responsibilities on the estates.

52. Armstead Robinson, "'Worser dan Jeff Davis': The Coming of Free Labor during the Civil War, 1861–1865," in *Essays on the Postbellum Southern Economy*, ed. Thavolia Glymph et al. (College Station, Tex., 1985), 26.

53. For a Brazilian case, see Stuart Schwartz, "Resistance and Accommodation in Eighteenth-Century Brazil: The Slaves' View of Slavery," *Hispanic American Historical Review* 57 (Feb. 1977): 78.

54. Laird Bergad, Fe Iglesias García, and María del Carmen Barcia, *The Cuban Slave Market, 1790–1880* (Cambridge, 1995). I am also indebted to Gwendolyn Midlo Hall for bringing differential prices to my attention by sharing quantitative data from her massive database on Louisiana slavery. See Philip D. Morgan, *Slave Counterpoint: Black Culture in the Eighteenth-Century Chesapeake and Low Country* (Chapel Hill, N.C., 1998), 345, on the relative dearth of drivers among runaway slaves.

55. Willie Lee Rose, *Slavery and Freedom* (New York, 1982), 32–33. See also Roswell King to Thomas Butler, 20 Sept. 1835, Wister Family Papers, box 33, folder 5, HSP.

56. In the Songhay empire, e.g., years before Columbus's first voyage, slave labor culti-vated grain on large estates under slave overseers.

57. David P. Geggus, "The Slaves of British-Occupied Saint Domingue: An Analysis of the Workforces of 197 Absentee Plantations, 1796–1797," *Caribbean Studies* 18 (April–July 1978): 31–33; Geggus, "Sugar and Coffee Cultivation in Saint Domingue and the Shaping of the Slave Labor Force," in *Cultivation and Culture: Labor and the Shaping of Slave Life in the Americas,* ed. Ira Berlin and Philip D. Morgan (Charlottesville, Va., 1993), 84–88.

58. John McDonogh to the editors of the *New Orleans Commercial Bulletin,* 10 July 1842, in *Some Interesting Papers of John McDonogh . . .,* ed. James T. Edwards (McDonogh, Md., 1898), 47.

59. Solomon Northup, *Twelve Years a Slave,* ed. Sue Eakin and Joseph Logsdon (Baton Rouge, La., 1968), 190. For the Nat Turner episode, see William Sidney Drewry, *Slave Insur-rections in Virginia (1830–1865)* (Washington, D.C., 1900), 54, although Drewry lauds Aaron's actions as loyalty to his master.

60. In addition to vols. 2–7, ser. 1, vols. 8–18, ser. 2, vols. 1–12, supplement, ser. 1, and vols. 1–10, supplement, ser. 2, of George Rawick, ed., *The American Slave: A Composite Autobiog-raphy* (Westport, Conn., 1972–79), I have used the narratives in Ronnie Clayton, ed., *Mas-ter Wit: The Ex-Slave Narrative of the Louisiana Writers' Project* (New York, 1990), and Charles L. Perdue Jr. et al., *Weevils in the Wheat: Interviews with Virginia Ex-Slaves* (Char-lottesville, Va., 1992).

61. Bryan Daniel McCann, "The Whip and the Watch: Overseers in the Paraíba Valley, Brazil," *Slavery and Abolition* 18 (Aug. 1997): 33.

62. William Kauffman Scarborough, ed., *The Diary of Edmund Ruffin,* 3 vols. (Baton Rouge, La., 1972–89), 1:391, 2:367. For another revealing example, from South Carolina in 1767, see Robert Olwell, *Masters, Slaves, and Subjects: The Culture Power in the South Car-olina Low Country, 1740–1790* (Ithaca, N.Y., 1998), 213–14.

63. Fogel, *Without Consent,* 43–44, makes a connection between increasing white plan-tation management and security concerns about the driver in the United States. In Cuba, after the conspiracy of La Escalera, see Rafael Mariscal del Hoyo to the Governor of Matanzas, 5 Nov. 1844, Matanzas Provincial Archive, Fondo Gobierno Provincial, Esclavos, legajo 23 (I am indebted to Sonia Labrador for a transcription of this document). For Suri-nam after a revolt of 1750, see the *London Magazine; or, Gentleman's Monthly Intelligencer* 19 (1750): 287.

64. Leonora Sneed, "Types of Rice Plantation Negroes," *Southern Workman* 32 (Feb. 1903): 109.

3

How the Low Country Was Taken to Task: Slave-Labor Organization in Coastal South Carolina and Georgia

PETER A. COCLANIS

THE GREAT South Carolina planter-sportsman William Elliott loved Cheeha more than any place else on earth. Located roughly forty miles southwest of Charleston, Cheeha was a low, swampy neck of land between the Ashley and Combahee rivers, a place that Elliott, renowned author of *Carolina Sports by Land and Water,* considered "the best hunting-ground" in the state.[1]

Elliott was also an absentee planter at Cheeha, but his passion for the area clearly owed more to white-tailed deer than to white or golden rice. As Theodore Rosengarten has recently pointed out, Elliott makes four separate trips to Cheeha in *Carolina Sports* but in so doing spends only two hours at his rice plantation there, and even then only rather grudgingly.[2] Nonetheless, one can gain important insights into low-country agriculture from Elliott's 1846 volume. Indeed, the well-educated and highly cultivated author, a man who refers to himself as Piscator and Venator in the book, might well have added Agricola—a pseudonym he used elsewhere.[3]

Not that Elliott goes on at length in *Carolina Sports* about matters agronomic. Moreover, when he does talk about agriculture, he does so rather whimsically, suggesting a certain casualness, if not insouciance. To be sure, much of this is artifice. Yet even after allowing for genre conventions and authorial self-fashioning, it is clear that Elliott illuminates much about the planter's world, whether intentionally or not.

In a chapter entitled "A Business Day at Chee-Ha," Elliott, who claims his motto is "Business before pleasure," makes a rare visit to his plantation to inspect his crops.[4] He arrives at the end of October, when the fetid swamplands at Cheeha are less dangerous to human health; even so, Elliott remarks that his overseer "crawled forth" to greet him, "pale and . . . feeble" with malaria.[5]

Elliott is in a hurry to hunt, but as this visit to Cheeha is his first of the year, he knows that he is obliged to look over his plantation operations. He rides quickly through his cornfield but, finding "that the grain had been gathered," asks, perhaps rhetorically, "Why should I pause to observe it narrowly?" and moves on. A bit later, while riding toward his cotton field, he decides that because "it lies out of [his] way, a distant coup d'oeil must serve" until such time that he can "examine it closely." Better to head home.[6]

Arriving back at the plantation yard, Elliott dismounts from his steed and climbs up into his rice-winnowing house; there his interrogation of his slave driver about the year's rice crop segues neatly into managerial meditation.

"Have you threshed out a rick?"
"Yes, sir," says the driver.
"What was the yield to the acre?"
"Sixty bushels sir."
"Was it your best rick?"
"N-o, sir."
"Mixed you any of the straw rice with this rick?"
"Y-es, sir, a lettle; but you kin see, maussa!"
and the driver brought me a sheaf from a rick hard by—thick, full-grained, heavy; a magnificent sample (if true sample it was) of a crop which was to reward my expectation. Alas, Venator! thou knewest not that the rick was *plated*, or rather *gilt;* and that while the outward and tangible sheaf was of such satisfactory quality, the light, and the mow-burnt, and the bird-pecked was safely bestowed, far from the reach of inquisitive eyes, in the very centre of those proud looking ricks! How like a honeymoon in the planter's life are the first brief visits of the fall, to the long deserted plantations! All then is bright and full of glorious promise; but winter comes, and at its close—the hours of disenchantment![7]

Then, after a rather awkward—and potentially confrontational—encounter with some of his slaves, Elliott hurries off his plantation to join his hunting group. "It is wonderful," Elliott observes in the chapter, "how we stride over the field of business, when we have hitched to the fence beyond, some favorite hobby which we are impatient to mount and ride!" Indeed.[8]

Now Elliott was obviously trying to be funny in this chapter, and in many ways he succeeded. He was, of course, more serious about planting than he allows in "A Business Day at Chee-Ha," writing knowledgeably on agriculture throughout the antebellum period and bringing in large crops of rice and Sea

Island cotton on a regular basis. According to some scholars, in fact, *Carolina Sports by Land and Water* was intended at least in part as a thinly veiled critique of the desultory practices of other low-country planters.[9] "A Business Day at Chee-Ha" is indispensable for our purposes in any case. In capturing certain raw, spare truths about the low country in slavery times—the highly mortal disease environment, the striking levels of planter absenteeism and inattention, and perhaps most importantly, the centrality of bound African-American labor—it affords a splendid opportunity to employ some relatively new analytical concepts from microeconomics to help reinterpret the low country's agricultural history, dare I say, from the ground up.[10]

To start at ground level in a place like the low country means to start with labor, largely black slave labor, organized for the most part by task rather than in gangs. It is difficult, in fact, to overstate the importance to the low country of tasked labor and the social patterns arising therefrom. Indeed, the so-called task system, which was far less common than the gang system, is frequently considered not merely the "central feature of lowcountry slave life" but the principal reason why slavery in the low country of South Carolina and Georgia seemed so different from slavery in other parts of the South.[11] The tendency of scholars (including this author) to "exoticize" the low country at times seems related, albeit in indirect ways, to the task system as well. For the system seemed to promote greater cultural autonomy and independence among an enslaved majority with non-European historical, if not necessarily genealogical, roots.

Under the task system, of course, a slave was responsible for a set amount of work—a certain number of tasks, as it were—upon the completion of which that slave was "free" to do as he or she so chose. Although some masters expected their slaves to produce part or all of their provisions during their "free" time, many slaves clearly were able to allocate part of their workdays or workweeks to labor for themselves.[12] Compared to the so-called gang system, the principal form of slave-labor organization, the task system allowed those working under it more physical and psychological "space," which at a minimum meant less direct or at least less immediate monitoring and supervision and a greater degree of control over work pace, rhythms, and routines. To be sure, in both the gang and task systems slaves were expected to work hard, but it is probably true that agricultural units organized under the gang system more closely resembled factories in the fields, and everything that this nineteenth-century metaphor connoted.

A word of caution should be sounded here, however, for it is both easy and tempting to idealize or reify the task and gang systems of slave-labor organization and to view these systems as not merely antipodal but quite possibly antithetical. In reality, the systems proved both more complex and indistinct than usually depicted. The systems, moreover, were sometimes combined, and hybrid organizational forms emerged as a result.[13] Still, the terms *task* and *gang*, however reduced and stylized, serve certain analytical purposes and are retained because the concern here is less with variation than with pattern, less with individual cases than with generalization. This concern leads logically to a consideration of the temporal, spatial, and occupational dimensions of these labor systems. More specifically, what accounts for the employment of one or the other system at certain times and in particular geographical areas or economic activities?

Obviously, one can find some examples of each of these labor systems wherever slavery existed and in virtually all economic activities in which slaves were involved. In several important articles Philip D. Morgan, for example, has documented the existence of tasking not only across the United States South but in both the Caribbean Basin and Brazil as well. Moreover, according to Morgan and others, the task system was sufficiently versatile and adaptable to be used in such diverse agricultural activities as coffee, sugar, hemp, and pimento cultivation, as well as in so-called forest industries such as timbering and naval-stores production.[14] In addition, a number of scholars, Charles B. Dew most recently, have demonstrated that the task system was employed at times in southern manufacturing establishments, and references to the task system can be found for still other activities including "grass picking" and even weaving and spinning.[15]

On the whole, these efforts have sharpened scholarly understanding of slave-labor organization, but in searching hither and yon for each and every reference to tasking—an exercise somewhat akin to "listing" in the world of bird watching—scholars may lose sight of the fact that the task system informed the economy of only one important region in the Western Hemisphere, the South Carolina–Georgia low country.[16] Elsewhere, the role of the task system was more limited. It was employed, for example, on a part-time basis in the production of minor staples and nonstaples and in marginal parts of the "extended Caribbean." The role of tasking in the Jamaican coffee industry and the Bahamian timber industry are cases in point. Moreover, because of ameliorationist sentiment or changing technology, or both, use of the task system sometimes became common even in major staples during the last years of slavery. For instance, the task system emerged in the 1820s and

1830s in the sugar colonies of Demerara, Essequibo, Berbice, and Martinique and in the 1840s in the cotton state of Mississippi.[17]

Nonetheless, the gang system—closely monitored labor in groups over set periods of time (sunup to sundown)—prevailed in most places and in the most important economic activities most of the time.[18] In light of this fact, one question immediately springs to mind: Why was the low country, in a manner of speaking, taken to task? Both contemporary observers and latter-day scholars have weighed in on this question; and out of a welter of explanations, three or four more or less distinct lines of argumentation can be discerned. According to one, often associated with U. B. Phillips, climate generally and malaria specifically were responsible. An inhospitable disease environment, that is to say, compelled low-country planters—the originators of the task system in this view—to impose a form of labor control that would at once allow for relatively regular and committed work on the part of unskilled slaves and relatively regular bouts of absenteeism on the part of planters.[19]

A second interpretive line, advanced most recently by Philip D. Morgan, attributes the task system's origins in the low country primarily to the technical requirements of rice cultivation. In this view, because rice "was a hardy plant, requiring a few relatively straightforward operations for . . . successful cultivation," and because in rice production the laborers' work efforts were subject to "inexpensive and efficient measurement," conditions were conducive for the emergence of the task system. If several other factors played some part, it was, according to Morgan, the "staple-crop requirements" associated with rice that, by minimizing the need for close managerial supervision, permitted the establishment of a labor regimen predicated largely on the self-paced performance of discrete, readily measurable tasks.[20]

To be sure, Morgan attributes the terms of the system, once established, in large part to the bargaining strategies employed by enslaved African Americans. Nonetheless, he tends to downplay the role of African Americans, let alone Africans, in the genesis of the system, unlike scholars such as Ira Berlin and, especially, Judith Carney.[21] To these scholars, the transfer of African agricultural technology was central not just to the several rice-cropping regimes that developed over time in the low country but to the establishment of the region's system of labor organization as well. Carney makes the fullest case regarding the latter point. After documenting the fact that the task system "was already a pervasive feature of African slavery along the Upper Guinea coast and its hinterland during the Atlantic Slave Trade," she concludes that this system, like other West African knowledge relating to risiculture, probably survived the Middle Passage and was, thus, available for and, in fact, deployed in the low-country rice industry.[22] In this Afro-centered view, then, the principal role of Europeans is to appropriate rather than to initiate a venerable and potentially profitable technology.

A final interpretive line remains to be discussed. Mounting an argument similar to but more theoretically rigorous than that of Morgan, the economist Jacob Metzer contends that the task system owed its origins to the efforts of planters to practice "precise and scientific management" wherever possible when "handling work routines and organizing field work." Given the "technical requirements" of rice cultivation—Metzer describes these requirements in basically the same way as Morgan—economically rational planters, operating with perfect information, are said to have turned, virtually homeostatically, to the incentive-laden task system in order at once to enhance efficiency, reduce shirking, and lessen their supervisory loads.[23] Clearly, complicated questions such as the origins of the task system do not pose much of a problem in the neat and tidy Walrasian world inhabited by Professor Metzer, if not by the rice planters of the low country.

Here, then, are the most important and influential explanations for the origins of the task system. Each of these explanations is the result of first-rate scholarship, yet each is incomplete in my view. One can, however, use the many insights contained in these four frameworks to construct a richer, denser, and more interpretively satisfying framework of our own. Some recent developments in microeconomics, particularly in the economics of information, can show us how.

That ideas have consequences is by now a truism. Just as paranoiacs sometimes do have enemies, however, even truisms can be revealing. Indeed, the contention here is that the most fruitful way to understand the role of the task system in the low country is through a set of ideas developed by economists over the past twenty-five years. These ideas, all of which are related in one way or another to the economics of information, offer us an elegant, even parsimonious way to reconcile hitherto unreconcilable scholarly points of view.

Until relatively recently almost all mainstream economists in the West, economists working, that is to say, from a conventional, neoclassical perspective, held to a rigorous set of assumptions about economic life. These assumptions are often associated in their purest and most insistent form with the French economist Léon Walras. Walras, one of the cofounders in the late nineteenth century of neoclassicism, is frequently disparaged today, somewhat unfairly, for his seemingly reductionistic assumptions that markets were "freely competitive," functioning almost as "organized auctions"; that they were unbounded and thus unaffected by space or time; and that the participants in markets were maximizers with both constant preferences and, more importantly for our purposes, perfect information.[24]

However useful and even necessary such assumptions are—general equilibrium as a theory and comparative statics as an analytical strategy are predicated in large part on these assumptions—both economists and economic historians have long known that they were quite unrealistic. Some of the problems with these assumptions were, in fact, pointed out early on, even in Walras's lifetime. Irving Fisher's suggestion in the 1890s that Walras had failed to consider time in his analysis is a case in point. Other problems, most notably those growing out of the assumption that markets are "freely competitive," have been targeted by economists through much of the twentieth century.[25]

That the Walrasian system was able to withstand such scholarly onslaughts was due in large part to the efforts of future Nobelist Kenneth Arrow. Indeed, Arrow's collaborative work forty-odd years ago with another future Nobelist, Gerard Debreu, work encapsulated in the so-called Arrow-Debreu or A-D model of competitive equilibrium, revivified the Walrasian approach and appeared for a time to settle residual questions about the original formulation. Ultimately, however, the clarity of the A-D model allowed critics to discover its own weaknesses and limitations, including its unrealistic assumptions about perfect information.[26]

Ironically, among the most effective of such critics was Arrow himself, who, along with James Mirrlees, George Akerlof, Stephen Ross, Joseph Stiglitz, and others, helped to weaken or, more precisely, to relax the rigid information assumptions of the Walrasian and A-D approaches.[27] In so doing, they introduced the concept of information asymmetry to economics, the implications of which have transformed research in the microeconomics field. Questions growing out of the recognition of information asymmetry—adverse selection, moral hazard, agency, and the like—are today considered among the most interesting in all of economics.[28] One of these questions, that referred to as the agency question, appears crucial to any satisfactory explanation of the role of the task system in the low country.

The agency question, however late-breaking in academic circles, is pervasive in economic life and has been recognized, if only casually, as far back as the eighteenth century.[29] In formal terms the question arises in situations involving two individuals, wherein the action or actions of one, designated the agent, affect not only his well-being, interest, or both, but that of another, designated the principal. In agency situations the principal, speaking formally again, possesses the power to prescribe the reward structure or compensation system to which the agent will be subject. The trick from the principal's perspective is to design a structure or system that will induce the agent to act in the principal's interest. The problem, again from the principal's viewpoint, is that in many real-world situations the principal lacks knowledge or, in other words, possesses imperfect information about what action the agent should undertake or has undertaken. The problem becomes more complicated—and more interesting—in agency situations characterized by pronounced information asymmetry between principal and agent, particularly when the latter possesses vital technical or specialized knowledge not available to the former.[30]

These problems of incomplete and asymmetrical information are embodied in principal-agent situations referred to in the literature as hidden action or moral hazard cases and as hidden information or adverse selection cases. In the former, some action on the part of the agent—typically effort—is of concern to the principal, who, for one reason or another, cannot completely monitor it. The principal's problem in this situation is to design a compensation system that will motivate an incompletely monitored agent to act in the principal's behalf. The principal's problem, alas, is exacerbated by the fact that even in cases when the agent's actions can be completely monitored, the final outcome or output may not be attributable to those actions alone, but to those actions in conjunction with some unobservable random variable or variables.[31]

In hidden information or adverse selection situations, other problems come to the fore. In such situations the principal lacks information important to his well-being or interest, and the principal knows the agent has it. The principal's problem here is somehow to motivate the agent to use such information in the principal's behalf, even though both the principal and agent know that the former is unable completely to judge whether the latter's actions, presumably based on such information, were appropriate.[32]

Now what does all of this have to do with the task system of slave-labor organization in the low country? Everything, I submit, for the insights and implications of the theoretical concerns outlined above—and, perhaps, only these insights and implications—can square the circle, as it were, and allow us to reconcile explanations of the task system emphasizing climate and disease, staple-crop requirements, African knowledge, and European managerial expertise.[33] That we hereinafter focus on agency—agency as explanatory theory rather than cri de coeur, expiatory ideology, or ex post rationalization—is an irony that, given the times, cannot be allowed to pass.[34]

In any case, in simple, stylized form, an agency interpretation of the role of the task system in the low country would go something like this: The key to the low-country economy, from the early eighteenth century on, was rice, and the central problem for the rice planters (the principals from this perspective) was to devise compensation systems (positive or negative incentives, or both) that would motivate individuals (bondmen and later freedmen) possessed with what economists call private information (about rice planting) to act in the principals' behalf.[35] This problem was rendered more difficult than might first appear not only because the planters often lacked specific, detailed knowledge about the "mysteries of the art" of rice planting but also because the unhealthy situation of the rice swamps and the pleasures of Charleston and, later, Savannah meant that their supervisory and opportunity costs were extremely high.

Over time planters found in the task system an integrated solution to this complex and multilayered problem. Whatever the prototype for tasked labor in the low country—Carney makes a good case, for example, that similar regimes existed in rice zones of West Africa during the early modern period—the system took hold or rather was allowed to take hold in the area because it seemed to economically rational planters to offer the best available solution to the difficulties arising from information asymmetry and high supervisory and opportunity costs.[36] That is to say, the employment of a compensation system with positive incentives in the form of self-regulation and free time and negative incentives in the form of the lash was in their view both necessary and sufficient to induce slave laborers in the low country to share their private information about rice planting and, while working, largely to monitor themselves.[37]

We can at once develop and historicize this argument by thinking a bit more about the process of technological transfer. Because transferring technology is generally a difficult and halting affair, it is likely that the hidden information (adverse selection) dimensions of the agency problem in the low country proved more acute in the eighteenth century than in the nineteenth century. It seems clear, that is to say, that for at least a good portion of the eighteenth century African and African-American laborers possessed private information about risiculture unavailable or only partially available to Europeans and Euro-Americans. Once such information was transferred to or appropriated by the latter groups, the agency problems posed by adverse selection considerations likely proved less compelling.

Agency problems resulting from hidden action or moral hazard situations, however, would not necessarily diminish in severity over time. Indeed, it is possible to argue that the supervisory and opportunity costs of monitoring slaves' behavior in the rice swamps rose as time passed, with the advent of tidal cultivation and, perhaps equally important, the elaboration and consolidation of cultural life in Charleston and Savannah.

To be sure, the task system, once in place, developed in ways not altogether to the liking of those responsible for its emplacement. Custom, as John Stuart Mill pointed out long ago, is the protector of the weak against the strong in agriculture, and over time customary practices sometimes were transformed through bargaining and negotiation into what might be called de facto or quasi rights.[38] As a result, moreover, the system gradually was carried over into other activities such as the production of long-staple cotton, where the economic rationale for tasking, at least in the low country, was less compelling.[39] In the last analysis, however, the prominence of the task system in the area was due to, first and foremost, the planters of rice.

According to some, of course, the agency approach, by its very nature, tends to privilege principals. In this case, though, I believe that such priority is justifiable on both theoretical and empirical grounds. Let us examine the theoretical case first.

Here, too, we must begin by reiterating the point that in recent years the economics profession has moved away from the assumption of perfectly competitive markets. As a result, few economists at this late date still subscribe to the Wicksellian notion, predicated on this assumption, that the employer-employee relationship could just as easily be described as one in which labor "hires" capital as vice versa.[40] Indeed, one of Marx's enduring contributions to economics was to call attention early on to the social embeddedness of exchange, that is to say, to the way in which exchange, "a relation between two wills," was structured by power.[41] This insight is extremely useful when studying labor exchanges between masters and slaves, for in such exchanges the priority—and power—of the former was formally encoded in law. Master-slave exchanges, in fact, would seem to be extreme forms of the "contested" exchanges analyzed recently by Samuel Bowles and Herbert Gintis.[42] In contested exchanges the parties involved therein have unequal access to what Bowles and Gintis call exogenous claim enforcement—comprehensive third-party (usually state) regulation of contracts—and the parties are perforce subject to "endogenous claim enforcement" mechanisms designed and controlled by the strongest party. Bowles and Gintis go on to apply their theory of endogenous claim enforcement to agency situations similar in many ways to that discussed here.[43] In such cases it seems clear that principals are, well, principal.

On the empirical level, too, there is strong support for an agency approach to the task system. Indeed, as suggested earlier, this approach can at once accommodate the findings of the other interpretations and plausibly answer questions left unanswered by scholars espousing alternative points of view. For example, although interpretations emphasizing alleged "technical requirements" of rice production are insightful—rice, ceteris paribus, is probably more conducive to tasking than, let us say, sugar—such interpretations fail to consider the vast differences in rice production techniques around the world, their varying levels of labor intensity, and the differential monitoring costs involved with each.[44] More to the point, they do not explain the failure of the task system of slave-labor organization to take hold in the commercial rice industry that grew up along the lower Mississippi in the antebellum period.[45] Could it be that the alleged "requirements" of rice production kicked in only in the presence of other factors specific, at least for a certain period of time, to the low country?

Moreover, although climate and disease are obviously important considerations in the history of the low country, the gang system rather than the task system was the dominant form of slave-labor organization in other parts of the Americas with equally arduous climates and disease environments. Perhaps the task system was not predicated solely on climate and disease, as some would have us believe. Still other interpretive problems remain. Approaches emphasizing African traditions or African-American labor bargaining, or both, fail to appreciate the implications of the fact that white planters held a near monopoly on state-sanctioned violence in the low country and were, thus, unlikely to respect any traditions inimical to their interests or to be consistently outwitted or outbargained by an outgunned and, apparently, divided slave labor force.[46]

None of this is to suggest, however, that the task system should be attributed to white managerial prowess alone. Despite some concern for organization and method, and occasionally even for time and motion, it would be a stretch to imply, as some do, that planters preternaturally introduced Taylorism to the ricefields.[47] What planters did do was to appropriate some knowledge, to which they added insights of their own, in establishing and le-gitimating a compensation system that allowed them to produce great quan-tities of rice with slave labor in a sickly climate, while minimizing their own supervisory and opportunity costs. They did as principals do, in other words.

The principal role of planters and, indeed, the planters' role as principals are suggested, finally, by the word *task* itself. According to the *Oxford English Dictionary*, the word derives from the Latin infinitive *taxare*—to rate, esti-mate, or value—and in medieval Latin the word came to mean to impose or exact a tax. Imposition and exaction have been associated with the word ever since, though over time the connotation has shifted from fiscal assessments to labor requirements, particularly requirements of a heavy or burdensome na-ture. "Alas poore Duke," Shakespeare writes in *Richard II*, "the taske he under-takes is numbring sands, and drinking Oceans drie." Three-quarters of a century later, Milton's Samson "grind[s] in brazen fetters under task," and in the mid-eighteenth century Samuel Johnson defined *task* tersely as "some-thing to be done imposed by another."[48]

From early on, the *OED* states, *task-work* denoted "forced labour; hence oppressive or burdensome work." Matthew Arnold captures this sense of bur-den well in his 1852 poem "A Summer Night":

> For most men in a brazen prison live,
> Where, in the sun's hot eye,
> With head bent o'er their toil, they languidly
> Their lives to some unmeaning taskwork give,
> Dreaming of naught beyond their prison-wall.[49]

With these images in mind, it is perhaps not surprising that a *taskmaster*, per-force, is "one who allots a duty, or imposes a heavy burden or labour." In the age of cultural studies, alas, it is probably de rigueur at this point to make a nod in that direction, too. Thus, it should be noted in closing that Kevin Sul-livan, who was one of the meanest and cruelest actors-grapplers in Ted Turner's World Championship Wrestling (WCW) stable, competed under the name "Taskmaster."[50] According to knowledgeable industry sources, he has also been the principal scriptwriter and choreographer for WCW bouts, fur-ther evidence, perhaps, that a task is a burden imposed.

The South Carolinian taskmaster William Elliott carried on an extensive correspondence throughout his adult life. Many of his letters are still extant, mainly in the Elliott-Gonzales Papers in the Southern Historical Collection at the University of North Carolina, Chapel Hill. In reading through this correspondence, one is struck by the many tensions in Elliott's life: between business and pleasure, between friends and family, and between travel and his beloved low country.

Such tensions are apparent in his career as a planter, too. He was avidly interested in and knowledgeable about rice and cotton cultivation but often complained that he lacked sufficient information to act decisively while his crops were in the ground. He claims to have loved the planting life but conceded that he lacked "the patience . . . to deal with mules & their partners the niggers" and was convinced that it was "unsafe to breathe the malarious air of a rice plantation in July." He distrusted his slaves, but knew he needed their expertise, and tried "to stimulate them by rewards."[51]

However well such stimulation may have succeeded in the rice and cotton fields, it seems to have bred little more than contingent loyalty. In August 1862, after the collapse of Confederate power in the Beaufort District, all of the prime hands on Elliott's Oak Lawn plantation "up and left," absconding en masse to the Yankees. Although they were ultimately caught and forced to return to Oak Lawn, it seems clear that what they were doing in a sense—a narrow economistic sense, to be sure—was attempting to reject one principal and one compensation package for others yet unknown.[52]

Notes

Earlier versions of this chapter were presented in 1997 at the Triangle Economic History Workshop, National Humanities Center, Research Triangle Park, N.C.; the Johns Hopkins University, Baltimore; and the St. George Tucker Society, Atlanta. I would like to thank those in attendance at each of these talks for their helpful criticism. In particular, I wish to acknowledge the suggestions offered by Robert E. Gallman, Lee Craig, Dean Lueck, Philip D. Curtin, Louis Galambos, Douglas Ambrose, David Moltke-Hansen, William K. Scarborough, and Mark Smith. I would also like to thank Robert L. Paquette and Louis Ferleger for their editorial assistance.

1. William Elliott, *Carolina Sports by Land and Water*, introd. Theodore Rosengarten (1846; Columbia, S.C., 1994), 152. On Cheeha, see Suzanne Cameron Linder, *Historical Atlas of the ACE River Basin, 1860* (Columbia, S.C., 1995), 111–22. Note that Elliott's holdings at Cheeha during the antebellum period actually consisted of four individual plantations—Bluff, Middle Place, Smilies, and Social Hall—each with a distinct land history.

2. Elliot, *Carolina Sports*, x. See also Linder, *Historical Atlas*, 112–17.

3. Elliot, *Carolina Sports*. Note that Elliott used the pseudonym "Agricola" for essays on agriculture as well as for essays on politics. For an example of the former, see Agricola [William Elliott], "Observations on the Present Condition of the Southern States," *Southern Agriculturist* 7 (June 1834): 287–93; for an example of the latter, see Agricola [William Elliott], *Southern Standard* (Charleston), 12 July 1851.

4. Elliott, *Carolina Sports*, 173–91 (quotation on 174). Note that this chapter originally was published as a sketch in the *Southern Literary Journal*, n.s., 3 (May 1838): 354–63.

5. Elliott, *Carolina Sports*, 176.

6. Ibid., 175.

7. Ibid., 178. Postcolonial literary scholars have recently called attention to some of the problems arising when subaltern groups are viewed through "imperial eyes." See, for example, Mary Louise Pratt, *Imperial Eyes: Travel Writing and Transculturation* (London, 1992). One can see some of these problems in *Carolina Sports*. In this work Elliott calls plantations "deserted" whenever he is absent from them; moreover, the slaves present on his hunting and fishing trips are largely invisible in his accounts of such trips.

8. Elliott, *Carolina Sports*, 175–81 (quotation on 175–76).

9. On Elliott as a planter, see ibid., ix–xliii; Lewis P. Jones, "Carolinians and Cubans: The Elliotts and Gonzales, Their Work and Their Writings" (Ph.D. diss., University of North Carolina, 1952), 16–29; Jones, "William Elliott, South Carolina Nonconformist," *Journal of Southern History* 17 (Aug. 1951): 361–81; Linder, *Historical Atlas*, 112–17. Note that according to the 1850 census Elliott "produced" over 200,000 pounds of (rough) rice on two of his Cheeha plantations alone in 1849 (MS returns, Seventh Census of the United States, 1850, Agriculture, Colleton District, St. Bartholomew's Parish, returns for William Elliott, Cheeha, SCDAH). In personal communications David Moltke-Hansen has suggested to me that in *Carolina Sports* Elliott may, in fact, have been engaging primarily in social commentary and criticism.

10. That there was widespread absenteeism among low-country rice planters, particularly those practicing tidal cultivation, is well known. See, for example, Frederick Dalcho, *An Historical Account of the Protestant Episcopal Church in South Carolina* (Charleston, S.C., 1820), vi; Basil Hall, *Travels in North America in the Years 1827 and 1828*, 3 vols. (Edinburgh, 1829), 3:188. For a broader view, see Lawrence Fay Brewster, *Summer Migrations and Resorts of South Carolina Low-Country Planters*, Historical Papers of the Trinity College Historical Society, ser. 26 (Durham, N.C., 1947), esp. 3–9, 109–22. For a recent demonstration and discussion of planter absenteeism in South Carolina and Georgia, see William Dusinberre, *Them Dark Days: Slavery in the American Rice Swamps* (New York, 1996), 78, 150 n. 90, 204, 215, 310–12. On Elliott's absenteeism, see *Carolina Sports*, xxi–xxvi; Beverly Scafidel, "The Letters of William Elliott" (Ph.D. diss., University of South Carolina, 1978).

11. Philip D. Morgan, "Work and Culture: The Task System and the World of Lowcountry Blacks, 1700–1880," *WMQ*, 3d ser., 39 (Oct. 1982): 563–99 (quotation on 564).

12. On the basic contours of the task system, see, for example, Lewis C. Gray, *History of Agriculture in the Southern United States to 1860*, 2 vols. (1933; rept. Gloucester, Mass., 1958), 1:550–56; Stampp, 54–56; Morgan, "Work and Culture"; Morgan, "Task System," in *Dictionary of Afro-American Slavery*, ed. Randall M. Miller and John David Smith (Westport, Conn., 1988), 715–16. Note that some scholars, most notably Michael Mullin, believe that the degree of "independence" achieved by low-country slaves may be overstated. See Mullin, *Africa in America: Slave Acculturation and Resistance in the American South and the British Caribbean, 1736–1831* (Urbana, Ill. 1992), 126–58.

13. Gray, *History of Agriculture* 1:550–56, Morgan, "Task and Gang Systems: The Organization of Labor on New World Plantations," in *Work and Labor in Early America*, ed. Stephen Innes (Chapel Hill, N.C., 1988), 189–220, esp. 190–202.

14. Morgan, "Work and Culture," 568–69; Morgan, "Task and Gang Systems," 190–211. See also B. W. Higman, *Slave Population and Economy in Jamaica, 1807–1834* (London,

1976), 21–25; Higman, *Slave Populations of the British Caribbean, 1807–1834* (Baltimore, 1984), 164–68, 179–88, Robert B. Outland III, "Slavery, Work, and the Geography of the North Carolina Naval Stores Industry, 1835–1860," *Journal of Southern History* 62 (Feb. 1996): 27–56.

15. See Charles B. Dew, *Bond of Iron: Master and Slave at Buffalo Forge* (New York, 1994), 108–21 and passim; Gray, *History of Agriculture* 1:551–52, 554; Elisha Cain to Mary Telfair, 20 Nov. 1836, Telfair Family Papers, Georgia Historical Society, Savannah. On the use of the task system in the cultivation of such crops as corn, groundnuts, and oats in the low country, see Walter Peyre Plantation Journal, 1812–1851, 332, SCHS.

16. See Mullin, *Africa in America*, 126–58; Peter A. Coclanis, "Slavery, African-American Agency, and the World We Have Lost," *Georgia Historical Quarterly* 79 (Winter 1995): 873–84.

17. Higman, *Slave Populations of the British Caribbean, 1807–1834*, 179; J. R. Ward, *British West Indian Slavery, 1750–1834: The Process of Amelioration* (Oxford, 1988), 8, 14–18, 61–118; Morgan, "Task and Gang Systems," 190–211; Emilia Viotti da Costa, *Crowns of Glory, Tears of Blood: The Demerara Slave Rebellion of 1823* (New York, 1994), 61–63, 79–80; Dale Tomich, "Une Petite Guinée: Provision Ground and Plantation in Martinique, 1830–1848," in *The Slaves' Economy: Independent Production by Slaves in the Americas*, ed. Ira Berlin and Philip D. Morgan (London, 1991), 68–91. By the early nineteenth century, aspects of the task system apparently had emerged in the sugar industry of northeast Brazil as well. See Stuart B. Schwartz, *Slaves, Peasants, and Rebels: Reconsidering Brazilian Slavery* (Urbana, Ill., 1992), 39–59. As for cotton, note that John Hebron Moore argues that in Mississippi, beginning in the 1840s, mechanization of some aspects of cotton cultivation led to use of a modified form of the task system in that crop too. See Moore, *The Emergence of the Cotton Kingdom in the Old Southwest: Mississippi, 1770–1860* (Baton Rouge, La., 1988), 95–98.

18. On the gang system, see Gray, *History of Agriculture* 1:550–57; Stampp, 54–56; Charles P. Roland, "Gang System," in Miller and Smith, *Dictionary of Afro-American Slavery*, 283–84.

19. Ulrich B. Phillips, "The Slave Labor Problem in the Charleston District," *Political Science Quarterly* 22 (Sept. 1907): 416–39, esp. 417–18. For a modern restatement of this position, see Julia Floyd Smith, *Slavery and Rice Culture in Low Country Georgia, 1750–1860* (Knoxville, Tenn., 1985), 50. On the relationship among climate, disease, and African-American slavery in the low country, see, for example, Elliott, *Carolina Sports*, xxv; James Habersham et al. to Benjamin Franklin, 19 May 1768, to the Earl of Hillsborough, 24 April 1772, in *The Letters of Hon. James Habersham, 1756–1775*, Collections of the Georgia Historical Society, vol. 6 (Savannah, 1904), 71–74, esp. 71–72, 173; Roswell King Jr. to Thomas Butler, 19 Feb. 1831, Butler Family Papers, HSP.

20. Morgan, "Work and Culture," esp. 568–69; Morgan, "Task and Gang Systems," 202–6.

21. On "bargaining" by slaves and the evolution of the task system, see ibid. See also Ira Berlin and Philip D. Morgan, "Introduction," in Berlin and Morgan, *The Slaves' Economy*, 1–27; Betty Wood, *Women's Work, Men's Work: The Informal Slave Economies of Lowcountry Georgia* (Athens, Ga., 1995), esp. 1–30. On the African role in the creation of the task system, see Ira Berlin, "Time, Space, and the Evolution of Afro-American Society on British Mainland North America," *American Historical Review* 85 (Feb. 1980): 44–78, esp. 59, 64–67; Judith A. Carney, "From Hands to Tutors: African Expertise in the South Carolina Rice Economy," *Agricultural History* 67 (Summer 1993): 1–30, esp. 26–28. On the broader

African role in the shaping of low-country rice technology, see Peter H. Wood, *Black Majority: Negroes in Colonial South Carolina from 1670 through the Stono Rebellion* (New York, 1974), 55–62; Wood, "'It Was a Negro Taught Them': A New Look at African Labor in Early South Carolina," *Journal of Asian and African Studies* 9 (July–Oct. 1974): 160–79; Daniel C. Littlefield, *Rice and Slaves: Ethnicity and the Slave Trade in Colonial South Carolina* (Baton Rouge, La., 1981), 74–114; Littlefield, *Rice and the Making of South Carolina: An Introductory Essay* (Columbia, S.C., 1995); Charles Joyner, *Down by the Riverside: A South Carolina Slave Community* (Urbana, Ill., 1984), 41–89; John Solomon Otto, *The Southern Frontiers, 1607–1860: The Agricultural Evolution of the Colonial and Antebellum South* (Westport, Conn., 1989), 34–37; William S. Pollitzer, "The Relationship of the Gullah-Speaking People of Coastal South Carolina and Georgia to Their African Ancestors," *Historical Methods* 25 (Spring 1993): 53–67; Amelia Wallace Vernon, *African Americans at Mars Bluff, South Carolina* (Baton Rouge, La., 1993), 119–23 and passim; Joyce E. Chaplin, *An Anxious Pursuit: Agricultural Innovation and Modernity in the Lower South, 1730–1815* (Chapel Hill, N.C., 1993), 227–76; Carney and Richard Porcher, "Geographies of the Past: Rice, Slaves, and Technological Transfer in South Carolina," *Southeastern Geographer* 33 (Nov. 1993): 127–47; Carney, "Landscapes of Technology Transfer: Rice Cultivation and African Continuities," *Technology and Culture* 37 (Jan. 1996): 5–35.

22. Carney, "From Hands to Tutors," 26–28 (quotation on 26).

23. Jacob Metzer, "Rational Management, Modern Business Practices, and Economies of Scale in the Ante-Bellum Southern Plantations," *Explorations in Economic History,* 2d ser., 12 (April 1975): 123–50, esp. 139–43. See also R. Keith Aufhauser, "Slavery and Scientific Management," *Journal of Economic History* 33 (Dec. 1973): 811–24.

24. See Léon Walras, *Elements of Pure Economics,* trans. William Jaffé (2 pts., 1874, 1877; Homewood, Ill., 1954). For an introduction to the Walrasian approach, see Donald A. Walker, "Léon Walras," in *The New Palgrave: A Dictionary of Economics,* ed. John Eatwell, Murray Milgate, and Peter Newman, 4 vols. (London, 1987), 4:852–63; Walker, *Walras's Market Models* (Cambridge, 1996).

25. Irving Fisher, "Translator's Note to Léon Walras, 'Geometrical Theory of the Determination of Prices,'" *Annals of the American Academy of Political and Social Science* 3 (July 1892): 45–47. For other problems with the Walrasian approach, see, for example, Walker, "Léon Walras," esp. 854–62; Henry William Spiegel, *The Growth of Economic Thought,* rev. ed. (Durham, N.C., 1983), esp. 552–55.

26. Kenneth Arrow and Gerard Debreu, "Existence of an Equilibrium for a Competitive Economy," *Econometrica* 22 (July 1954): 265–90. See also John Eatwell, Murray Milgate, and Peter Newman, "Preface," in *The New Palgrave: Allocation, Information, and Markets,* ed. Eatwell, Milgate, Newman (New York, 1989), xi–xii.

27. See Kenneth Arrow, "Uncertainty and the Welfare Economics of Medical Care," *American Economic Review* 53 (Dec. 1963): 941–73; Arrow, "The Organization of Economic Activity: Issues Pertinent to the Choice of Market versus Nonmarket Allocation," in Joint Economic Committee, U.S. Congress, *The Analysis and Evaluation of Public Expenditures: The PPB System,* vol. 1 (Washington, D.C., 1969), 47–64; George A. Akerlof, "The Market for 'Lemons': Quality Uncertainty and the Market Mechanism," *Quarterly Journal of Economics* 84 (Aug. 1970): 488–500; James Mirrlees, "Notes on Welfare Economics, Information, and Uncertainty," in *Essays in Economic Behavior under Uncertainty,* ed. M. S. Balch, D. L. McFadden, and S. Y. Wu (Amsterdam, 1974), 243–58; Mirrlees, "The Optimal Struc-

ture of Incentives and Authority within An Organization," *Bell Journal of Economics* 7 (Spring 1976): 105–31; Stephen A. Ross, "The Economic Theory of Agency: The Principal's Problem," *American Economic Review* 63 (May 1973): 134–39; Joseph E. Stiglitz, "Incentives and Risk Sharing in Sharecropping," *Review of Economic Studies* 41 (April 1974): 219–55; Stiglitz, "Incentives, Risk, and Information: Notes towards a Theory of Hierarchy," *Bell Journal of Economics* 6 (Autumn 1975): 552–79.

Alternatively (or additionally), one can trace the genealogy of the principal-agent approach to Ronald Coase, Oliver Williamson, Harold Demsetz, and others emphasizing the importance of institutions and transaction costs in economic life. The rich work of Douglass North comes immediately to mind in this regard. See North, *Structure and Change in Economic History* (New York, 1981); North, *Institutions, Institutional Change, and Economic Performance* (New York, 1990).

28. See, for example, Eatwell, Milgate, Newman, *The New Palgrave: Allocation, Information, and Markets;* Jack Hirschleifer and John G. Riley, *The Analytics of Uncertainty and Information,* Cambridge Surveys of Economic Literature (Cambridge, 1992); Donald E. Campbell, *Incentives: Motivation and the Economics of Information* (Cambridge, 1995).

29. See Adam Smith's statement of the basic agency problem in *An Inquiry into the Nature and Causes of the Wealth of Nations,* ed. Edwin Cannan (1776; New York, 1937), book 5, chap. 1, pt. 3, pp. 699–700.

30. See Ross, "The Economic Theory of Agency"; Kenneth J. Arrow, "The Economics of Agency," in *Principals and Agents: The Structure of Business,* ed. John W. Pratt and Richard J. Zeckhauser (Boston, 1985), 37–51; Joseph E. Stiglitz, "Principal and Agent," in Eatwell, Milgate, and Newman, *The New Palgrave* 3:966–72.

31. See, for example, Arrow, "The Economics of Agency," 38–45; Yehuda Kotowitz, "Moral Hazard," in Eatwell, Milgate, and Newman, *The New Palgrave* 3:549–51; Campbell, *Incentives,* 78–136.

32. Arrow, "Economics of Agency"; Charles Wilson, "Adverse Selection," in Eatwell, Milgate, Newman, *The New Palgrave: Allocation, Information, and Markets,* 31–34; Campbell, *Incentives,* 137–207.

33. For somewhat similar approaches, which is to say, approaches employing transaction-costs models in analyzing American slavery, see Stefano Fenoaltea, "Slavery and Supervision in Comparative Perspective: A Model," *Journal of Economic History* 44 (Sept. 1984): 635–68; Yoram Barzel, *Economic Analysis of Property Rights* (New York, 1989), 76–84; Charles Kahn, "An Agency Approach to Slave Punishments and Rewards," in *Without Consent or Contract: The Rise and Fall of American Slavery, Technical Papers,* ed. Robert William Fogel and Stanley L. Engerman, 3 vols. (New York, 1992), 2:551–65.

34. On the overuse of the concept of agency by historians of American slavery and emancipation, see Coclanis, "Slavery, African-American Agency, and the World We Have Lost."

35. In reality, of course, there are actually several layers of principal-agent problems here, involving field workers, drivers, overseers, and planters and their relationships to one another. For simplicity's sake I have reduced a much more complex set of principal-agent problems to one involving only two parties: planters and enslaved field workers. One should also note that the principal-agent approach assumes—correctly, in my view—that all parties involved are seeking to optimize, subject to their respective constraints.

On the low country's economic history and the place of rice and slaves therein, see, for example, Peter A. Coclanis, *The Shadow of a Dream: Economic Life and Death in the South Carolina Low Country, 1670–1920* (New York, 1989); Smith, *Slavery and Rice Culture;* Mart A. Stewart, "Rice, Water, and Power: Landscapes of Domination and Resistance in the Lowcountry, 1790–1880," *Environmental History Review* 15 (Fall 1991): 47–64; Stewart, *"What Nature Suffers to Groe": Life, Labor, and Landscape on the Georgia Coast, 1680–1920* (Athens, Ga., 1996).

36. Carney, "From Hands to Tutors," 26–27.

37. Note that the principal-agency approach employed here is not necessarily inconsistent, much less incompatible, with interpretations emphasizing paternalism, ameliorationism, or hegemony.

38. John Stuart Mill, *Principles of Political Economy,* 4th ed., 2 vols. (London, 1857), 1:292–99. On the task system, customary practices, and de facto rights in the low country, see Morgan, "Work and Culture." Olmsted, one should note, was a bit ambiguous on the role of custom in the low-country task system. In *A Journey in the Seaboard Slave States . . .* (New York, 1856), 435–36, he wrote: "In nearly all ordinary work, custom has settled the extent of the task, and it is difficult to increase it." Later in the same passage, however, he added: "Notwithstanding this, I have heard a man assert, boastingly, that he made his negroes habitually perform double the customary tasks. Thus we get a glimpse again of the black side. If he is allowed the power to do this, what may not a man do?" For the record, I personally do not believe that the task system was ever as "fixed" as some scholars—Philip Morgan most notably—believe. For evidence of the open and contingent nature of the task system even in the antebellum period, see, for example, Alexander Telfair, Rules & Directions for my Thorn Island Plantation . . ., 11 June 1832, Rule 5, Telfair Family Papers, Georgia Historical Society; A Practical Farmer, "Observations on the Management of Negroes," *Southern Agriculturist* 5 (April 1832): 181–84; entry, 28 May 1841, Plantation Journal, 1838–1842, Davison McDowell Papers, SCL; Francis S. Holmes, *The Southern Farmer and Market Gardener* (Charleston, S.C., 1842), 230–32; William Elliott to Ann Elliott, [Spring 1849], Elliott-Gonzales Papers, SHC; S. D. Wragg, "Overseeing," *Farmer and Planter* 5 (June 1854): 141–42 and (Sept. 1854): 229–30; A. M. H. Jr., "Rice Culture," *Southern Cultivator* 24 (Dec. 1866): 278–79; interview with Uncle Ben Horry, Aug. 1937, in George P. Rawick, ed., *The American Slave: A Composite Autobiography,* 19 vols. (Westport, Conn., 1972), vol. 2, pt. 2, p. 302; interview with Uncle Gabe Lance, n.d., ibid., vol. 3, pt. 3, p. 92; interview with Prince Smith, n.d., ibid., pt. 4, p. 117; interview with Sam Polite, n.d., ibid., pt. 3, pp. 271–72. For more on the variability of tasking, see Peter Coclanis, "Thickening Description: William Washington's Queries on Rice," *Agricultural History* 64 (Summer 1990): 9–16.

39. Morgan, "Work and Culture." On "tasking" in the cultivation of Sea Island cotton in particular, see, for example, T. J. Woofter Jr., *Black Yeomanry: Life on St. Helena Island* (New York, 1930), 30; John Solomon Otto, *Cannon's Point Plantation, 1794–1860: Living Conditions and Status Patterns in the Old South* (Orlando, Fla., 1984), 34–37.

40. In terms of "purity," Wicksell's conception of economic relationships was similar to that of Walras. See Spiegel, *Economic Thought,* esp. 590–92. On the formulation mentioned in the text, see Stiglitz, "Principal and Agent," 967. For Paul A. Samuelson's acceptance of this formulation in the mid-1950s, see Samuelson, "Wages and Interest: A Modern Dissection of Marxian Economic Models," *American Economic Review* 47 (Dec. 1957): 884–912, esp. 894.

41. The quote in the text is from Karl Marx, *Capital,* ed. Frederick Engels, trans. Samuel Moore and Edward Aveling, 3 vols. (1867–94; New York, 1967), 1:94. To Marx, obviously, a given "relation between two wills" need not be equal.

42. Samuel Bowles and Herbert Gintis, "Contested Exchange: New Microfoundations for the Political Economy of Capitalism," *Politics and Society* 18 (June 1990): 165–222.

43. Ibid., 166–67 and passim.

44. The calibrated, gridlike layout of most rice fields in the low country and the relatively discrete nature of cultivation activities—activities punctuated by three or four flows of water over the fields—probably rendered labor there easier to grade than was the case for labor in the sugarcane fields of Jamaica, Cuba, or Louisiana. This does not mean that the costs for whites of monitoring labor in the rice fields were low; indeed, the disease environment in the low country rendered such costs quite high.

Note, too, that it is dangerous to speak categorically, as some do, about the "technical requirements" of rice or any other crop. Rice can be grown in many different ways. In more labor-intensive cultivation systems—systems employing nurseries and transplanting, for example—labor-monitoring costs would likely be greater than in systems such as that in the low country of South Carolina and Georgia. See, for example, Clifford Geertz, *Agricultural Involution: The Processes of Ecological Change in Indonesia* (Berkeley, Calif., 1963), esp. 28–37; Lucien M. Hanks, *Rice and Man: Agricultural Ecology in Southeast Asia* (Arlington Heights, Ill., 1972), 16–68; Francesca Bray, *The Rice Economies: Technology and Development in Asian Societies* (Oxford, 1986). See also Raymond E. Crist, "Rice Culture in Spain," *Scientific Monthly* 84 (Feb. 1957): 66–74, and the works by Carney cited in note 21 above.

45. See James Pitot, *Observations on the Colony of Louisiana from 1796 to 1802,* trans. Henry C. Pitot (Baton Rouge, La., 1979), 68–69, 77; Timothy Flint, *A Condensed Geography and History of the Western States, or the Mississippi Valley,* 2 vols. (Cincinnati, 1828), 1:522–23; R. A. Wilkinson, "Production of Rice in Louisiana," *De Bow's Review* 6 (July 1848): 53–57; "Rice Culture in Louisiana," ibid., 3d ser., 21 (Sept. 1856): 290–92; entries, 15 July 1862, 1 Aug. 1862, Isaac Erwin Diary, Hill Memorial Library, Louisiana State University, Baton Rouge; "Rice Culture in Louisiana," *Southern Cultivator* 32 (Oct. 1874): 395–96; Armando A. Calleja, "Agronomic Practices and Their Influence on the Development of the Louisiana Rice Industry" (M.S. thesis, Louisiana State University, 1938), 15–28; Mildred Kelly Ginn, "A History of Rice Production in Louisiana to 1896," *Louisiana Historical Quarterly* 23 (April 1940): 544–88, esp. 549–54; Gray, *History of Agriculture* 1:65–66, 2: 722–23; Chan Lee, "A Culture History of Rice with Special Reference to Louisiana" (Ph.D. diss., Louisiana State University, 1960), pp. 89–150; Joe Gray Taylor, *Negro Slavery in Louisiana* (Baton Rouge, La., 1963), 78; Henry C. Dethloff, *A History of the American Rice Industry, 1685–1985* (College Station, Tex., 1988), 60–62. On the problems of one would-be rice planter in southern Louisiana, see J. Blodget Britton to Mother [Julia Ann Allen Britton], 1 June 1854, 7 Dec. 1856, Britton and Moore Family Papers, SHC. On the role of Africans in the early history of the rice industry in Louisiana, see Daniel H. Usner Jr., "From African Captivity to American Slavery: The Introduction of Black Laborers to Colonial Louisiana," *Louisiana History* 20 (Winter 1979): 25–48; Gwendolyn Midlo Hall, *Africans in Colonial Louisiana: The Development of Afro-Creole Culture in the Eighteenth Century* (Baton Rouge, La., 1992), 121–24. The gang system of slave-labor organization seems to have predominated in all

agricultural activities in southeastern Louisiana. On its prevalence in sugar cultivation there, see Frederick Law Olmsted, *The Cotton Kingdom . . .*, ed. Arthur M. Schlesinger (1861; New York, 1953), 254–55; Roderick A. McDonald, "Independent Economic Production by Slaves on Antebellum Louisiana Sugar Plantations," in Berlin and Morgan, *The Slaves' Economy,* 182–208, esp. 184–85.

46. On divisions within the slave communities of the low country, see Dusinberre, *Them Dark Days,* 190–206, 342–49; Larry E. Hudson Jr., *To Have and to Hold: Slave Work and Family Life in Antebellum South Carolina* (Athens, Ga. 1997), 181; Lawrence T. McDonnell, "Slave against Slave: Dynamics of Violence Within the American Slave Community," paper presented at the annual meeting of the American Historical Association, San Francisco, Dec. 1983.

47. See Metzer, "Rational Management." Some planters did call for "clock-work" discipline, uniformity, and system, of course. See, for example, Anon., "On the Management of Slaves," *Southern Agriculturist* 6 (June 1833): 281–86, esp. 283–84, 286; Strait Edge, "Plantation Regulations," *Soil of the South* 1 (Feb. 1851): 20–21 and (May 1851): 68; St. Geo Cocke, "Plantation Management-Police," *De Bow's Review* 14 (Feb. 1853): 177–78. See also Mark M. Smith, "Time, Slavery, and Plantation Capitalism in the Ante-Bellum American South," *Past and Present,* no. 150 (Feb. 1996): 142–68. Note that R. Keith Aufhauser makes the most explicit and forceful case for Taylorism as a useful concept for analyzing labor-management relations in American slavery. See Aufhauser, "Slavery and Scientific Management."

48. William Shakespeare, *Richard II* (1593) 2.2.145; John Milton, *Samson Agonistes* (1671), line 35; Samuel Johnson, *A Dictionary of the English Language,* 2 vols. (1755).

49. Matthew Arnold, "A Summer Night" (1852), lines 37–41.

50. On Kevin Sullivan, see, for example, George Napolitano, *The New Pictorial History of Wrestling* (New York, 1990), 118–19.

51. See, for example, William Elliott to Ann Elliott, 4 Nov. 1847, 15 Nov. 1851, to Phoebe Elliott, 11 Oct. 1852, 16 Aug., 9 Nov. 1854, to Emily Elliott, 7 Aug. 1858, Elliott-Gonzales Papers, SHC. The quoted passages are from William Elliott to Ann Elliott, 24 Nov. 1829, 10 Aug. 1856, and n.d. [Spring, c. 1850–53], ibid.

52. William Elliott to William Elliott Jr., 26 Aug. 1862, to General [Johnson Hagood], n.d. [late Aug. 1862], ibid.

PART II

SECESSION

4.

"Free Trade: No Debt: Separation from Banks": The Economic Platform of John C. Calhoun

CLYDE N. WILSON

The conservatives of the Old South believed that the preservation of a society's spiritual and moral values depends to a significant extent upon the nature and form of its property.

—Eugene D. Genovese, *The Southern Tradition: The Achievements and Limitations of an American Conservatism* (1994)

IT IS CURIOUS how little attention has been paid to John C. Calhoun's economics. Between the resolution of the nullification conflict (1833) and the Wilmot Proviso (1846)—fully a third of his career—the greater part of his public life was directed toward matters of economics. He paid some attention in this period to foreign affairs and to threshold defenses against the as-yet-weak threat of abolitionism, but Calhoun devoted more study and more major speeches to economic questions than all other subjects put together.

In so doing he developed comprehensive programs, distinct from those of both the Whigs and the Democrats, in regard to the tariff, government finance, the public lands, internal improvements, and especially currency and banking—all the vexed issues of the "Jacksonian" era. His program won adherents and admirers from both parties and was regarded by many thoughtful Americans, as much or more in the North as the South, as exemplary of true republican statesmanship.

The issues were all interrelated, of course, and all integral to the great theme of the period as Calhoun saw it, the maintenance of prosperity and harmony in the wake of a vast expansion and development of the Union. Many at the time thought that Calhoun's platform came closer to being principled and reasoned than did the often expedient positions of the two parties. In a speech of 1842 Calhoun summarized his position: "Free Trade: Low Du-

ties: No Debt: Separation from Banks: Economy: Retrenchment: and Strict
Adherence to the Constitution." This was used by his supporters as a slogan
in his campaign for the 1844 Democratic presidential nomination and was
emblazoned on the front page of the Washington *Spectator*, the campaign
newspaper.

The neglect of Calhoun's economics is even more surprising when one remembers that as long ago as 1957, Bray Hammond, generally considered the
best historian of banking, praised Calhoun's understanding as superior to
that of the other statesmen of the time.[1] Of Calhoun's numerous biographies
and book-length commentaries, only one has given any significant attention
to his banking and currency proposals—the central issue of the period. That
was the 1903 work by Gustavus M. Pinckney, a South Carolina lawyer and am-
ateur scholar.[2] Some authors—Coit, Wiltse, Styron, Marmor[3]—have paid attention to Calhoun's thought in the broad sense of a philosophic defense of
an agrarian economy and society, but even these have not consistently and
thoroughly examined how his principles were formulated and defended in
the legislative battles of the time, though there have been a few specialized articles on some aspects.[4]

In fact, one may say that "Jacksonian" historians as a group have done an
abysmal job of explaining the economic issues of the period. There are many
reasons for this, in addition to the complexity of the subject. For a long time
Federalist/Republican historiography reigned supreme, dismissing southern
opposition to the northern version of economic nationalism as simply stupid
and evil, just as Calhoun's opponents sometimes did in his day.

Later, an influential school of historians tended to promote a romanticized
version of "Jacksonian democracy," portending the New Deal. Historians
such as Bowers, Schlesinger, Remini, and Niven have adopted the negative
and minimizing view of Calhoun held by the Free-Soil wing (a minority) of
the Democratic party. Remini, for instance, pictured Calhoun as grinding his
teeth over his "own foolish mistakes," and Niven portrays him as "out of
touch with reality."[5] Neither has paid any attention to his bills or speeches,
which reveal him to be not the Marx of the Master Class, as Richard Hofs-
tadter wrote, but in many ways a better "Jacksonian" than his principal Democratic opponents—whose adherence to free trade or opposition to the
national bank were sometimes compromised by political expediency and disguised profiteering as well as inconsistencies that Calhoun never exhibited.
(Democratic senators from New York, Pennsylvania, and lower New England,
pledged to a free trade platform, always voted to raise tariffs, as Calhoun
often pointed out.)

By the time serious historians had undermined the romantic myth of antibusiness Jacksonians, attention had shifted massively to slavery, in the light of American preoccupation with racial issues in the 1960s and 1970s, leaving no market for a close examination of Calhoun as economist.

Of course, economics is a very imperfect "science." As a correspondent once observed to Calhoun, in economics "sequences are not always consequences." Multiple variables are always at work, and there are always political and ideological incentives to make claims for sequences as consequences of particular ideas, policies, or conditions, or of the supposed virtues of particular politicians. And it is as often in the interest of politicians to obfuscate as to clarify—as Calhoun frequently pointed out in debate.

These difficulties perhaps explain why historians in general have tended to portray the Jacksonian controversy over banking and currency in terms of stale political polemics rather than pursue its complexities to the bottom. There have been a number of original contributions, such as Hammond's emphasis on the influence of expansive New York banking interests behind the allegedly "hard-money" Jacksonian attack on the second Bank of the United States and Peter Temin's discovery of the critical impact of Mexican silver on the American currency situation.[6] But general accounts of the era have shown little impact of these or other complicating insights.

I cannot presume here to fully explicate the tortured issue of banking and currency and the other economic questions that Calhoun addressed. However, they can be somewhat illuminated by close attention to Calhoun's ideas and positions because Calhoun, always casting himself in the role of high statesman, was engaged in clarifying the issues for his own time, in providing alternatives to party gimmicks, and in clearing away common political distortions and public misunderstandings that stood in the way, in his view, of truth and the harmonious progress of the Union. Whatever else may be said of Calhoun, his arguments were never superficial or expedient.

Thus an examination of Calhoun's economic arguments and legislation should enrich our understanding of the "Jackson" period and of the mind of the Old South. And a proper understanding of these matters will be seen to support nicely in nearly every aspect the description of the worldview of the planter class that has been developed by Eugene Genovese in recent books—its interest in material progress, but a progress morally centered and preservative.

One of the great paradoxes of American history is that the conservative South has often been the fount and mainstay of "liberal" and "democratic" movements. Without the South there would have been no Jeffersonian

democracy and no Jacksonian democracy in the forms that occurred (not to
mention later populist uprisings)—as the most casual glance at voting statistics will prove. The conservative regime of the South has often been the chief
obstacle to the bourgeois conservatism of the business classes. The latter
needed a strong national government for protected markets, credit expansion, infrastructure expenditures, and much else. This has led to a permanent
confounding in American discourse (as Russell Kirk has pointed out) of the
"conservative tendency" with the often incompatible "acquisitive instinct."[7]

   This mistake the South never made. The South's organic conservatism was
complete, in a sense, at the plantation level, and no activist government was
needed. Eugene Genovese has explicated with great depth and subtlety the
organic conservatism that reached its heights in the South in the 1850s after
Calhoun's death. One can see an early sign of this in Calhoun when he told
the Senate in 1838:

> The Southern States are an aggregate, in fact, of communities, not of indi-
> viduals. Every plantation is a little community, with the master at its head,
> who concentrates in himself the united interests of capital and labor, of
> which he is the common representative. These small communities aggre-
> gated make the state, in all whose action, labor, and capital is equally repre-
> sented and perfectly harmonized. Hence the harmony, the union, and
> stability of that section, which is rarely disturbed except through the action
> of this Government. The blessing of this state of things extends beyond the
> limits of the South. It makes that section the balance of the system; the
> great conservative power, which prevents other portions, less fortunately
> constituted, from rushing into conflict.[8]

   In his economic and constitutional views Calhoun was free to remain essentially an eighteenth-century Jeffersonian republican. Indeed Calhoun's
mature program coincides almost exactly with the views of the Old Republicans and the later Jefferson, as expressed in Jefferson's elaboration of his famous avowal that the "earth belongs in usufruct to the living."[9] Jefferson's
statement implied the "liberal" economic freedom of the current generation,
but also a "conservative" moral responsibility to future generations in regard
to public debt.

   If Calhoun's goal was the defense of an organic society, that did not imply
a reactionary state on the European model or a mercantilist state on the
British and northern pattern. In fact, a loose republican confederation with a
limited central power was the best possible government for an organic society. The South required only free markets and a purely local labor discipline.

Thus Calhoun's political economy expressed economic liberalism and a society of independent though morally responsible freeholders—an ideal that had powerful appeal to many Americans beyond the South. This ideal is why Calhoun was the preferred national leader of many radical libertarian Locofocos and moderate independent commercial gentlemen of the North. Not as Marx of the Master Class but as the best representative of a true republican polity.

Though it has never been examined except in passing, a substantial number of labor leaders and libertarian thinkers gave their allegiance to Calhoun. Orestes Brownson's youthful discipleship is well known. Less well known but even more steadfast supporters of this type were Condy Raguet of Philadelphia and Fitzwilliam Byrdsall of New York. Interestingly, these men accepted the South's position not only on economic questions but also on the superiority of southern society to northern in the preservation of liberal principles. They agreed that the South was a necessary restraint to acquisitive mercantilism and deprecated abolition as a form of hypocritical Puritan mania.

This was a constant theme in letters received by Calhoun from sympathizers. One of these, Ellwood Fisher, an Ohio Democratic leader and a Quaker, wrote in the Cincinnati *Enquirer* in 1846 of the moral superiority of slave society to capitalist society: "The money power, like every other kind of power, aims to be paramount and exclusive. It aims at a showy form of civilization of its own . . . luxury collected from every clime where money finds its slaves."[10] Raguet (1784–1842) has received some attention from twentieth-century libertarian scholars as an able advocate of free trade and "free banking." It has not been noted that in the several publications he edited, he vehemently defended South Carolina on nullification and repeatedly contrasted the tolerant, gentlemanly virtues of the South to New England WASP prejudice and hypocrisy. (He was of French descent.)[11]

Byrdsall, author of *The History of the Locofoco or Equal Rights Party of New York*, fought hard against both Tammany and Free-Soil Democrats and would write in a typical letter to Calhoun: "In short, my dear Sir, I am satisfied that the salvation of this confederacy from the evils which now beset it, depends entirely upon the Southern States." And again on abolitionists: "The peaceful teachings of the Gospel are abandoned to get up a crusade of falsehood slander dissention disunion throughout the Confederacy, in short the press the pulpit the monarchists the aristocrats the demagogues of Europe and the States are as zealously engaged in the work of wickedness as if they were serving both God & man. And yet they are no friends of the negro. . . .

He has no real friends but in the Southern States."[12] And again:

> The South is bound by every motive sacred and dear to the heart of man to maintain intact her own social organization, for it is far preferable to that of Europe and the free states. The latter is calculated for nothing so much as the uttermost development of all the selfish properties of human nature. Every man is in competition with his fellow men, to build himself up on the ruin of others . . . upon the dog eat dog principle. . . . I for one as a member of a Christian church will never consent to change it [the southern social system] for the heartless, selfish, vice misery and crime producing social system of the North. Besides, such is the intense dislike of the proletaires toward the non-producers in the free States in consequence of the wealth and luxury which they create but cannot partake or enjoy, that discontent and hatred exists to an extent scarcely imaginable.[13]

Byrdsall told how he had encountered an industrialist who was gleeful over the Mexican War, which he thought would leave a debt of a hundred million dollars and thus compel restoration of a high tariff: "This man is but one of a numerous class whose selfish interests over[r]ule all considerations of the loss of life . . . as well as . . . patriotism or common justice. And yet it is very probable that he (as well as most of the class he belongs to) is a member or elder of a Christian church—a praying and hymn singing man."[14]

Calhoun also found allegiance among moderate Whig members of the merchant class, those who agreed with him that national prosperity was a matter of reciprocity rather than ruthless sectional aggrandizement as in the tariff. Charles Augustus Davis, a New York City merchant and well-known writer under the pen name "Major Jack Downing," conducted a long correspondence with Calhoun on the injustice of the tariff, the need for nationally unifying measures, and the willingness of northern capitalists to invest in southern transportation. There were a number of other New York mercantile men who felt the same way.

In response to such supporters, Calhoun was always ready to seek reform gradually in economic matters. Thus in 1834 he said he was willing to extend the charter of the Bank of the United States another six years to allow a gradual transition to another system. In 1842 he actually opposed certain reductions in the tariff because he thought they were politically motivated and would involve the South in reneging on the gradual reductions that had been agreed to in the Compromise of 1833.

Such agreements between the sections were to him morally binding. However, the ineluctable flaw in this approach was that in a system of political operatives and shifting majorities, reciprocity could not be maintained. He was pursuing the impossible, seeking a permanent consensual basis of agreement (as he was later to do on slavery) that was simply not going to be kept by the other side. As Merrill Peterson has pointed out, "Calhoun's whole tendency . . . was to approach issues theoretically rather than practically and to seek resolution the hard way, on principles, rather than by balancing interests and accommodation to circumstances." [15]

As a part of his strategy of meeting the sensible men of the North halfway and in good faith, Calhoun always blamed bad economic legislation not on businessmen but on politicians. It was the politicians who made the tariff and Bank into issues so polarized and obfuscated that they could not be settled by reason. His scorn for capitalists was muted; that for northern Democratic politicians who supposedly were committed to free trade but in fact voted for tariff bills and engaged in the logrolling for special interests that this involved, was unstinted.

But so thorough was Calhoun's commitment to free trade in principle that he refused to countenance even retaliatory duties. "If other countries injured us by burdensome exactions," he remarked, "it was no reason why we should do harm to ourselves."[16] "Free trade," he said on another occasion in words reminiscent of the late twentieth century, is "destined to work the greatest and most happy change. . . . Its reaction on politics, morals and religion will be powerful and most salutary." Again: Free trade "is, in my opinion, emphatically the cause of civilization & peace."[17] And he refused to come out for "incidental protection" as a part of a mostly revenue tariff, a political expedient adopted by several Democratic presidential contenders and often urged upon Calhoun by supporters.

It is curious how indifferent historians have been to the South's complaint about the tariff, often dismissing it as a scapegoat for the section's own economic shortcomings or as a disguised form of slavery conflict. But the plain truth is that Calhoun was entirely correct in his opposition to the tariff. Debates about the actual macro- and micro-economic effects of antebellum protection are beside the point. The South, providing the bulk of the Union's exports, sold in an unprotected world market, while all American consumers bought in a highly protected one. And this was to the benefit of one class, no matter how plausibly disguised as a public boon. Such exactions are hard to justify at any time, but especially so in a federal Union in which economic interests are regionalized in such a way that the exploitive effect is concentrated. Americans had fought a revolution for smaller grievances. Not to mention, as

Calhoun pointed out in the *South Carolina Exposition,* to the agreement of free traders, that the tariff's "tendency is, to make the poor poorer and the rich richer."

But the tariff, like abolition, was also a question of honor. The disingenuous arguments of the protectionists tended, like those of the abolitionists, to dwell upon the moral inferiority and stupidity of southerners in comparison with wise, righteous, industrious New Englanders. Calhoun did not engage in that type of polemic, but he replied to it, again in the *Exposition:* "We are told, by those who pretend to understand our interest better than we do, that the excess of production and not the Tariff, is the evil which afflicts us. . . . We would feel more disposed to respect the spirit in which the advice is offered, if those from whom it comes accompanied it with the weight of their example. *They* also, occasionally, complain of low prices; but instead of diminishing the supply, as a remedy for the evil, demand an enlargement of the market, by the exclusion of all competition."

Calhoun had supported the tariff of 1816 as a measure of justice to those New Englanders whose interests had been dislocated by government action in Embargo and war. This support was part of his pursuit of harmony and reciprocity. When he was later attacked as inconsistent, he pointed out that he had viewed the tariff of 1816 as temporary. He had not foreseen that it would become a permanent, ever-tightening system, that even after the retirement of the national debt, the duties would not come down.

Given his political inheritance and the clear interest of those he represented, Calhoun could have taken no other position than to view the tariff as oppression and a violation of the bargain of the Union. Had reciprocity been forthcoming from the other side, how different might the course of American history have been. Indeed it is clear that in 1861 a large part of support for the war against the South came from a fear of free trade and the loss of revenue from the South.[18] Condy Raguet had been eloquent about the smooth and ruthless "lobbyists" of the "Yankee" capitalists who haunted the outer rooms of Congress. With the South gone they indeed had the upper hand.

In regard to the public lands, which were the American people's endowment as well as the largest source of government revenue after the tariff, Calhoun made farseeing though unsuccessful legislative efforts. In 1837 he first proposed and later often reintroduced a bill to cede the public lands that remained unsold after ten years on the market to the western states in which they were situated. Some of any future revenue would go to the government, and the lands would still get into the hands of legitimate settlers. The advantages would be to free the federal government from a major source of expense, corruption, and contention and to free the "new states" from vassalage, putting them on the same basis as the "old states" in regard to their lands.

Further, and here we see Calhoun's pursuit of moral and harmonious progress once again, it would be a gesture of generosity from the East to the West that would cement the bonds of Union. It was in the same spirit by which the old states had generously turned over their western claims as a common treasure of the Union.

The hallowed Jeffersonian policy was that the lands be sold off at moderate prices to legitimate settlers, thus obviating the need for direct taxes. During the Jacksonian period two popular contrary ideas took hold. One was the homestead act favored by some Democrats and later taken up by the Republicans with disastrous consequences in the West — give the land away to individuals and to corporations to encourage development ("Vote Yourself a Farm"). The other policy, particularly popular with Whigs, was called "Distribution," by which the revenue derived from sale of public lands would be distributed as a "surplus" to all the states. This was politically popular because all states were to be paid off on the basis of their federal population. These Whig "conservatives" thus would dissipate the public treasury, requiring more taxes (an indirect pressure for a higher tariff) and making the states dependent upon congressional largesse.

To Calhoun such plans were immoral in all aspects — squandering the endowment of the Union, breaking faith with the states that had given up their claims to provide a source of revenue for the government, providing an excuse to raise the tariff, continuing all the expense and corruption inherent in federal administration of the lands, and encouraging states to take on irresponsible debts in the expectation of "a windfall."

A distribution bill passed in 1841 and soon after had to be suspended. The whole project proved a disaster, throwing many states into disgraceful defaults, as Calhoun had predicted. The South Carolina General Assembly, alone among all the states, had refused to accept its portion of the "surplus."

Calhoun's proposal was too simple, too good, to be adopted, requiring as it did the federal politicians to give up certain advantages for the greater good. By Calhoun's plan the western states would have had a secure endowment which they could have used as they wished. The plan would have put the means for internal improvements directly into the treasuries of the states, helping to remove another troublesome and corrupting issue from Congress. Young Abraham Lincoln, then a member of the Illinois legislature, wrote his congressman in enthusiastic support of Calhoun's proposal.[19]

Had Calhoun been successful on this and on other issues, it is possible to imagine a different scenario for some aspects of American history. There would have been some corruption in the states, but nothing that could have matched the vast land giveaways to corporations by the Republicans after 1861. The states and thus genuine federalism would have been measurably strengthened. Calhoun took a statesmanlike and farseeing position, though opposed by the "practical" politicians of both parties.

Calhoun's earliest peacetime fame came from his relationship to his country's dreams of development and progress. He was, after all, the young patriot who had declared, "Let us conquer space." Calhoun appears with advantage, compared with other leaders of the time, in his efforts, persistently renewed, to make federal internal improvements into a truly constructive and unifying force rather than the egregious example of logrolling they increasingly became as the century wore on.

He contended as a young congressman, as secretary of war, and later, that if the federal government was to engage in subsidy of internal improvements (setting aside the constitutional issue for the moment), there should be a master plan that would truly benefit all of the Union, or at least large regions of it. Whether it was constitutional or not, he added, Congress never had abandoned the power and never would abandon it.

President Madison had vetoed Calhoun's original plan on his last day in office in 1817, approving the plan but insisting on the need for a constitutional amendment to clarify federal power. Monroe had taken a similar position. John Quincy Adams had scorned constitutional scruples and had failed. Jackson had assumed a presidential prerogative of determining, with the veto, which projects were constitutional and which were not, and had provided no real leadership on the issue, as usual.

In this stalemate of more than three decades, Congress legislated continuously for projects here and there, without any plan that embraced ends "appropriately called federal," in Calhoun's words. It merely responded to the most effective special interests. The expenditures had not been "systematic, judicious, and efficient."[20] If Congress did possess any power in this area, then surely it was for "federal" and not for local objects, Calhoun contended. As usual, many "practical" politicians found Calhoun's "metaphysical" distinction incomprehensible.

In 1828, justifying a casting vote as vice president to limit certain appropriations, he remarked: "If the system of Internal Improvement cannot be confined, in practice, to objects of really national importance, as contemplated by the act of 1824; and if it must degenerate into those merely local, having no reference to the powers and duties of the general government, it would, and ought, to fall into disrepute."[21]

It was clear to Calhoun that as a matter of equity and justice, which he always saw in the concept of Union, the demands of the growing West had to be satisfied in some way. The Old Northwest in the 1840s was filling with population around the Great Lakes and was in the midst of unprecedented expansion. Its greatest need was for transportation to markets. And the Southwest had been almost entirely neglected by Congress. The West sooner or later would have its way. Better and wiser to concede generously at once.

In 1843, speaking of the Tennessee River valley, he asked if a Senate committee "would inquire how far this great river was entitled to their attention; and that they would establish some principle upon which the navigation of these great internal seas—for such, to all intents, they were—might be improved."[22]

After serving as president of the Southwestern Commercial Convention in Memphis in 1846, Calhoun undertook to provide the principle himself. What could and ought the general government do in this area that would achieve a relatively wide consensus and serve legitimate "Federal" purposes? His report for a Senate select committee gave his answer. The Congress had clear constitutional power over interstate and foreign commerce. This power was without doubt among those delegated by the states, and it had been construed from the beginning as allowing the government to engage in improvements of navigation—harbors, lighthouses, and other federally constructed navigational aids dotted the Atlantic and Gulf coasts.

Calhoun reasoned that the Mississippi River and its tributaries were a great inland sea—an artery of an immense volume of interstate and foreign commerce over which no state could exercise jurisdiction. Thus the government could legitimately engage in improvements of navigation in the Mississippi Valley. And for this purpose he introduced a bill to develop a systematic survey. He did not touch on the issue of land transport except to hint that some assistance might be given for roads and railroads (as was in fact already the common practice) by means of defense and mail contracts.

Another proposal had to do with the public lands. Did not the Congress, in its capacity as proprietor and trustee of the public lands, have the right or even the duty to join with the states and private enterprise in encouraging improvements that would enhance the value of the lands and thus the nontax revenue of the government? Especially when this involved no expenditures but merely donations of some land, as was already the practice, to encourage development and thus increase the value of the rest and the revenue to be derived. Such grants, he stressed, would have to be carefully limited and supervised to prevent exploitation of the public, but judiciously applied on the basis of a master plan, they could be of universal benefit. And he renewed his suggestion that unsold lands be turned over to the western states. This practice would both bolster the dignity of the states and provide them with a source of development capital. And, Calhoun pointed out, Congress itself was responsible for hindrances to development: tariff protection for Pennsylvania iron interests added $2,000 per mile to the costs of railroad construction.

Calhoun's 1846 plan failed of adoption. Instead the Congress passed an immense logrolling "rivers and harbors" bill with forty-nine local projects, mostly for the Midwest. President Polk properly vetoed this, on good constitutional and expedient grounds. However, as Calhoun pointed out, Polk and his party provided no leadership on the issue—no alternative to satisfy legitimate demands. One can reasonably argue that this event, along with the 1846 tariff reductions, began the unraveling of Democratic strength and the rise of Free-Soilism in the Midwest and the mid-Atlantic states and thus led inevitably to the eventual crack-up of the Union. Suppose Calhoun's conciliatory program had been adopted, dampening down the northern belief that southern politicians thwarted the North's legitimate interests?

Two questions can only be touched on briefly here: Calhoun's opposition to a federal bankruptcy law and his guarding of the treasury from unnecessary expenditures. His great speech of 2 June 1840, against a proposed federal bankruptcy act—which was essentially a form of bailout for banks and other corporations—is an eloquent argument against the abandonment of public virtue for special interests.

And for his last fifteen years in the Senate, Calhoun was on the watch for expenditures that were unnecessary or unauthorized. Though he always maintained that those things the government had a duty to do, it should do well, time and again he pointed out that expenditures which seemed plausible or appealed to the sympathies of legislators created unwholesome precedents, exceeded Congress's authority, and, most importantly, involved an abuse of the people's labor. Like the tariff, such actions invariably transferred wealth from one group to another and so should be kept at a minimum. "We robbed the People in levying taxes. It was plunder and nothing more, and reform and retrenchment could be accomplished in no other way than by correcting the erroneous doctrines which had grown up." "Economy and accountability," he said on another occasion, "are virtues belonging to free and popular Governments, and without which they cannot long endure."[23] His defense of the agrarian version of republican virtue never wavered, and many Americans, North and South, honored him for the consistency of principle.

Money is that great Mystery the love of which is near universal and the root of all evil. One needs only to think of "Not worth a Continental," "the Monster Bank," "the Cross of Gold," and beyond, to be reminded of the large and controversial part it has played in American political history. Historians in general have seen the recurrent conflicts over money largely in terms of capitalist/agrarian and creditor/debtor conflict. Much discussion has rested on the empirically false assumption (apparently derived from the late nineteenth-century battles over bimetallism) that capitalists are always in favor of "hard money" and agrarians always in favor of inflation or "cheap money." The actualities are quite a bit more complicated because capitalists, or some of them, have often been in the forefront of promoting currency expansion and inflation. Money is indeed a great Mystery, not only involving the interest of every member of society but surrounded by strong emotions and (often man-made) clouds of confusion.

Calhoun perhaps appears in his best light as a national statesman when we follow his course through the banking and currency conflicts of his time. It is difficult, I think, to find here the mere sectional politician that so many wish to see him to be.

Financial disarray brought on by the War of 1812 and the difficulties of financing the war led the Madison administration to revive the idea of a national bank. The first United States Bank of Hamilton, which the Republican party had come into existence opposing, had expired in 1811. Calhoun, as an administration leader in the House of Representatives, was asked to manage the bill to revive the Bank, a task he accepted, feeling strongly the obligation that he, as an advocate of the declaration of war, had to achieve good results. "This," Calhoun later observed, "was my first lesson on banks. It has made a durable impression on my mind."

When he looked at the plan. "I had not proceeded far before I was struck with the extraordinary character of the subject; a bank of $50,000,000, whose capital was to consist almost exclusively of Government credit in the shape of stock . . . to furnish the Government with loans to carry on the war! I saw at once that the effect of the arrangement would be, that the Government would borrow back its own credit, and pay six per cent per annum for what they had already paid eight or nine."[24] Calhoun had put his finger on the bottom line of modern government finance, the alliance of government and great capital that had been designed by Hamilton.

Yet how else deal with the existing "embarrassment of the Treasury" when the Bank was the only remedy on the table: "I cast my eyes around, and soon saw that the Government should use its own credit directly, without the intervention of a bank; which I proposed to do in the form of Treasury notes, to be issued in the operations of the Government, and to be funded in the subscription to the stock of the bank."[25]

The chartering of the Second Bank of the United States was a complicated struggle extending over several sessions of Congress, but Calhoun was generally considered the rightful father of the bill, it having been extensively amended by him to ensure that "the capital of the bank should consist of funded Treasury notes; and that instead of a mere paper machine, it should be a specie-paying bank, so as to be an ally instead of an opponent in restoring the currency to a sound condition."[26]

Treasury notes were paper issued by the government in payment of its expenditures. They were receivable in payment of government obligations, as at the customshouses and land offices, and were redeemable in specie, usually after the passage of one year. A great many things intersected here, in Calhoun's observation. For the rest of his career he advocated, not only in the case of the bank's capital but in the case of all government expenditures, the use of Treasury notes. Why should the government go into the market to borrow money at high rates, with no risk to the lender, when it could issue its own promises to pay? (Interestingly, the same Whigs (like Webster) who regarded a debt as a blessing and advocated loans, attacked Calhoun's issues of Treasury notes as piling up a dangerous debt!)

Calhoun had observed that the soundness and acceptability of the notes made them a circulating medium. Because they were known to be sound, they did not have to be redeemed but could circulate in the private economy as a currency. This not only was a boon to the government, saving interest charges, but went far toward meeting the Congress's constitutional obligation to provide the currency of the country in the absence of a sufficient amount of specie and given the inconvenience of coin.

In 1832, responding to a variety of ideas and impulses, Andrew Jackson vetoed Henry Clay's early renewal of the Second Bank of the United States's twenty-year charter, which was to expire in 1836. Then Jackson's Treasury Department withdrew the government funds from their legal resting place in the Bank and put them into a variety of private, state-chartered banks picked by his own administration. This withdrawal inaugurated a struggle between advocates and opponents of a National Bank that seesawed back and forth until the Civil War. During this struggle Calhoun pursued an independent and elevated course.

In the Senate, Calhoun analyzed with merciless logic and clarity the illegality and sophistry of Jackson's proceedings and supported Clay's resolutions of censure. Whatever the faults of the Bank, it had acted, on the whole, responsibly, and it was the law. The "pet banks" that now held the government funds were a vast spoils system which the executive had created for itself and a danger to the economy as well.

Thus far he agreed with the Whigs. But in a great speech of 21 March 1834, he indicated that although an opponent of Jackson's proceedings, he was no longer an advocate of a Bank of the United States, though he was willing to see it continue for a few more years to provide a gradual transition.

He presented a history of banking, indicating the study he had put into the subject since 1816, and put his finger on the real issue. It was not a question of Bank or no Bank but a question of the control of the currency. Even with the Bank of the United States out of the picture, the government was still deeply involved with the banking system. Why? Because Alexander Hamilton, in a little-noticed executive order, which had been casually validated by 1816 legislation, had begun accepting the notes issued by banks as if they were equivalent to specie. Since then the banking system had grown exponentially. On the one hand, the Bank of the United States had some control over the banks in that it could regulate their practices by receiving their notes at various degrees below face value. On the other hand, the banks made use of the government's validation to back their paper. People, observed Calhoun, still thought of banks largely as places of deposit and had not noticed the explosion of "banks of discount," what was later to be called "fractional reserve banking." The banks now had vast power to expand or contract the credit of the country by the issuing of notes.

The banks were lending far out of proportion to their specie reserves, thus creating what would later be called the business cycle—boom followed by bust. (Calhoun accurately predicted the panic of 1837 three years in advance.) Jackson's actions had greatly aggravated the situation, encouraging the pet banks to even greater expansion and removing the power of the Bank of the United States to curb them.

Calhoun noted issues that were being neglected in the smoke and din of party warfare over the Bank. It was the Congress's constitutional duty to provide a sound circulating medium. There was no reason this duty had to be performed by delegating power to a national bank. The states were forbidden by the Constitution to emit bills of credit, but state-chartered private institutions had been encouraged by the federal government to do what the states were forbidden to do and thus were performing the duty of Congress. Further, control of the currency and credit of the country was the most powerful instrument that had ever been developed for transferring wealth from one group to another. Currency of all sorts made up only one-twenty-fifth or one-thirtieth of the wealth of the country, "and yet this small proportion of the property of the community regulates the value of all the rest, and forms the medium of circulation by which all its exchanges are effected."

He added:

> Place the money power in the hands of a single individual, or a combination of individuals, and, by expanding or contracting the currency, they may raise or sink prices at pleasure; and . . . may command the whole property and industry of the community, and control its fiscal operations. The banking system concentrates and places this power in the hands of those who control it, and its force increases just in proportion as it dispenses with a metallic basis. Never was an engine invented better calculated to place the destiny of the many in the hands of the few, or less favorable to that equality and independence which lie at the bottom of all free institutions.[27]

In 1836 Calhoun played a leading role in forming and passing a Deposit Act which regulated and legalized the pet bank system — forcing the banks to pay for the privilege of using the government funds and guarding against the fraud and defaults that had taken place. In addition, the act provided for surplus treasury funds to be distributed to the states rather than held in the banks for their use. Calhoun approved of this distribution, which was not linked to the sales of public lands but was aimed at disposing of the huge surplus created by the tariffs of 1828 and 1832.

In defending this provision he pointed out that the Jacksonians, who called themselves the friends of the people, had shown no hesitancy in distributing public funds among favored banks and public lands among favored speculators but were opposing the distribution of the surplus to the states: "Were they to leave it with the banks, as an instrument for political purposes? Why should gentlemen recommend so extraordinary a course, so unequal, so partial, to avoid returning it to the people to whom it belonged? Why were they so averse to such a distribution? Was it to prevent the people from being corrupted? Were the people alone capable of being corrupted? Were the Government and banks all pure, while the people, the people alone, were corrupt and corruptible?"[28]

On 18 September and 3 October 1837, Calhoun made in the Senate two great speeches supporting the Independent Treasury or Subtreasury plan that Van Buren had put forward. Thus he put aside his opposition to Van Buren and rejoined the Democratic party for the national crisis of the panic. And he expanded his analysis of the history and nature of banking.

It was time, Calhoun maintained, that Congress directly undertook its constitutional responsibility over the currency and separated the government and the currency from private privilege, profit, and control. But it was necessary not only to set up the Independent Treasury. This did not really divorce the government from the banks as long as the government accepted and dealt in the notes issued by private state-chartered banks. He offered an amendment to the Independent Treasury that would have gradually eliminated the government's reception of banknotes, which involved the government in support of the banks and their power over the credit supply of the country. He desired to separate the government and the banks and let each go its own way. (Thus the slogan "Separation from Banks.") The market would regulate banknotes without the artificial support of the government. His amendment to this effect passed. The Independent Treasury passed the Senate but failed to be acted on in the House at that time, though it was established in 1846.

Calhoun's economic analysis, I would argue, reflected brilliant insight and high statesmanship. He cut through the demagoguery and superficiality of political conflict in an attempt to discern the public good. And his arguments always came back to the ethics of the community—the moral degradation and the undermining of republican virtue that resulted from interested legislative manipulations. The alliance of bankers and government was an imposition on honest farmers and merchants, a threat to their independence and to the moral climate that was necessary to sustain free government. His eloquence on these matters is still moving. Calhoun once remarked, "I do not hesitate to say, if Genl. Hamilton had not issued his circular directing bank notes to be received as gold & silver in the publick dues, and if the Bank of the United States had not been created, the whole course of politics under our system would have been entirely different."[29] Another time he declared, "It has justly been stated by a British writer that the power to make a small piece of paper, not worth one cent, by the inscribing of a few names, to be worth a thousand dollars, was a power too high to be entrusted to the hands of mortal man."[30]

Hear Calhoun on the moral effects of the banking system:

If a community be so organized as to cause a demand for high mental attainments, they are sure to be developed. If its honors and rewards are allotted to pursuits that require their development by creating a demand for

intelligence, knowledge, wisdom, justice, firmness, courage, patriotism, and
the like, they are sure to be produced. But, if allotted to pursuits that require inferior qualities, the higher are sure to decay and perish. I object to
the banking system, because it allots the honors and rewards of the community, in a very undue proportion, to a pursuit the least of all others favorable to the development of the higher mental qualities, intellectual or
moral, to the decay of the learned professions, and the more noble pursuits of science, literature, philosophy, and statesmanship, and the great
and more useful pursuits of business and industry. With the vast increase
of its profits and influence, it is gradually concentrating in it itself most
of the prizes of life. . . . The rising generation cannot but feel its deaden-
ing influence.[31]

Calhoun demonstrates thoroughly what Eugene Genovese writes of the
slaveholding class: that they "did place great weight on the quantitative
progress of morality and did see material progress as its handmaiden." Many
historians have attributed to them, therefore, a "basically bourgeois worldview to which they merely tacked on an opportunistic defense of slave
property." Of such historians, Genovese remarks, "They err."[32]

Forrest McDonald has ascribed to the Founding Fathers two different
versions of republicanism.[33] Puritanical republicanism saw the state as the
instrument of promoting and preserving virtue. The agrarian republicanism
of the South relied upon independence of the citizen for the preservation of
virtue and regarded the government as an enemy to be watched and limited.
The triumph of puritanical republicanism has been nearly complete, though
it has shifted its emphasis from material progress to distribution and more
lately to political correctness. The type of discourse represented by Calhoun
has all but disappeared from the American public dialogue and perhaps not
all for the good.

Calhoun was the chief public man of the Old South, and his economics
were the South's. Those things in which the Confederate Constitution differed from the United States Constitution were provisions governing the economic behavior of government, along the lines Calhoun had laid down.
Interestingly enough, the two constitutions differed hardly at all on the question of slavery.

Calhoun's philosophy represented the last gasp of agrarian republicanism,
of which only the faintest echoes remain in the American consciousness. But
it also represented an effort to adapt that ideology to the prospects of material and moral progress of the nineteenth century without sacrificing it, and
also to adapt it to the more organic concepts of man and society that ap-

peared in the post-Enlightenment era. This intellectual effort took place, as the works of Eugene Genovese have so profoundly demonstrated, in a society necessarily committed to the defense of its unique historical burden of slavery.

Notes

1. Bray Hammond, *Banks and Politics in America: From the Revolution to the Civil War* (Princeton, N.J., 1957), 37, 111, 234–37, 367–68, 427–29, 609.

2. Gustavus M. Pinckney, *Life of John C. Calhoun: Being a View of the Principal Events of His Career and an Account of His Contributions to Economic and Political Science* (Charleston, S.C., 1903).

3. Margaret L. Coit, *John C. Calhoun: American Portrait* (Boston, 1950); Charles M. Wiltse, *John C. Calhoun*, 3 vols. (Indianapolis, 1944–51); Arthur M. Styron, *The Cast-Iron Man: John C. Calhoun and American Democracy* (New York, 1935); Theodore R. Marmor, *The Career of John C. Calhoun: Politician, Social Critic, Political Philosopher* (New York, 1988).

4. Noteworthy are Magdalen Eichert, "John C. Calhoun's Land Policy of Cession," *South Carolina Historical Magazine* 55 (Oct. 1954): 198–209, and John L. Larson, "'Bind the Republic Together': The National Union and the Struggle for a System of Internal Improvements," *Journal of American History* 74 (Sept. 1987): 363–87.

5. Robert V. Remini, *Martin Van Buren and the Making of the Democratic Party* (New York, 1951), 184; John Niven, *John C. Calhoun and the Price of Union: A Biography* (Baton Rouge, La., 1988), 178–99. See also Claude G. Bowers, *Party Battles of the Jackson Period* (1922), and Arthur M. Schlesinger Jr., *The Age of Jackson* (1945).

6. Peter Temin, *The Jacksonian Economy* (New York, 1969).

7. Russell Kirk, *The Conservative Mind: From Burke to Eliot*, 4th ed. (New York, 1968), 80.

8. Remarks, 10 Jan. 1838, *The Papers of John C. Calhoun*, ed. Robert L. Meriwether et al., 25 vols. to date (Columbia, S.C., 1959–), 14:84–85.

9. Jefferson's ideas in regard to public debt and currency coincide nearly exactly in spirit and specifics with those elaborated by Calhoun. See especially his letters to John Wayles Eppes, 24 June 1813, and to Samuel Kercheval, 12 July 1816, *The Works of Thomas Jefferson*, ed. Paul Leicester Ford, 12 vols. (New York, 1905), 11:297–306, 12:3–15. See also Carey M. Roberts, "The Great Compact, Dual Federalism, and Nullification: The Conservatism of Patrick Henry, John Randolph, Nathaniel Macon, and John C. Calhoun" (M.A. thesis, University of South Carolina, 1995). Schlesinger's scenario in *The Age of Jackson* portrays the Old Republicans passing on their legacy to such figures as Van Buren and Benton rather than to Calhoun. It should be clear, however, who gave lip service to their ideas and who creatively carried them out. See also Donald F. Swanson, "'Bank-notes Will Be But as Oak Leaves': Thomas Jefferson on Paper Money," in *Virginia Magazine of History and Biography* 101 (Jan. 1993): 37–52.

10. "John C. Calhoun" by [Ellwood] F[isher], Cincinnati *Enquirer*, as reprinted in the Tallahassee, Fla., *Floridian*, 9 Jan. 1847.

11. Raguet's journals were the *Free Trade Advocate and Journal of Political Economy*

(Philadelphia, 1829); *Banner of the Constitution* (Washington, D.C., 1829–33); *Examiner, and Journal of Political Economy* (Philadelphia, 1833–35). An extended circle of pro-Calhoun intellectuals in Philadelphia is well described in H. Arthur Scott Trask, "The Constitutional Republicans of Philadelphia, 1818–1848: Hard Money, Free Trade, and State Rights" (Ph.D. diss., University of South Carolina, 1998).

12. Byrdsall to Calhoun, 7 May, 23 July 1849, Calhoun Papers, Clemson University.

13. Byrdsall to Calhoun, 11 Feb. 1850, Calhoun Papers, SCL.

14. Byrdsall to Calhoun, 4 Aug. 1846, *Papers of John C. Calhoun* 23:387.

15. Merrill D. Peterson, *Olive Branch and Sword—The Compromise of 1833* (Baton Rouge, La., 1982), 60.

16. Remarks, 27 Jan. 1841, *Papers of John C. Calhoun* 15:474.

17. To Francis Wharton, 25 Dec. 1843, to the Manchester Anti-Corn Law League, 24 March 1845, ibid., 17:642, 21:445.

18. See Kenneth M. Stampp, *And the War Came: The North and the Secession Crisis, 1860–1861* (Baton Rouge, La., 1950), and the more recent Charles Adams, *For Good and Evil: The Impact of Taxes upon the Course of Civilization* (New York, 1992).

19. Lincoln to John T. Stuart, 1 Jan. 1840, in *The Collected Works of Abraham Lincoln,* ed. Roy P. Basler, 8 vols. (New Brunswick, N.J., 1953), 1:135–38, 181.

20. Report on the Memphis Memorial, 26 June 1846, *Papers of John C. Calhoun* 23:193–228.

21. Remarks, 9 April 1828, ibid., 10:369.

22. Remarks, 17 Jan. 1843, ibid., 16:614.

23. See Clyde N. Wilson, ed., *The Essential Calhoun* (New Brunswick, N.J., 1992), 163–88, esp. 183–84, 187.

24. Speech, 3 Oct. 1837, *Papers of John C. Calhoun* 13:609, 612.

25. Ibid., 610.

26. Ibid., 611. The "inconsistent" and "opportunistic" Calhoun made exactly the same proposals thirty years later on the financing of the Mexican War. See Remarks of 18 July and 4 Aug. 1846, ibid., 23:335–36, 391–92.

27. Ibid., 602.

28. Remarks, 28 Feb. 1837, ibid., 13:480.

29. To James H. Hammond, 16 May 1840, ibid., 15:228–29.

30. Remarks, 29 Dec. 1841, ibid., 16:25.

31. Speech, 3 Oct. 1837, ibid., 13:603.

32. Eugene Genovese, *The Slaveholders' Dilemma: Freedom and Progress in Southern Conservative Thought, 1820–1860* (Columbia, S.C., 1992), 33.

33. Forrest McDonald, *Novus Ordo Seclorum: The Intellectual Origins of the Constitution* (Lawrence, Kans., 1985), 70–77.

5

Statism in the Old South: A Reconsideration

DOUGLAS AMBROSE

I N *The World the Slaveholders Made,* Eugene Genovese noted how proslavery ideologue George Fitzhugh "ridiculed those Jeffersonian notions of weak government which were still so strong in the official political ideology of the South." Although Fitzhugh favored the decentralization of political power, he nonetheless advocated, in Genovese's words, "the vigorous exercise of power" and dismissed the prevalent "nonsense about the best government governing least."[1] Twenty-five years later, in *The Southern Tradition,* Genovese reminded his readers that not all antebellum southerners conformed to the popular image of jealous defenders of personal freedom from all but the most minimal exercise of governmental authority. Most may have shared John C. Calhoun's "effort to provide constitutional foundations for resistance to a Leviathan central government," but many, like Calhoun himself, "favored strong government within prescribed constitutional limits," for government performed the "special function of reining in the evil tendencies in human nature and strengthening the good."[2] Genovese's recognition that southern attitudes toward state power consisted of more than simple "notions of weak government" has remained largely underexplored. Many students of the slave South still believe that antebellum white southerners were suspicious of and indeed hostile to "the vigorous exercise of power."[3]

Yet these southerners, during the course of the Civil War, vastly expanded the scope of state governments and built the most powerful central government America had ever seen. Most historians who have pondered these remarkable phenomena have rightly focused on how the exigencies of war forced southerners into statist policies. Only the desperate desire to win the first modern war led southerners to embrace what they had traditionally considered one of their greatest threats. Southerners, notwithstanding their wartime actions, remained committed antistatists in principle.[4]

Several recent studies, although hardly rejecting the notion that most southerners sought to minimize state authority, suggest that as the war demonstrated, many may have been practical rather than principled antistatists.[5] The use of law, whether at the local, state, or national level, appealed to southerners who desired social reform. The idea that the exercise of governmental power threatened slavery and other precious liberties was, in effect, turned on its head as some important and influential southerners argued that the state was a vital instrument in the organization and defense of slavery and southern society. By regulating slavery and social relations, these southerners believed that the South would not only combat its opponents more effectively but, more important, make the South a more perfect society. They saw the state as a positive force that would shape society and prevent the social corruption that resulted from the irresponsible actions of unregulated individuals.

No one expressed these positive views of the state more enthusiastically or boldly than Henry Hughes of Port Gibson, Mississippi, whose statism was a central feature of his thought.[6] Few southerners, however, could accept Hughes's embrace of a Leviathan state, at least not before the war. But Hughes's ideas, although extreme and hardly representative, found support throughout the South, albeit in less explicit form.[7] One influential southern intellectual who shared some of Hughes's ideas on the state was the great Presbyterian divine James Henley Thornwell. An examination of Hughes's and Thornwell's ideas of the state hardly establishes the presence of a strong statist element in antebellum southern thought, but it does force us to reconsider the degree to which the wartime experience of southerners constituted a dramatic deviation from southern principles. Hughes's strongly secular argument and Thornwell's religious defense of state action suggest that southerners could draw upon more than simple expediency in their justifications for and creation of an activist state. Although the war forced southerners to expand state authority, it did not necessarily require them to jettison their principles. Rather, it permitted them to exercise what some intellectuals had all along insisted was the legitimate, even necessary role of the state in southern society.

Henry Hughes's statism grew out of his synthesis of classic and contemporary social thinkers and his desire to defend the South from northern political and ideological threats. He read broadly, especially among his contemporaries, including Charles Fourier, John Stuart Mill, Thomas Carlyle, John C. Calhoun, and Auguste Comte. But Hughes did not adopt one conception of the state from these or any other writer. Rather, his understanding remained distinctly his own.[8] Although he never systematically developed his ideas into a comprehensive, internally consistent theory of the state, his writings, most notably his *Treatise on Sociology,* establish the activist, nearly all-powerful state as the essential basis of any proper social order.

The *Treatise,* Hughes's most important work, vigorously denounced social contract theory and argued instead that man's nature and God's law compelled individuals to live in and belong to society. "The origin of rational association," he wrote, "is morally, not in a compact or agreement of the associates. Because the association is not free but commanded. It is a duty or law of God." Such a duty, he asserted, required individuals to comply; one's will had to be subordinated to one's duty: "And the will is not free to do or not to do, a duty. There is no choice. Duty is without alternative." But although duty compelled individuals to live in society, it was not sufficient to ensure society's proper functioning. Hughes strenuously maintained that all societies had one "primary, capital, necessary, overriding and supreme" goal: "the subsistence of all." All societies therefore had to develop the necessary means to ensure that every individual received "a comfortable sufficiency of necessaries for health and strength."[9]

Hughes posited that only an "orderly" society could fulfill the fundamental task of providing universal subsistence. "Anarchy is impotence. Men, therefore, must be orderly; the whole power of society, must be orderly" (51). But order could only be realized through unequal social relations. "In every society," Hughes wrote, "there must . . . be both orderers and orderees. Some must order; some, be ordered. These are subordinates; those, superordinates." At the top of any society that sought to realize its essential goal was "the supreme orderer . . . the sovereign power." This power, for Hughes, could be "either monarchical, oligarchical, aristocratic, republican, or democratic." It preserved order and attended to society's primary obligation through the "association, adaptation, and regulation" of society's members. The natural association that all human beings are born into differed from the association achieved by the sovereign power. "Association is not gregation. It is more than that. It is gregation adapted to an end; it is rational gregation" (51). But even this rational gregation could not adequately realize society's goal. "Rational gregation is insufficient for the existence and progress of all. To these ends, the adaptation and regulation of society, are necessary" (176). Thus, although human beings were naturally drawn together, they then had to devise rational systems to ensure universal subsistence, the only proper end of any association.

For Hughes, association, adaptation, and regulation were the means by which the sovereign power maintained the order needed for society to realize this end. "Association makes men ruly; adaptation makes their rules, and regulation makes them ruled" (52). The order that resulted from this process of association, adaptation, and regulation could not occur through individual choice; it could only be achieved through the exercise of sovereign power. "Sovereign order is therefore warranted. It is not natural or accidental; it is necessary or certain. It is not from choice, but from duty. It is ordained and established. It is authoritative. It is magisterial. It is not private; it is publicly organized; it is municipal" (54). Only a state capable of making and enforcing rules could warrant order and thereby provide the necessary basis for the pursuit of universal subsistence.

Society thus had to associate, adapt, and regulate its members so that order was maintained and universal subsistence realized. Not surprisingly, Hughes's argument led directly to an emphasis on the relations of production. Only a society that produced sufficiently could provide for its members. Hughes viewed labor as a social duty that all individuals owed society. "Everybody ought to work. Labor whether of mind or body, is a duty. We are morally obliged to contribute to the subsistence and progress of society." But this obligation, although moral, could not be left to individual conscience. Because the failure to fulfill this obligation jeopardized society's ability to realize its primary task, society had to ensure that everyone did his duty. "The obligation of every consumer to produce, may, as any other moral obligation, be if necessary, civilly enforced" (95). Hughes's emphasis on the "civil enforcement" of anyone's moral duties necessarily required that the state be able to exercise near total control of the productive process.

He stated that "the three economic classes are simple-laborers, skilled-laborers, and capitalists." Although each class had a different function within society, all contributed to the productive process, and accordingly, each was subject to state directive. "These three classes may, in a system, be civilly enforced to work, or do their economic duty." Based on its assessment of the economy, the state would decide whether one, two, or all three classes would require civil enforcement. The economy, because of its vital role in providing subsistence, was necessarily subject to state control. "The function of subsistence," Hughes pointed out, "is the economic system; but because existence is the right of all, and because the function of right or justice is the State or civil organization; the economic system is an implement of the State" (178). The civil enforcement of labor represented but one aspect of the state's prerogative to do whatever it needed to ensure subsistence. The freedom of individuals to do as they pleased must be subordinated to their need to fulfill their duty, either by moral or civil means. Hughes's elevation of social duty, and of the state's fundamental right to enforce that duty, severely restricted the personal freedom of individuals: "A man has not a right to use his mind and body as he will. . . . Man must do what he ought. . . . He cannot as he wills, work or be idle; pursue one, another, or no calling; be dissociate, unadapted or irregular. . . . The freedom of every man is therefore, qualified by a duty. That duty is to use it, as a social being ought. But a social being ought to use his labor socially, or for the existence and progress of all" (186). And, Hughes constantly reminded his readers, the state had to guarantee that every man did "what he ought." "The powers, rights, duties, and responsibilities of laborers and capitalists, must be adapted and regulated by law; their private relations superseded; public relations, ordained and established" (204).

The *Treatise* does not describe the South of 1854. Hughes wanted both to defend the South from outside attack and to urge internal reform. The *Treatise* thus contained his vision of what the South would hopefully become, and as the logic of his argument regarding society, duty, and the state makes evident, that vision necessitated fundamental changes in southern society. Throughout the *Treatise* Hughes argued that the social organization of the South was not slavery but "warranteeism." He never explicitly defined the term, but for him it was a set of social and economic relations and, by extension, the governing principle of political relations. Although some historians have dismissed warranteeism as simply a euphemism for slavery, Hughes's elaboration revealed instead a fundamentally different social order in which a powerful activist state controlled nearly all social activity.[10] For Hughes, the evolution of southern society from slavery to warranteeism consisted of recognizing through law the essentially "public" character of the master; his "powers, rights, duties and responsibilities" originated not from ownership of property but from the state's "transferral" of them to a "deputy."

Hughes's emphatic insistence that warranteeism differed from slavery centered in the state's role in each system. Following William Paley, whom he had read as a student at Mississippi's Oakland College, Hughes defined slavery as the "obligation to labor for the benefit of the master, without the contract or consent of the servant." Whereas slavery represented a private relation between a master who owned a slave, warranteeism was a system in which the state sanctioned and regulated a public relation between a "warrantor" and a "warrantee." "Warranteeism," he asserted, "is a public obligation of the warrantor and the warrantee, to labor and do other civil duties, for the reciprocal benefit of, (1) the State, (2), the Warrantee, and (3), the Warrantor." Unlike the slave, whose obligation was to the master, the warrantee's obligation was owed the state. "Nor is it [warranteeism] an obligation without the contract or consent of the servant. That consent is due of the State. It is the State's right. The servant consents, because he ought to consent. That is his duty." But Hughes made it clear that the "State's right" to the labor of the warrantee differed in no way from the state's right to the warrantor. "Both warrantor and warrantee, are economic lieges of the State." The entire relation between warrantor and warrantee constituted nothing more than a state creation.

In contrasting slavery and warranteeism, Hughes expressly rejected one of the essential characteristics of slavery: property in human beings. "The parties to the warrantee-obligation, have no property in each other. Property in man, is absurd. Men cannot be owned." What gave the warrantor authority over the warrantee was not his property right to the labor of another but the power conferred on that warrantor by the state. "The warrantee is obliged by the State in favor of the warrantor; but the warrantor is reciprocally obliged by the State, in favor of the warrantee" (167). Everyone was obligated to labor; the form that obligation took was up to the state. The state, in effect, determined how best to structure social relations so that everyone met his obligation and thereby preserved the proper functioning of society. "The obligor is the State. . . . All the powers, rights, duties, and responsibilities of the obligation issue from it. It is the economic sovereign, or lord-paramount. All are its lieges. . . . Justice is its only limit; and it is the judge of that. Parties to the labor-obligation, have no rights, duties, or powers, which the State does not authorize; over which the State has not jurisdiction; and which the State may not according to justice, amend, remedy, enlarge or restrain" (166). The state's ultimate and primary responsibility to ensure subsistence required that it create whatever social relations it deemed expedient. Whatever "rights" either warrantors or warrantees had, they had because the state granted them, not because they inhered in them as individuals. Individuals had, ultimately, but one right, the right to subsistence. But the state's need to ensure that right effectively eliminated the free exercise or even possession of any other right.

Hughes's statist vision had serious implications for all members of society, but it most forcefully confronted the slaveholders' position. Although warranteeism would have preserved the hierarchical and inegalitarian form of southern society, it would have radically transformed its substance and direction. Most notably, the master's power, over his laborers and even over his own actions, would derive from state-delegated authority. Thus, a vast expansion of state authority, although limiting individual slaveholders, would actually strengthen the unfree labor system and society of the South.

Hughes's persistent claim throughout the *Treatise* that "subsistence ought to be warranted to all" and that "everything ought to be stopped, till that is done," necessarily led him to propose state subordination of all individuals and classes (81). The state in warranteeism did not so much regulate relations between warrantors and warrantees, it created them. The state enabled a warrantor to "purchase" the labor obligation of another, who thereby became a warrantee. This fundamental relation, therefore, was not natural but civil and thus subject to state direction. Hughes, in fact, considered the warrantor a public officer, created to implement state policy; he was not an individual free to do what he willed. For Hughes, the public character of the warrantor proved crucial to his entire conception of warranteeism and the future of southern society. He desired, above all, to eliminate the personal power of masters by making them subject to state control.

"The warrantor capitalist or master," Hughes wrote, "is not the obligor of the warrantee labor-obligation. He is an agent of the State; nothing more. He is the State per proxy. The State is supreme and principal warrantor. The capitalist is deputy warrantor. That is a public office. The master is a magistrate" (166). As the mere "agent of the State," the warrantor possessed no "rights" to his warrantees, he simply exercised state-delegated authority over them. Hughes repeatedly reminded his readers that "all warrantors are special government-officers. Their official powers issue from the State, are subject to the State, and under review and visitation of the State. The State is supreme and supervising. It is the fountain of power" (227).

Clearly Hughes was not describing the contemporary South, even though all southern states in various ways regulated masters' power. Like many reformers who called for the legalization of slave marriage, the preservation of slave families, and the lifting of bans on slave literacy, Hughes urged southerners to expand the state's role in the master-slave relation, although he did not endorse these specific reforms. He differed from those reformers, however, in seeking to establish that critical social relation on fundamentally different principles. Hughes, in essence, redefined property. No longer would masters possess an absolute or even a qualified right over their laborers. Instead, control of labor and, by extension, all property represented a social trust. The basis of the state's intervention into social relations thus would not constitute an extraordinary action in which an individual's property rights were limited by social necessity; rather, the state would simply modify, as it saw fit, a relation that it created and controlled. When Hughes reiterated that all warrantor "rights, duties, powers, and responsibilities issue from the law, pursue the law, are limited by the law; and are created, continued, modified or terminated by the law" (212), he envisioned a South in which masters continued to command labor but did so under the watchful eye of an activist state. Nothing less than such a state could ensure the order and productivity that the law of universal subsistence demanded.

After the *Treatise*'s appearance in 1854, Hughes moved away from writing book-length theoretical works and focused more on the practical concerns facing the South. But even though he no longer wrote about warranteeism as a formal system, his writings continued to advance the southern need for a powerful regulatory state. Hughes labored strenuously to convince southerners that only the proper uses of state power could simultaneously strengthen unfree labor in its ongoing struggle with the forces of free labor and enable the South to fulfill the goal of universal subsistence.

Although Hughes's later writings frequently concentrated on slavery as opposed to warranteeism, he occasionally reiterated the vast differences between them. At times he argued that the South had already moved from slavery to warranteeism, but more frequently he continued to see warranteeism as a goal that the South was moving toward. As in the *Treatise,* he unceasingly viewed the expanded role of the state and the correspondingly diminished power of the master as the key distinctions between slavery and warranteeism. In his "Report on the African Apprentice System," which he presented at the 1859 Southern Commercial Convention in Vicksburg, Hughes noted that the "master's private power" most clearly characterized the slavery that had existed in America at the time of the adoption of the Constitution. Although "some statutes prohibiting the wanton slaughter of slaves" had partially mitigated the "inhumanity and injustice" of this system, the "master's powers" remained "sovereign, irresistible, unlimited, and irresponsible." Only the efficacious and therefore forceful use of state power could transform such a system into one that protected laborers from rapacious masters. Returning to his central argument in the *Treatise,* Hughes argued that the "State to whom economic allegiance for the subsistence of all" was due "associates, adapts and regulates the master's powers, rights, duties and responsibilities." The source of the master's authority lay not in property rights, for "the State entrusts to the masters" only the "labor-obligations" of laborers. "Thus," he concluded, "the masters are the State's deputies, public officers or magistrates to administer in responsibility to the State the public powers and duties transferred to them."[11]

Although Hughes took advantage of opportunities to articulate the fundamental principles of warranteeism, he also commented on specific policies and proposals that he believed might advance those principles. Thus in 1858, when Robert H. Purdom, editor of the Jackson-based newspaper *The Eagle of the South,* invited Hughes to comment on measures before the Mississippi legislature, he readily accepted. He strongly urged the enactment of the "African Contract-labor Immigration Bill," which would have permitted the state to import from Africa laborers who had "voluntarily" contracted to come work in Mississippi. Hughes argued that "within the last year Africans have been introduced" into the South and "are now at work on plantations in this or neighboring States." This unregulated introduction of laborers demanded state intervention. "The true issue," he stated "is not whether the supply of African labor shall be opened, but whether this supply already opened . . . shall be legitimated, regulated and equalized."[12] Throughout the late 1850s Hughes focused on this question of the state's role in controlling and regulating the influx of African labor. In an 1857 article he addressed the concern that the importation of African laborers would lead to a dangerous imbalance in the ratio of whites to blacks. The acquisition of such laborers, he maintained, would not be determined by the market but by the state. "Legislation," he assured his readers, "can systematically make it [the proportion of whites to blacks] more or less. For when the slave population shall have reached some certain limit, a tax on slaves introduced will regulate the introduction. . . . Thus taxation will be regulation, and each State can adapt to its need the number of its laborers." Hughes's use of the word *systematically* points to his frequent claim that state planning could solve existing social problems and avoid future ones. States that carefully examined conditions and needs could, through legislation, implement orderly and beneficial change. For Hughes, population ratios were not only legitimate matters of state concern but, like most social facts, capable of state manipulation and control. The proportion of whites to blacks, he confidently explained, "is, of course, . . . perfectly variable to the exigency. If need be, the law can as efficiently ordain one white to every five as well as one to every fifty blacks."[13] On practical concerns such as the race ratio, Hughes demonstrated his confidence in the activist state and sought to impart to his readers an understanding of the state as the efficient and logical instrument for the promotion of orderly social change.

Hughes's efforts to reopen the Atlantic slave trade provided him several opportunities to present this extremely positive view of the state's ability to implement beneficial social changes. In 1859, responding to the objection that an increase in the number of slaves would lead to the overproduction of cotton, he again insisted that the state could prevent such an occurrence. He reasoned that the state had a variety of options available that would enable it to import new laborers and yet maintain current levels of cotton production. Not only could the state adopt import restrictions, it could also regulate the type of labor performed by imported African laborers. Hughes explicitly called for the state to restrict the type of labor a master could demand of a slave. "Can the African Labor Supply be so restricted that only menials be introduced and our cotton force not directly or indirectly increased? Nothing is easier." Citing a litany of means other governments have historically employed to regulate economic activity, including "trade restrictions, regulation of employment, [and] limitations of laborers," he assuredly claimed that "only judicious legislation is needed" to ensure desired effects. "A statutory proviso," he proclaimed, "that all Africans and their descendants here shall be restricted to menial service or extra labor, and shall not directly, indirectly or by substitution become cotton hands, will prevent any supposed increase in the production and supposed decrease in the price of cotton."[14]

Hughes recognized that such a program of labor control required a vast expansion of the state's enforcement mechanisms. Not surprisingly, he welcomed such a development. "For the regulation of servants[,] employments, the customary governmental method is Classification, Registration and Identification. Each negro by this method is in law, first identified, then classified as a cotton hand or an extra hand, and then duly registered." Hughes had no doubt that "the identification of our negroes will not be difficult. Public officers if necessary may be ordained and sworn to identify. If necessary bloody letters may by State authority, be branded on the negroes cheeks and chins." Viciously criticizing "rampant, free-labor philanthropy," he proceeded to suggest that "in humorous contempt, in delightful and deliberate detestation of sanctimonious meddlers, let us . . . mark them like hogs and brand them like beeves." Hughes's harsh proposal should not obscure his statist vision. The "public officers" acting under "State authority" would ensure that laborers worked not as their master desired but as the state commanded. The regulatory system, Hughes excitedly related, would provide the state with information that would enable it to go far beyond restricting certain activities. "The sage statesman," he wrote, "will recognize that such restriction may by State classification, registration and identification be easily operated." But he "will also recognize that State classification and registration have for other purposes, superior advantages. Of these the chief is State information, for information must always precede reformation, and statistics ought to be the basis of all legislation." Hughes moved from the hypothetical questions of how to accommodate a reopened slave trade to urging that the collection of "State information" be accomplished regardless of whether or not the trade was re-opened. "The State by classification and registration will always be informed of the conditions, the proportions and the progress of its negro laborers, and even without the Labor Supply, such information is essential to right legisla-tion." Hughes thus concluded that the state had to pursue policies, such as the classification and registration of all slaves, that would enable it to function properly. The acquisition of accurate statistics, which itself would require a formidable bureaucratic apparatus, would provide the state with the infor-mation it needed to pursue social reformation through "right legislation." Such logic led inexorably to a vast expansion of state intervention into nearly every aspect of society.[15]

Although it may seem strange to pair the South's leading antebellum the-ologian with the rather obscure Hughes, aspects of James Henley Thornwell's thought, especially those that relate to his understanding of the state, make such a pairing instructive. Long recognized as an important leader of "Old School" Presbyterianism, Thornwell was president of South Carolina College, editor of the *Southern Presbyterian Review* and the *Southern Quarterly Re-view,* professor at Columbia Theological Seminary, and a prominent educa-tional reformer. All who have studied Thornwell have noted his prosouthern and proslavery convictions (although he opposed nullification and resisted secession until the last moment), best expressed in his well-known moniker "the Calhoun of the Church." His 1850 sermon *The Rights and the Duties of Masters* contains a classic exposition of the Christian defense of slavery.[16] Un-like Hughes, Thornwell never aspired to public office and devoted little pub-lic attention to specific political questions. And although he never developed an elaborate, complex vision of a statist southern society, he repeatedly dis-cussed the state in a number of his writings. Thornwell took pains to insist that as a minister of the church, his sphere of influence remained distinct from that of the state. But time and again the spheres overlapped, and Thorn-well did not shy away from public issues if they concerned moral questions. Slavery, intemperance, and profaneness necessarily involved the church, and its ministers, in the affairs of state. Thornwell's writings on these and similar issues reveal an understanding of the legitimacy, indeed moral necessity, of state activity. Far from viewing the state as a human institution to be feared, Thornwell endorsed the state as a divine ordinance bound by God's law to ex-ercise moral authority over man.

Regarding the nature and function of the state, Thornwell followed Calvin quite closely. As Calvin made clear in his chapter "On Civil Government" in the *Institutes of the Christian Religion,* the state is a divine creation that receives its authority directly from God. Men were to acknowledge that "the authority possessed by kings and other governors over all things upon earth is not a consequence of the perverseness of men, but of the providence and holy ordinance of God, who has pleased to regulate human affairs in this manner."[17] Thornwell echoed Calvin by frequently reminding his readers and listeners that "states and governments are the instruments of God, ordained in their respective departments, to execute His schemes."[18] In an 1848 article in the *Southern Presbyterian Review,* Thornwell reiterated his belief that "the State is a Divine ordinance, a social institute, founded on the principle of justice, and it has great moral purposes to subserve."[19] Thornwell's insistence on the divine origin of states carried with it a strong rejection of any notion that man was the author of governments. States, he asserted, "are a part of that series of Providential arrangements, by which the moral purposes of God, in reference to the race, are conducted to their issue—and as much the appointments of His will as the family, or the Church." Although human beings might decide what form the state might take, the essence was from God. "There is not the same direct interposition in the organization of civil and political communities as in the constitution of the Church—but the necessity of the State is founded in the nature of man. . . . It is the spontaneous offspring of a social state—and in the same sense the creature of God, that the society from which it springs and from which it cannot be severed is the Divine ordination." Thornwell's emphatic rejection of social contract theory, like Hughes's, rested on the belief that human beings were never isolated individuals who contracted with one another to leave a state of nature but were instead social beings designed by God to live in society and under government. "There never was an absurder, and I may add, a more mischievous fiction," he maintained, "than that political communities are conventional arrangements, suggested by the inconveniences of a natural state of personal independence, and deriving their authority from the free consent of those who are embraced in them." Thornwell saw in social contract theory another glaring example of the usurpation by man of God's majesty. Thornwell's understanding of the basis of states remained firmly grounded in his overarching belief in God's intimate role in human relations and his consequent insistence that man recognize his limited power over even seemingly temporal matters such as the origins of government. "Political societies are not artificial combinations to which men have been impelled by chance or choice, but the ordinance of God, through the growth and propagation of the species, for the perfection and education of the race."[20]

Human institutions — the family, the visible Church, and the state — both acknowledged God's power and contributed to the progress of humanity. The state thus represented both man's fallen state and the means by which he would move toward redemption. "The State," he wrote, "is an ordinance of God as God is in Christ reconciling the world unto Himself." The state was "an element of God's moral administration — and to secure his favour it must sedulously endeavor to maintain the supremacy of right."[21] Thornwell therefore understood that the proper performance of the state was a necessary precondition for the coming of Christ.[22] The state was no mere institution to facilitate the mundane affairs of men; its divine origins and function demanded that it be recognized, like the family, as an institution that had to follow God's will or risk his wrath. As Thornwell noted in his 1860 "Sermon on National Sins," "If the State is a moral institute, responsible to God, and existing for moral and spiritual ends, it is certainly a subject capable of sin." Like individuals, states had duties that flowed from God; "the State exists under a law which defines its duty. It is a means to an end, which limits its powers and determines its functions. It is the realization of an idea."[23] And like individuals, states that violated their duty deserved punishment.

Thornwell, in this sermon and in other writings, urged his audience, especially politicians, to recognize the social danger posed by the state that acted contrary to the commands of God. In an 1854 sermon Thornwell implored the South Carolina House of Representatives to remember "that the personal character of those who are placed in authority, have much to do, from the very nature of moral government, with the prosperity of the State." Rulers, including the legislators listening to him, "are the representatives of the land, and in God's word no more tremendous judgement is threatened against any people than the sending among them of ignorant, debauched and wicked counsellors." And although "to make a great people, you must make a pure people, and every man must begin with himself," Thornwell rejected the idea that individual reformation would produce social happiness. The state had to act, through law as well as example, in order to prevent sin and thereby protect society. "But next to this inquiry into our own State, the judgements of God should direct our attention to those forms of inequity which most extensively prevail in the land." Thornwell contended that a state that failed to correct pervasive "inequities" neglected its divine duty and thus tempted God's wrath: "When God's judgements are abroad in the land, they put us

upon general inquiry. They proclaim the fact of sin, and that sin we are to
search out and expel wherever we find it, whether in our own hearts, or in the
customs and usages of the people."[24] Law, in his view, not only expressed the
state's will, it more importantly displayed to God the degree to which that
will coincided with God's will. As Thornwell wrote in the early days of the
Confederacy, "Let us guard, in this new Confederacy, against the fatal delusion that our government is a mere expression of human will. It is, indeed, an
expression of *will,* but of will regulated and measured by those eternal principles of right which stamp it at the same time as the creature and institute of
God."[25] Only by designing legislation that conformed with God's will and
sought to "expel" sin from among a people could a state avoid rightful punishment. A state therefore had to scrutinize its actions carefully so as to avoid
the collective punishment God would impose on all within the state. "When
the State fails, or transgresses, its offenses are . . . abominations in the sight of
God. . . . the misconduct of the State is rebellion against God, and . . . a nation
which comes short of its destination, and is faithless to its trust, is stained
with sin of the most malignant dye." Such sin, Thornwell argued, could result
both from a state that acted beyond its rightful scope of authority or from
one that failed to exercise its rightful authority. Again echoing Calvin, who
wrote that a permissive government was worse than an overly authoritarian
one, Thornwell argued in his sermon to the house of representatives that "one
other instance of sin . . . calls for humiliation and correction." This sin was
"the deplorable extent to which our laws, especially in the punishment of
crime, are prevented from being executed. It is a lesson which pervades the
Bible, that States and communities may be dealt with as guilty of crimes
which they refuse or neglect to punish." Only a state that vigorously enforced
the law, that exercised its righteous will among the people, could fulfill its
providential duty. Thornwell contemptuously dismissed "a sickly and mawk-
ish benevolence . . . a feeling of pity and of childish tenderness to the person
of the criminal" that "prevents any adequate expression, and, in many instances, any expression at all, of indignation and horror at the crime." "In
such cases," he warned, "the community assumes the guilt." "There is no principle which is more plainly stated, more clearly illustrated, more frequently
exemplified in the sacred Scriptures, than that the punishment of malefactors
is a duty. It is not discretionary; not a thing of expediency or policy; it is a
duty."[26] Failure to fulfill this duty would violate the state's primary function
and, consequently, would produce disorder. "Freedom must degenerate into
licentiousness unless the supremacy of right is maintained. We must co-oper-
ate in our spirit and temper and aims with the great moral ends for which the

State was instituted, if we would reach the highest point of national excellence and prosperity."[27] "*There* only is security," he warned in another sermon, "where the law is supreme; and the worst of all social evils is where the populace is stronger than the law."[28]

Just as "national excellence and prosperity" resulted from the state's maintenance of "the supremacy of right," Thornwell, like Hughes, understood social chaos to arise, at least in part, from the state's failure to understand its fundamental responsibility and act accordingly. Whereas for Hughes that responsibility was universal subsistence, for Thornwell it was obedience to divine will. "To absolve the State," he wrote, "from a strict responsibility to the Author and Source of justice and law, is to destroy the firmest security of public order, to convert liberty into license, and to impregnate the very being of the commonwealth with the seeds of dissolution and decay."[29] Although he repeatedly claimed that church and state remain separate, he nonetheless insisted that the state acknowledge its Christian duty to follow God's word. Thus, although "the Church has no right to construct or modify a government for the State, and the State has no right to frame a creed or polity for the Church,"[30] "a State . . . which does not recognize its dependence upon God, or which fails to apprehend, in its functions and offices, a commission from heaven, is false to the law of its own being." For Thornwell, "every state, therefore, must have a religion, or it must cease to be a government of men." Not only must the state have a religion, "it is equally necessary, in order to an adequate fulfillment of its own idea, that it have the true religion."[31] Such a view necessarily compelled the state to act in accordance with Christian principles. When Thornwell thundered that the punishment of malefactors "was not discretionary; not a thing of expediency or policy" but a "duty," he laid bare the extent to which the state's Christian character mandated its actions, which "limits its powers and determines its functions."[32] Maintaining "the supremacy of right" called not for passive Christian legislators who acted only when un-Christian laws were proposed but for active ones who legislated in order to remedy sin. Thornwell claimed that the "will of God, as revealed in the Scriptures . . . does not prescribe the things to be done, but only forbids the things to be avoided. It only conditions and restrains the discretion of rulers within the bounds of the Divine law."[33] Nevertheless, his writings insist again and again that legislators ensure that the divine law be followed. Although he often framed the relation of Christianity to the state as a negative one that set limits on rulers, he just as often expressed it as a positive one that commanded rulers to act. Even the notion that Christianity prevented legislators from voting against God's will led to the corresponding demand that they vote for it. "As every legislator is bound to be a Christian man, he has no right to vote for any laws which are inconsistent with the teachings of the Scriptures. He must carry his Christian conscience into the halls of legislation."[34] But once in those halls, that Christian legislator was "bound" to vote for laws that would fulfill the state's obligation to God. It is in the calls for state action to remedy social defects that Thornwell's positive view of the state surfaces most clearly.

Thornwell identified three areas in which the state had to take positive action in order to eliminate or at least minimize social sin. Intemperance and profaneness represented cases of individual sins that had become so widespread that they constituted "national sins." Slavery posed a rather different dilemma. Individual slaveholders, like drunkards and profaners, committed sinful acts. But slaveholders, according to Thornwell, directly violated the rights of slaves who, as Christians and as human beings, also possessed rights that the state had to protect. Thornwell encouraged the state to expand its scope so that it could effectively address all three sins. His calls for state regulation of intemperance and profaneness, although revealing his positive view of the state, nonetheless would have kept the state on the margins of most southerners' lives. His call for an expanded role of the state in the master-slave relation, however, brought him, like Hughes, to envision a fundamentally different social order than that which had hitherto prevailed.

Thornwell posited that "there are . . . forms of sin which, though not national in the sense that they pertain to the administration of the government, are national in the sense that they are widely diffused among the people. . . . Conspicuous among these is the sin of profaneness."[35] Six years earlier he had made the same accusation in his sermon to the South Carolina house: "Profaneness and intemperance," he claimed, "deserve to be called national sins."[36] Although the state may have been unable to eradicate every individual profane or drunken act, as part of its divine duty it had to act both to correct the individual transgressor and to ensure that the state did not participate in the sin itself. Thus, regarding profaneness, Thornwell charged that "the government is implicated in the sin," because it "encourages the desecration of the Lord's Day by the companies which carry its mails."[37] The government, he therefore argued, had to bar Sunday mail deliveries or be guilty of sin and thereby risk collective divine punishment. The logic here compelled the state, as a Christian institution, to legislate not according to popular mandate but according to Christian principle. Thornwell's hostility toward democracy, a sin he referred to as "the *deification* of the people" and "the worst of all governments," grew directly out of his belief that states were bound by divine truth, not popular will. The state had to resist the temptation to satisfy the people; it instead had to maintain its commitment to its higher providential purpose. In his sermon to the South Carolina house Thornwell stated, "This legislature is not a congregation of deputies, or ministerial agents, and you have, and know that you have, higher functions to perform than merely to inquire what do the people think." Although popular opinion should be considered, he insisted "that the true and legitimate end of government is not to accomplish their will, but to do and enforce what reason, conscience, and truth pronounce to be right. . . . The will of the people should be done only when the people will what is right, and then primarily not because they will it, but because it is right."[38] This denunciation of democracy flowed from Thornwell's view of the state as not only a divinely ordained institution but one that had to "do and enforce" what was right in the eyes of God. The only "legitimate end" of government was fulfilling its divine duty, which required that it act aggressively, if need be, to minimize sin. "A Commonwealth is magnanimous," he wrote, "when it comprehends the vocation of a State, when it rises to the dignity of its high functions, and seeks to cherish a spirit in harmony with the great moral purposes it was ordained to execute."[39] Profaneness, therefore, whether committed by individuals or by the state, had to be punished and corrected. This process whereby individual actions became state concerns because they violated that which the state was duty bound to protect—God's will—was even more apparent in Thornwell's comments on intemperance.

Thornwell, like countless other antebellum Americans, considered intemperance an immense evil. Demonstrating the intimate connection between personal behavior and social effect, he viewed intemperance, like profaneness, as one of those sinful "customs and usages of the people" that the state had "to search out and expel." "In its influence upon society," he instructed the South Carolina house, "hardly less disastrous [than the consequences of widespread profaneness] are the ravages of intemperance." The individual drunkard, Thornwell reasoned, not only defied God, but his actions also inhibited society's ability to progress. The collective need and duty of society, therefore, required that it discipline the individual drunkard. "Refinement proceeds upon a principle that drunkenness directly contradicts, and, as it is the end of civilization to develop and carry out this principle, the drunkard stands in the way, a monument of degradation and of barbarism."[40]

The obstacle of the individual drunkard illuminates Thornwell's logic of state action. If individual actions conflicted with or violated society's adherence to divine duty, then those actions became the legitimate target of state action. Thornwell, like Calvin, claimed that states could do whatever they wanted "so long as they keep within the limits of the Divine Law."[41] Although intended primarily to check the role of the church in state affairs, the commitment to ensure that the state did not violate divine law became the basis for the expansion of state authority into society generally and, in the case of intemperance, into the lives of individuals in particular. Yes, the state was free to do what it willed as long as its actions did not contradict divine law. Allowing Sunday mail deliveries was a state action that directly violated Scripture and was thus illegitimate. But when the state permitted individuals to act profanely or intemperately, Thornwell argued, it also violated its duty. Only by acting, by legislating to correct individual actions that corrupted society and invoked God's wrath, could states fulfill their obligation to God. Thornwell told the legislators that the "drunkard is not the object of peculiar sympathy or compassion. He is as truly criminal, though it may be not in the same degree, as the robber or the assassin. And this sin never will be put down until it is placed on the footing of other crimes, and visited according to the demands of justice."[42] His explicit equating of sin and crime drove home the fundamental function of the Christian state: "to search out and expel" sin. Such a task necessarily broadened the legitimate scope of the state to a near limitless extent. Because individual behavior had social ramifications that jeopardized the state's ability to realize God's will, the state was obligated to regulate or, if need be, eliminate that behavior. Like the efforts of Hughes's warrantee state to ensure universal subsistence, the duty of Thornwell's Christian state to enforce "the supremacy of right" led it into nearly every aspect of social life. In the antebellum South, of course, no aspect of social life mattered more than slavery. And here too, Thornwell's view of the state's legitimate role paralleled Hughes's and, like Hughes's, transformed slavery from a property relation to a state-regulated one between two persons.

Thornwell, like Hughes and many other southerners, rejected the notion that masters possessed unlimited authority over their slaves. Following William Paley, again like Hughes, Thornwell insisted that slavery be defined as "the obligation to labour for another, determined by the Providence of God, independently of the provisions of a contract." Under such conditions, he continued, "the right which the master has is a right, not to the *man,* but to his *labour.*"[43] Thornwell repeatedly insisted that slaves were men and, like Hughes, totally rejected the idea that slaves were property. "The idle declamation about degrading men to the condition of chattels and treating them as oxen or swine, the idea that they are regarded as tools and instruments and not as beings possessed of immortal souls, betray a gross ignorance of the real nature of the relation."[44] But it is important to note here that Thornwell did not simply state that slaves were treated like men; he was not defending practice so much as establishing principle. Slaves had to be treated as men because they "possessed . . . immortal souls." Thornwell's Christian convictions demanded that he reject any notion of slavery that compromised the slave's essential humanity. He was thus led to or, rather, eagerly embraced the notion of slave rights. Just as Hughes acknowledged that slaves, as people, possessed the right to subsistence, Thornwell held that slaves, as people, possessed souls and the rights that accompanied them. He found support for this belief, as he did for so many others, in the Bible: the apostles "treat him [the slave] as a man—possessed of certain rights, which it was injustice to disregard." But the Bible not only established that slaves had rights, it also demanded that Christians protect those rights. Thus did Thornwell establish the basis for intervention in and regulation of the master-slave relation. The apostles, he asserted, "make it the office of Christianity to protect these rights by the solemn sanctions of religion—to enforce upon masters the necessity, the moral obligation, of rendering to their bondmen that which is just and equal."[45]

These words echoed what many southerners, ministers in particular, had been saying for decades. But unlike most of them, Thornwell was not content with the hope that Christians, either individually or through their churches, would "enforce upon masters" their "moral obligation." The logic that led him to call for state responses to the "national sins" of profaneness and intemperance, led him with even greater force to call for state action against sinful masters.[46] For slavery involved relations between and among people, as moral agents, and because the "necessity of the State . . . springs from the moral relations of individuals," no human relation could exist totally outside of state supervision.[47] In his sermon on *The Rights and the Duties of Masters,* Thornwell left no doubt that law, as well as right religion, was vital to the security of slave rights: "In treating slavery as an existing institution, a fact involving most important moral relations, one of the prime duties of the State is to protect, by temporal legislation, the real rights of the slave."[48] Thornwell knew well that there already existed laws that regulated the actions of masters vis-à-vis their slaves. He also probably knew, along with many Americans, North and South, and modern historians, that those laws were infrequently enforced.[49] He therefore coupled his call for law with an insistence that the state enforce that law. Although the "moral sense of the country acknowledges them [slave rights]—[and] the religion of the country to a large extent, ensures their observance," nonetheless "until they are defined by law and enforced by penalties there is no adequate protection of them."[50] Thornwell was by no means talking through his hat. The entire logic of his understanding of the state compelled him to demand the vigorous enforcement of the law. States that failed to execute laws were "guilty of the crimes which they refuse or neglect to punish."[51] A state, "like an individual, . . . may sin by defect in coming short of its duty." "The moral law is one, and the State is bound to do its duty"; therefore, "when the State fails, or transgresses, its offences are equally abominations in the sight of God."[52]

Thornwell's Christian understanding of slaves as moral beings and his Christian understanding of the state's critical role in protecting the rights that inhered in all moral beings necessarily led him to endorse an activist, interventionist state that would have seriously limited the master's authority over his slaves. Thornwell's conception of slave rights reveals the extent to which the state would have to insert itself into the master-slave relation. In his "Sermon on National Sins," he asked the slaveholding states to inquire "whether we have rendered unto our servants that which is just and equal." Such an inquiry could not be limited solely to personal behavior. "Is our legislation in all respects in harmony with the idea of Slavery? Are our laws such that we can heartily approve them in the presence of God?" Once again, notwithstanding his claim that "political and social relations . . . are not within the province of her [the Church's] immediate labours," Thornwell believed that the laws regarding the social relation of slavery had to conform to the will of God.[53] "Have we sufficiently protected the person of the slave? Are our provisions adequate for giving him a fair and impartial trial when prosecuted for offences? Do we guard as we should his family relations? And, above all, have we furnished him with proper means of religious instruction?"[54]

Such a vision of slavery, in which legislation protected slaves from mistreatment, guaranteed fair trials, preserved families, and ensured religious instruction, required a vast expansion of the state and a corresponding restriction of masters' personal authority. Indeed, like Hughes, Thornwell envisaged a social order in which the state's need to ensure that social relations corresponded to God's law superseded a master's "property right" to his slave's person and even to his labor. Thornwell did indeed recognize slave rights, and that recognition did lead him away from slavery, even though he, unlike Hughes, continued to use the term. But Thornwell's "idea of Slavery" represented something substantially, even fundamentally, different from actual southern practice. Slavery, as it existed in the antebellum South, had to be transformed so that it concurred with God's will. If the South continued to allow violations of slave rights or failed to enforce the laws meant to prevent such violations, it would be guilty of sin and worthy of divine chastisement.

Thornwell recognized that only by establishing a different basis for unfree labor could southern society avoid God's wrath. That basis would be the authority granted to masters by a state that considered first and foremost the dictates of divine law. Government should only extend authority that proved consistent with the will of God, and it should further legislate to ensure that masters exercised that authority properly. The individual master would be subject to supervision and correction. In short, Thornwell's conception of the state as a divine ordinance "bound to reverence the gospel" and his conviction that slaves, as persons, were "bone of our bone, and flesh of our flesh," and thereby deserving of Christian treatment, produced a vision of southern society in which the state, not the master, reigned supreme.[55] For Thornwell, even slaveholder control of the government would not affect this vision, because "God will bring" all rulers "into judgement for their public and official conduct.... God demands of them a supreme regard for justice, truth and religion." By establishing a transcendent standard of "justice, truth and religion," much like Hughes's universal subsistence, Thornwell attempted to free state policy from "selfish schemes" and ground it in divine law. The state, and whatever parties controlled it, "cannot expect the patronage of heaven to schemes of injustice and wrong."[56] To hope that individual masters would protect slave rights was "wrong," as was any social system that refused to recognize and correct such an abdication of governmental responsibility. As the South headed into its experiment in independent nationhood, Thornwell hoped that now it could firmly establish the only legitimate social order, legitimate because it conformed to God's word. In a Christian Confederacy, Thornwell hoped to see a society in which the state exercised the authority God granted it to ensure "the supremacy of right."

Thornwell and Hughes differed in many respects regarding their views of the state. Thornwell, for instance, never approached Hughes's enthusiastic certainty that the state was the source of rights and the fountain of all power. Hughes, for his part, appealed more to his own understanding of natural law than to the Bible and thus did not commit himself to Thornwell's belief that the state was limited as well as sanctioned by the higher authority of God. Notwithstanding these differences, however, Hughes and Thornwell shared an underlying conviction that the state had to occupy and exercise a central role in southern society. In particular, they advocated that the state regulate individual behavior in order to fulfill its essential responsibilities. Both men, in effect, saw the state as the primary vehicle by which the South would preserve those elements that deserved preservation — order, hierarchy, justice — and eliminate those that threatened it, especially the irresponsible, selfish master. For both men, the state possessed the power to punish and thus minimize the negative social consequences of freedom. Hughes and Thornwell ultimately agreed that the activist state was the necessary and beneficial alternative to the free individual. They thus both believed that only through the state, and not in freedom from it, could the South realize, in Thornwell's words, "the perfection and education of the race."[57]

Notes

1. Eugene D. Genovese, *The World the Slaveholders Made: Two Essays in Interpretation* (New York, 1969), 210, 207.

2. Eugene D. Genovese, *The Southern Tradition: The Achievement and Limitations of an American Conservatism* (Cambridge, Mass., 1994), 28, 64.

3. Those who see a strong "republican" element in southern political culture suggest that southerners, especially Democrats, viewed state power with suspicion and fear. See, for example, J. Mills Thornton, *Politics and Power in a Slave Society, Alabama, 1800–1860* (Baton Rouge, La., 1978).

4. The most thorough study of statism in the Confederacy is Richard Franklin Bensel, *Yankee Leviathan: The Origins of Central State Authority in America, 1859–1877* (New York, 1990).

5. See, for example, Eugene Genovese's comments on William H. Trescot in *The Slaveholders' Dilemma: Freedom and Progress in Southern Conservative Thought, 1820–1860* (Columbia, S.C., 1992); William W. Freehling "Beyond Racial Limits: Paternalism over Whites in the Thought of Calhoun and Fitzhugh," in his *The Reintegration of American History: Slavery and the Civil War* (New York, 1994), 82–104; and, more broadly, Mark V. Tushnet, *The American Law of Slavery, 1810–1860: Considerations of Humanity and Interest* (Princeton, N.J., 1981).

6. On Hughes, see Bertram Wyatt-Brown, "Modernizing Southern Slavery," in his *Yankee Saints and Southern Sinners* (Baton Rouge, La., 1985), and Douglas Ambrose, *Henry Hughes and Proslavery Thought in the Old South* (Baton Rouge, La., 1996).

7. The two most prominent southerners who resembled Hughes in this respect were George Fitzhugh and William H. Trescot.

8. For Hughes's readings, see his diary in the Henry Hughes Papers, Mississippi Department of Archives and History, Jackson. See also Ambrose, *Henry Hughes*. The relation of Hughes's statist ideas to those of nineteenth-century European statists is complex, as are all questions of intellectual genealogy. Hughes's eclectic borrowing and his own original notions of the state's proper role in social and economic life produced a vision that defies easy comparisons with other thinkers. A larger, separate study will examine southern views of the state within the context of Western statist thought.

9. Henry Hughes, *Treatise on Sociology, Theoretical and Practical* (Philadelphia, 1854), 176, 81, 122 (words quoted). Hereafter, page references in the text are to this book.

10. For examples, see Louis Hartz, *The Liberal Tradition in America: An Interpretation of American Political Thought since the Revolution* (New York, 1955), 149, and Eric L. McKitrick, *Slavery Defended: The Views of the Old South* (Englewood Cliffs, N.J., 1963), 51.

11. Henry Hughes, "A Report on the African Apprentice System" (1859), in *Selected Writings of Henry Hughes: Antebellum Southerner, Slavocrat, Sociologist*, ed. Stanford M. Lyman (Jackson, 1985), 177.

12. Henry Hughes, "Letter to R. H. Purdom" (1858), ibid., 147–48.

13. "St. Henry" [Henry Hughes], "'Re-opening of the Slave Trade: Sectional and State Security Argument' Number IV," Jackson *Mississippian and State Gazette*, 2 Dec. 1857; also in Lyman, *Selected Writings*, 100.

14. "St. Henry" [Hughes], "Re-opening of the African Labor Supply—Number Seven—Wealth Argument," Jackson *Semi-Weekly Mississippian*, 4 Oct. 1859.

15. Ibid. In an 1854 article Hughes urged that "it is now time that the Southern States should commence the collection of slavery statistics." "Statistical information," he asserted "is the very best. It is received without prejudice. It impresses. It is reliable." Hughes believed that, armed with such information, the South could command "a new verdict of the world on the slavery question." See Hughes, "New Duties of the South," Port Gibson *Southern Reveille*, 18 Nov. 1854, clipping, in Hughes Scrapbook, Hughes Papers.

16. In 1852 John Patillo of Emory College wrote to Thornwell to request a copy of his sermon. See Patillo to Thornwell, 9 Nov. 1852, Thornwell Papers, SCL; see also Freehling, "Thornwell's Antislavery Moment."

17. John Calvin, *Institutes of the Christian Religion*, trans. John Allen, 2 vols. (Philadelphia, 1936), 2:774.

18. James Henley Thornwell, *Thoughts Suited to the Present Crisis: A Sermon, on Occasion of the Death of Hon. John C. Calhoun* (Columbia, S.C., 1850), 28–29.

19. Thornwell, "The Ruling Elder: Being a Review of Two Speeches of Dr. Breckinridge," in *The Collected Writings of James Henley Thornwell*, ed. John B. Adger and John L. Giradeau, 4 vols. (1871–73; rept. Carlisle, Pa., 1974), 4:58.

20. Thornwell, *Thoughts*, 29.

21. Ibid., 37, 34.

22. It should be noted here that Thornwell, unlike Hughes, was not utopian. As a Calvinist, Thornwell rejected the idea of earthly perfection. The perfection that would result was because of God's will, not man's design. "The Gospel," he insisted, "does not propose to make our present state a *perfect* one—to make our earth a heaven. Here is where the philanthropists mistake" (Thornwell, *The Rights and the Duties of Masters* [Charleston, S.C., 1850], 32).

23. Thornwell, "Sermon on National Sins," in Adger and Girardeau, *Collected Writings* 4:521.

24. Thornwell, *Judgements, a Call to Repentance. A Sermon Preached by Appointment of the Legislature in the Hall of the House of Representatives* (Columbia, S.C., 1854), 11–13.

25. Thornwell, "The Relation of the State to Christ," in Adger and Girardeau, *Collected Writings* 4:551.

26. Thornwell, *Judgements*, 20–21.

27. Thornwell, *Thoughts*, 35.

28. Thornwell, "Sermon on National Sins," in Adger and Girardeau, *Collected Writings*

4:535. Here, and elsewhere, Thornwell leveled heavy attacks on democracy. "Representatives are appointed," he insisted, "not to ascertain what the will of the people actually is, but what it ought to be." Like Hughes, Thornwell endorsed a republican form of government, but he warned that obedience to right, not to popular opinion, had to guide state activity.

29. Thornwell, "Our Danger and Our Duty," in Benjamin Morgan Palmer, *The Life and Letters of James Henley Thornwell* (Richmond, 1875), 588.

30. Thornwell, "An Address of the General Assembly of the Presbyterian Church in the Confederate States to all the Churches of Jesus Christ throughout the Earth" (1861), in Adger and Girardeau, *Collected Writings* 4:449. See also Thornwell, "Speech on African Colonization, [1859]," ibid., 475–76.

31. Thornwell, "Sermon on National Sins," ibid., 515–16.

32. Ibid., 521.

33. Thornwell, "The Relation of the State to Christ," ibid., 553. See also Thornwell, *Report on the Subject of Slavery, Presented to the Synod of South Carolina* (Columbia, S.C., 1852), 8; and Thornwell, "Church Boards and Presbyterianism," in Adger and Girardeau, *Collected Writings* 4:259.

34. Thornwell, "Sermon on National Sins," in Adger and Girardeau, *Collected Writings* 4:517.

35. Ibid., 537.

36. Thornwell, *Judgements*, 13.

37. Thornwell, "Sermon on National Sins," in Adger and Girardeau, *Collected Writings* 4:538.

38. Thornwell, *Judgements*, 17–18. It should be noted that Thornwell, like Calhoun, denounced "mass" or "numerical" democracy. Both supported the "republican" or "constitutional" democracy.

39. Thornwell, "Sermon on National Sins," in Adger and Girardeau, *Collected Writings* 4:546.

40. Thornwell, *Judgements*, 15.

41. Thornwell, *Report*, 8. Also see "Sermon on National Sins," in Adger and Girardeau, *Collected Writings*, 4:517.

42. Thornwell, *Judgements*, 16.

43. Thornwell, *Rights and Duties*, 24. The definition of slavery is practically the only aspect of Paley's thought with which Thornwell agreed. For his criticisms of Paley, see Benjamin R. Stuart's 1853 student notebook, "Notes on Paley's Moral Philosophy," Thornwell to William Preston [President of South Carolina College], 23 Nov. 1846, and Thornwell to Preston, 1 May 1847, all in Thornwell Papers. The *Collected Writings* also contain lengthy criticisms of Paley.

44. Thornwell, "Sermon on National Sins," in Adger and Girardeau, *Collected Writings* 4:541. See also Thornwell, *Report*, 10, and Thornwell, *Hear the South! The State of the Country: An Article Republished from the* Southern Presbyterian Review (New York, 1861) 15–16.

45. Thornwell, *Rights and Duties*, 19.

46. William Freehling has examined this aspect of Thornwell's thought with particular insight. Although I differ with him on certain questions, his essay has significantly influenced my analysis. See Freehling, "Thornwell's Mysterious Antislavery Moment."

47. Thornwell, *Thoughts*, 29.

48. Thornwell, *Rights and Duties*, 46.

49. On the enforcement of laws regulating master-slave relations, see especially Andrew Fede, *People without Rights: An Interpretation of the Fundamentals of the Law of Slavery in the U.S. South* (New York, 1992).

50. Thornwell, *Rights and Duties*, 46.

51. Thornwell, *Judgements*, 20.

52. Thornwell, "Sermon on National Sins," in Adger and Girardeau, *Collected Writings* 4:521–22.

53. Thornwell, "Review of the General Assembly [Presbyterian Church] of 1847," ibid., 502.

54. Thornwell, "Sermon on National Sins," ibid., 543. The question of fair trials for slaves had concerned Thornwell personally some years earlier. See his 3 May 1854 Report to the Board of Trustees of South Carolina College, Thornwell Papers.

55. Thornwell, *Thoughts*, 20; Thornwell, "Sermon on National Sins," in Adger and Girardeau, *Collected Writings* 4:543.

56. Thornwell, *Thoughts*, 26, 34.

57. Ibid., 29.

6

Moment of Truth: A Woman of the Master Class in the Confederate South

DREW GILPIN FAUST

THE CIVIL WAR, Eugene Genovese wrote in 1974, forced the slaveholders of the South into a "confrontation with themselves." The conflict was, as he described it, a "moment of truth" for the master class, compelled to witness the erosion not just of slavery but of the very assumptions on which both the peculiar institution and the southern social order had been based. The ideological structures of power in the slave South have been central to Genovese's scholarly concerns, and his conceptualizations of hegemony have demonstrated the ways in which the master class sought to naturalize its rule over both slaves and lesser whites, to govern by holding brute force in reserve while wielding ideas as everyday weapons.[1]

Critical to any such interpretation of power relations is a deep and nuanced understanding of the master class's vision of itself, of its justifications, its own delineation of the logic and legitimacy of its rule. In the crisis of Civil War, this logic, like the world it was designed to explain, met its severest test. For many of the South's ruling elite, the Confederate years were not just a time of physical suffering and emotional anguish caused by the demands and losses of war. The era was a moment of ideological upheaval as well, as the privileges of antebellum years were called into question and the prerogatives of the master class laid bare, even as their foundations began to disappear.

The wartime journal of one elite southerner offers a textured glimpse into the day-to-day negotiation of this privilege and its foundations in racial, religious, class, sectional, and gender assumptions. Removed from the fullest exercise of power by her womanhood, Catherine Edmondston of North Carolina was nevertheless advantaged in every other possible way—by both her own and her husband's family background and wealth, by her whiteness and her position as mistress of eighty-eight slaves, by her education, and by her insulation from war's severest hardships. Perhaps the contradiction between her subordination as female and her prerogatives as wealthy and white made her a sharper and more vehement defender of the privileges she did possess. She was an acute observer—and grateful beneficiary—of the world the slave-holders made. Yet unlike George Fitzhugh or Henry Hughes, she did not make her commentary "in the abstract" but in the context of the daily events of a war waged to destroy that very world.[2]

Catherine Anne Devereux Edmondston was thirty-seven years old when the Civil War broke out. Married since 1846 to Patrick Edmondston, descendant of a prominent Charleston family, she lived with her husband and their slaves on a nearly two-thousand-acre cotton plantation in Halifax County, North Carolina, adjacent to the residence of her father and stepmother. Childless, the Edmondstons focused their emotional lives almost exclusively upon one another, and Catherine thus approached the separations and dangers of war with particular trepidation.

From the outbreak of the secession crisis, the couple shared fervent sectionalist views that in part reflected Patrick's South Carolina origins and ties. Lincoln's election in November 1860 precipitated considerable friction between the Edmondstons and Catherine's father, a loyal Whig of strong Unionist leanings. When Catherine voiced her support for southern independence, her stepmother was horrified, proclaiming her a "terrible traitor." Catherine was deeply troubled by this disagreement within her family. "This difference of opinion with Father has been very sad to me, for I think I can honestly say that it is the first time in my life that my judgment and feelings did not yield to him." But she did not believe herself to be simply choosing her husband over her father. She regarded herself as an informed and astute political analyst. Her long-standing intellectual interests now concentrated themselves on current events; poetry seemed trivial, Ruskin's "aesthetics of painting" irrelevant. "Public affairs," she declared, "absorb all our interest."[3]

Catherine Edmondston's understanding of the issues dividing North and South reveals much of her social as well as her political philosophy. The Confederacy represented the embodiment and the guarantor of her status; the North threatened the very assumptions that shaped her world. Catherine Edmondston never doubted that the Civil War was about slavery. "We want," she explained, "simply to be left alone & allowed to manage our own domestic institutions in our own way." She defined Yankees as "vile" creatures who "exalt the negro & debase the white man." After the Emancipation Proclamation, she began simply to refer to them as the "Abolitionists," underlining her belief that the North was fighting not for the Union or the Constitution but for the destruction of slavery.[4]

The North's antislavery stance, its foolish sentimentality about African Americans, its false abolitionist "philanthropy" seemed to Catherine Edmondston but a piece of a larger and still more pernicious misconstruction of the world. The North's racial views were an aspect of broader "leveling" tendencies that marked Yankees as a threat to the multiple hierarchies on which Catherine Edmondston believed any civilized society must rest. "That is just the difference between us," she remarked early in the war. "Our army is composed mainly of gentlemen. . . . Theirs is the riff raff." This distinction appeared even more clearly, she believed, in the contrast between Union and Confederate leaders. Jefferson Davis was a man of "good breeding," while Abraham Lincoln's backwoods humor betrayed the vulgarity of his origins. None of the North's politicians and generals had been raised with the much vaunted southern "habit of command." "Neither Lincoln, Halleck, Stanton, McClellan, Burnside or Hooker," she proclaimed in 1863, "understand the first principles of a gentleman . . . they know not what is due themselves from their subordinates or their subordinates from their own hands. Faugh! they disgust me." The attributes of the southerner's class status would provide the means for its own preservation. The gentleman, Catherine Edmondston argued, was both the justification for southern civilization and its best weapon of defense.[5]

In practice, however, Patrick Edmondston proved to be not much of a weapon at all. Although he had attended West Point and possessed considerable military knowledge, Patrick spent most of the war at home with his beloved wife, not risking his life for the Confederacy. Patrick's secessionism translated in the first months of war into an effort to raise a company of volunteers under his command. In June 1861 this troop departed to defend the Carolina coast. Catherine stifled her anguish in deference to her devotion to the Cause she had so enthusiastically embraced. Although wives of the common soldiers "wept, sobbed, and even shreiked aloud," she was determined to display a demeanor befitting her position as the captain's wife. "The sentiment of exalted Patriotism which filled my heart found no echo in Lamentations, no vent in tears." Reproducing the rhetoric of male service and female sacrifice that propelled men across the South into arms, Catherine wrote: "He is gone, gone in the exercise of man's highest & holiest duty. Yet I would not have him here, would not have him fail in one duty, falter in one step."[6]

Within weeks, the couple was reunited, for Catherine arranged to move in with friends living on the coast near Patrick's command. Camp visits were "short, unsatisfactory & tantalizing," but far better than the anxiety and lone-liness of prolonged separation. By fall Patrick had returned home, resigning his commission because of the enlistees' discontent with his leadership.[7]

From this time forward, Catherine's patriotism and self-sacrifice, her will-ingness to give her husband up to the Cause, were eclipsed by personal im-peratives, by her dread not just of separation from Patrick but of his possible injury or death. When the first Confederate conscription act passed in April 1862, she reassured herself that now a bountiful supply of young men made Patrick's service unnecessary. A proposal in the fall to extend the act to make Patrick, at age forty-three, subject to the draft seemed to Catherine "like the sword of Damocles over my head." Eager to stay out of the ranks, Patrick began again to try to raise a company. In October the Confederate Congress passed an act popularly known as the "Twenty Nigger Law," because it ex-empted supervisors of twenty or more slaves from the draft. Catherine greeted the controversial measure with undisguised relief, for "as we own more than eighty," Patrick would be freed from service. In face of widespread criticism of the act as class legislation, Catherine invoked her husband's deli-cate aristocratic constitution as justification for his immunity from conscrip-tion. "As an officer he can take care of himself, have a horse & a servant, & the exposure is not so great." But service as a common soldier would require a "change in his habits" that she feared "would be fatal to him." Yet every anx-ious wife and mother in the South confronted exactly that terror. Enrollment in the Confederate army did indeed prove fatal to hundreds and thousands of southerners who, unlike Patrick Edmondston, found themselves unwilling or unable to avoid the ranks.[8]

At home with a delighted and grateful Catherine, Patrick assumed a prominent role in local defense, mobilizing the aged and unfit of his commu-nity against Yankee raids that threatened the North Carolina coast. This post shielded him when his exemption under the "Twenty Nigger Law" was called into question. And when he was voted out of his leadership position in the Home Guard in February 1865, a surgeon's certificate of disability assured his immunity to the draft for the remaining weeks of war.

Motivated by the misery she felt during the brief period of their separation in 1861, Catherine abandoned her early declarations of patriotic loyalty and public obligation for the personal satisfactions of marital love. But she justi-fied this behavior in the language of class prerogative. The privileged life Patrick had always led, his "talents," and his "habit of command" fitted him only for an officer's position, not for the lot of the common soldier. Cather-ine's "grateful thankfulness" that Patrick was spared "the dangers and hardships of the battle field" did not diminish her sense of entitlement to that protection. When she bemoaned the loss of eleven acquaintances in the Gettysburg campaign of 1863, it was for "young men of family, education, & position slaughtered in this horrible manner" that she mourned. In both her actions and her words, Catherine Edmondston wholeheartedly embraced the principle of a rich man's war and a poor man's fight.[9]

Gradually abandoning the rhetoric of self-sacrifice as the potential cost of Patrick's military service became clear, Catherine Edmondston ultimately welcomed the use of elite privilege to keep him out of the ranks. Yet the sacrifice demanded of Confederate women encompassed more than just giving up their men. Women were called upon to renounce luxuries, even necessities, as well as to work actively in support of southern armies. In 1861 Catherine Edmondston responded to these public exhortations. While Patrick attempted to fill the ranks of his company, his wife joined the ladies of the community in a sewing circle to make needed uniforms. Under their mistress's direction, seven Edmondston slave women undertook the heavier task of stitching Patrick's tent. Catherine was delighted by the demonstrations of female patriotism all around her. "Thousands of Ladies," she wrote in May 1861, "who never worked before are hard at work on coarse sewing all over our whole country."[10]

Yet these communal energies, or at least Catherine's engagement with them, were apparently short-lived. Her trips to follow Patrick's company and her long visits to her father or other relatives during her husband's absences broke up her "regular habits." By the fall of 1862, Catherine had begun to berate herself for her failure to live up to both Confederate ideology and her own standards. "I am lazy and that is the fact." Her most consuming endeavor had become chess, which she played for hours each day in a never-ending match with her father. Yet she feared the game was producing a "dissipation of mind and a frittering away of the moments," and she proclaimed herself determined to find "some regular steady occupation" to fill her days.[11]

Catherine Edmondston was an accomplished knitter, and she began to try to produce a sock a day for the soldiers. She found the endeavor satisfying and not unduly tedious, for as a young girl she had taught herself to knit and read at the same time. "It is a great blessing to be able to work so, to see the work grow under your hands," she reported once she had begun her new regime. "It is heartsome & encouraging, & it is all a matter of habit. After all any one can do it who gets in the way of moving her fingers rapidly."[12]

Yet such work did not fill her days. The leisurely and comfortable character of Catherine's life did not change dramatically even as war grew more

intense. "How many hours do I daily waste in bed in the morning," she wondered. "N'importe. *I do not think it healthy to get up early*," she protested in
August 1863. "I accomplish very little daily," she observed the following summer. "True I spend hours at chess with Father . . . but I must manage better
and read more." Catherine often reported to her diary the schedule of her
busiest days, for she wanted to record her pride in her accomplishments. Yet
these achievements are telling, for they display the ways in which the prerogatives of slave ownership continued to shape and limit her involvement in the
work of war.[13]

Severe shortages of cloth plagued the blockaded South, and in the postwar
years many Confederate women's memoirs described female dedication and
ingenuity in producing homespun garments. Catherine Edmondston reported in December 1864, "We wear homespun only." But it was the Edmondston slaves, not their mistress, who were skilled in spinning and weaving. "I
have never," Catherine reported with relief, "been forced to lay my hand to the
distaff." Similarly, as the lack of candles prompted the Edmondstons to take
up domestic production, it was the slaves who did the work. "Fanny will make
the candles," Catherine wrote, "but 'Missus' must see her & arrange the wicks
in the moulds. Cuffee is not up to that yet, tho she soon shall be for I am fully
of the old opinion that there is no use in having a dog and barking for one's
self."[14]

Despite a professed longing to "be able to do something to show my devotion to my country in this her hour of need," Catherine did very little "barking" for herself. Instead, much of the work she proudly detailed consisted of
what might most generously be called supervisory efforts. She described one
morning, for example, spent reading "Literature du Midi" in a plantation
storeroom while slaves nearby pickled meat and packed flour. "Finding it tires
me waiting on them & my bodily presence being needed when so many valu-
ables as I have there were exposed, I sat down . . . and sent for my book." A
journal entry from November 1864 eloquently represents the relationship between Catherine Edmondston's understanding of work and accomplishment
and its—literal—foundation in racial privilege and exploitation. "Set with
my own hand," she wrote proudly, "608 (six hundred & eight) splendid blossoming bulbs." But then she continued parenthetically and revealingly,
"(Owen [a domestic slave] dug the holes)."[15]

After an initial flurry of sewing for the soldiers, Catherine engaged in little
work intended to benefit those outside her own immediate household. The
new sorts of endeavors the war necessitated on the Edmondston plantation—
production of candles, homespun, ink—were intended for internal con-

sumption and family survival, not as contributions to the larger Confederate cause. Self-preservation once again proved more compelling an imperative than self-sacrifice. Except for the knitting of socks, Catherine Edmondston made few tangible offerings to southern victory. And many of war's demands were met primarily by extra labor or sacrifice from the Edmondston slaves. Across the South thousands of slaves took advantage of war-born opportunity to flee to Union lines and freedom. The Edmondston slaves, however, remained on the plantation during the conflict, largely because, Catherine believed, the Edmondston property was so isolated that it made flight especially difficult and risky. Whatever the reason for the slaves' continuing presence, its result was a significant mitigation of war's hardships for their masters. Just as the presence of slaves had helped, under the provisions of the "Twenty Nigger Law," to keep Patrick with Catherine and out of active military service, so the labor of slaves shielded Patrick and Catherine from war's severest demands. The Edmondstons' membership in the master class blunted the material impact of social, political, and military upheaval.[16]

"We have not wanted for a comfort," Catherine Edmondston wrote in early 1863, "scarcely a luxury" — except, she added almost as an afterthought, she had ceased ordering her cook to prepare any desserts but baked apples. But Catherine resisted explaining her good fortune as the result of social privilege or even of simple good luck. God, she believed, had favored her. "I feel almost ashamed," she sometimes mused, "that I suffer so little for the Cause, the glorious Cause of our country's freedom." But she more often than not translated her uneasiness into a prayer of thanks, investing God with direct and seemingly self-conscious responsibility for her privileges and immunities. It was God, she believed, "who hath made me to differ," who has "blessed me beyond others."[17]

Across the South, Confederates struggled to understand why they, like Job, had been chosen for the trials of hardship, deprivation, and mounting military losses. Catherine Edmondston similarly regarded herself as chosen, but as one selected to be passed over rather than to be tried, to be by divine as well as by military provision largely exempted from the war. "Our Lot," she concluded, "has been truly blessed."[18]

Catherine's views about slavery and racial differences reinforced her conception that social arrangements must reflect divine plan. Edmondston commented frequently on racial matters, offering a generalized, indeed stereotyped "Cuffee" to embody her views about the black race. Catherine Edmondston objected to the invocation of social circumstance or experience as explanation of human behavior or capacity, seeking instead more essentialist stereotypes of race and breeding. Her reading of *Les miserables* in the middle of the war prompted her to articulate her own social philosophy by noting her differences with Victor Hugo's revolutionary views. In celebrating an "ignorant convict"—Jean Valjean—and a prostitute—Fantine—and portraying them as the heroic victims of social injustice, the book, she believed, worked to "deify impurity & excuse it because it is the fault of society." This was too close to the kind of sentimental and false philanthropy prevalent in the North, which blamed the social arrangements of slavery for the ignorance and immorality of southern blacks. Edmondston insisted upon firm and hereditary racial differences and hierarchies that underlay the logic and justice of the southern social order. "Cuffee" possessed inherent traits—childishness, laziness, simplicity—that prescribed permanent inferiority but at the same time, Edmondston believed, encouraged the southern master's paternal affection. "Ah! Cuffee! Cuffee!" Edmondston wrote after her slave Owen prolonged a carriage trip several hours by careless mending of a harness, "You are no manager, & yet I love you. Faults & all I accept you & prefer your carelessness & affection to the best groom that England ever sent forth!" Yet that very affection depended upon maintaining both hierarchy and difference. Miscegenation, Edmondston explained, "disgusts & revolts my whole nature."[19]

Because Catherine Edmondston regarded the practice of slavery and racial subordination as both the essence of the South's social order and its national purpose, she was horrified by Confederate proposals to arm slaves in the last months of the war. "Think of it, armed negroes," she wrote in dismay. "Think what it means! And this is the nineteenth century!" The progress of human knowledge had, she believed, firmly established both a religious and a scientific basis for white superiority. Yet in their desperate search for military manpower, Confederate policymakers seemed bent on ignoring those very truths. In Edmondston's view such shortsightedness threatened the very ideals for which the Confederacy was fighting. "We give up a principle when we offer emancipation as a boon or reward," she wrote late in 1864, "for we have hitherto contended that Slavery was Cuffee's normal condition, the very best position he could occupy, the one of all others in which he was the happiest, & to take him from that & give him what we think misery in the place of it, is to put ourselves in the wrong essentially." She summarized both her social philosophy and its roots in emphasizing her position on African-American soldiers. "No! freedom for whites, slavery for negroes, God has so ordained it!"[20]

But Catherine Edmondston's endorsement of hierarchy as the foundation of the southern social order prescribed her support not just for black subordination but for her own. White and wellborn she might be, but she was also female. In her wartime journal Edmondston explored the logic of the South's system of gender hierarchy, affirming its legitimacy and occasionally revealing more than she perhaps intended in justifications that like those of the queen in *Hamlet* seemingly protested too much.

Catherine spoke out against the changes war forced upon many women in circumstances less fortunate than her own. When the necessities of widowhood compelled her sister to open a boardinghouse, Catherine was horrified. "I can neither comprehend or have any patience with it—this pretence of Independance." Yet when her own servants grew careless and ill behaved during one of Patrick's absences, Catherine dared to voice her dissatisfaction both with the new burdens war was imposing on her and with Patrick's failure to appreciate the difficulties she faced in managing their household. "What a drag it sometimes is on woman," she complained, "to 'lug about' the ladder upon which man plants his foot & ascends to the intellectual heaven of peace in ignorance of the machinery which feeds his daily life." But she caught herself up short, retreating from her objections into an almost stylized affirmation of gender difference and hierarchy. "Rightly managed, prayerfully taken, women also may ascend, using each of their petty cares as an advance toward that 'heaven' which is gained by self conquest, self abnegation." Men and women did not just live in separate spheres on earth but apparently expected to rise into different heavens.[21]

But Catherine Edmondston had come only slowly to accept the notion that the female self was fulfilled through self-denial; she had had to learn that, as she now solemnly intoned, "obedience is a wife's first duty." She had only gradually understood her proper place in marriage, had only reluctantly abandoned the ambition that her early education had fostered. "How many of my youthful aspirations have I 'come down' from," she mused in early 1862. "Do you remember, Madam," she reminisced about the beginning of her marriage, "how you wept and cried the first year?" Catherine had been "pained & mortified" by Patrick's insistence that cooking—by which he meant ordering food and arranging menus—was a wife's highest mission. "Was it for *this*," Catherine asked herself, "that you had been educated?" She had no desire to "undervalue" domestic duties, "but the pedestal on which he placed them debased all else. You could not worship at such a shrine! and yet . . ." And yet, Catherine conceded, apparently accepting the entire correctness of Patrick's views, "Have you not long years ago seen and confessed that your husband was right?; that a well ordered table . . . was the keystone to health, happiness and usefulness?"[22]

Ultimately, however, it seems to have been Plutarch, not Patrick, who persuaded Catherine of the point. It was not the authority of her husband that
she found most convincing but a voice from the intellectual world she valued
so highly. Only by invoking the transcendence of learning could she comfort-
ably accept her female role. "Remember how you exulted in a passage in
Plutarch's Paulus Emilius that it required more genius to order a feast than to
marshal an Army," she asked herself. Plutarch satisfied her not just by validat-
ing the realm of achievement to which she felt herself consigned but by establishing its equality with the most esteemed accomplishments of men.
Plutarch seemed to ignore and thus undermine any notion of a separate and
subordinate sphere into which the management of food might be relegated.
Planning a feast was like leading an army. By accepting woman's mission as
"cook" on such terms, Catherine approached a celebration of equality, a de-
nial of the distinctiveness of spheres and of the subordination in which she
professed to believe.[23]

It was, as the doubts she expressed about the purpose of her education
suggest, her intellectual gifts and aspirations that caused Catherine Edmondston the most uneasiness with the principles of gender hierarchy and, in particular, with the assignment of the life of the mind to the male sphere.
Catherine's sister, Mary Devereux Clarke, was in fact an accomplished poet
and periodical author who helped support her family with her writings.
Catherine had direct evidence for the possibility of female literary achievement. Yet she tried to dampen her ambition to see her own work in print. Be-
littling her poetry as "mediocre," she simultaneously revealed that she at heart
thought it far more worthy, voicing her aspirations, even as she struggled
against them. "But beware. O! beware of stepping out of your sphere & publishing them. Then indeed you would forget a woman's first ornament, modesty. Women have no business to rush into print; so wide an arena does not
become them." Catherine Edmondston cloaked her literary ambition in a
conventional diffidence and self-effacement that befitted her abstract notions
of an appropriate female role.[24] But her behavior suggested more unconven-
tional aspirations. "With Patrick's consent," she decided to send a long poem
she had written on the death of General A. S. Johnston to Jefferson Davis. Eagerly she composed a covering letter. Patrick declared her note unnecessary
and unseemly, and Catherine yielded to his views, forwarding the poem without annotation. In her journal she negotiated her disappointment at having
to suppress her identity and lose her opportunity for recognition. She
mocked her aspirations, even as she expressed them. "Ah! Mrs Edmondston, I

fear me you are a vain woman and have a hankering after dignities, for even tho' your name was not to be signed to the letter, you wished to write to the President!" Catherine Edmondston's journal served in part as a vehicle through which she worked to reconcile her desires with the constraints of her social position.[25]

But before long, Catherine Edmondston was submitting poetry for publication without Patrick's knowledge or "consent." Yet she mounted no direct challenge to his authority, instead devising an elaborate justification for her action, one that fit neatly with prevailing gender prescriptions. She sought, she explained, her husband's unbiased opinion of her poems and could achieve that only by having him happen across her work in print, where he would feel free to comment upon it. By the time her poem on Beast Butler appeared in a Richmond newspaper in January 1863, she either had abandoned her ruse or at least failed to record Patrick's reaction to it in her pleasure at seeing her work actually appear.

After the war Catherine did in fact publish a book. *Morte d'Arthur: Its Influence on the Spirit and Manners of the Nineteenth Century* extolled, as Edmondston had during the war, the chivalric and aristocratic origins of Confederate behavior and contrasted it with the debased and barbaric practices of the Yankees. Like many women of the Civil War era, Edmondston embraced literary accomplishment as the least dangerous arena for female achievement. Only one's words, not one's body, advanced into the public sphere and the public eye, and even these could be clothed in the garb of anonymity. The title page of the *Morte d'Arthur* listed no author.[26]

For all the tensions that lurked within Catherine's embrace of female subordination, she, overtly at least, supported the South's gender hierarchy, as she did its racial and class hierarchies. Although this seeming acceptance of her female status presented her with constraints and disabilities rather than the privileges and immunities she received from her wealth and her whiteness, she understood these systems of stratification and subordination to be of a piece, based in broader principles of natural hierarchy. She also understood her own very favorable situation. She had, she recognized, been "blessed . . . beyond others." The requirements of female sacrifice did not for Catherine seem to entail any very significant erosion of the benefits of her class and racial prerogatives.

By the last months of the war, Catherine had begun to harbor doubts about Confederate leadership and policies, but not about the larger Cause she had defined as the war's purpose. Early in 1865 she remarked upon the "growing distrust with which all men view 'the Government.'" "It is," she observed, "getting to be considered an instrument of oppression & tyrany because it does not keep faith with its citizens." Like the misconceived attempt to turn slaves into soldiers, the Confederacy's centralizing policies—taxation, conscription, impressment—challenged the very principles of racial hierarchy and class prerogative for which the war was being fought. Yet although she criticized the president and his cabinet as "imbecile," she did not abandon her faith in these larger principles, and she greeted defeat with disbelief and despair. "I seem as tho' in a dream," she wrote after Lee's surrender. "I sleep, sleep, sleep endlessly . . . I think of it, but I cannot grasp it or its future consequences. I sit benumbed." "I seem," she observed revealingly, "to grope after my own ideas, my own identity, & in the vain attempt to grasp it I fall asleep." Without the social order that had defined her, Catherine Edmondston was no longer certain she knew who she was.[27]

Her summary of the first months of Reconstruction focused on its challenge to the foundation of that old social order. The narrative of Yankee rule, she explained, was "but a tiresome repetition of the same story, to wit, a preference of the Negro to the white man, a deliberate attempt to debase the latter in a vain endeavor to elevate the former." Her disgust at the growing assertiveness of her own slaves, at their refusal to work on Patrick's terms, at their demands for improved material conditions, at the abrupt departure of some of those she had thought most devoted, was mitigated only by the continuing faithfulness of Owen and his wife Dolly. At her death Catherine would reward their loyalty with the bequest of a house, an acre of land, ten dollars each, and an annual allotment that echoed the rations of slavery days: two hundred pounds of pork and five barrels of corn.

Owen and Dolly would not have to wait as long as they might have expected for their legacy. Patrick died in 1871, and bereft without her beloved companion, Catherine survived only until January 1875. She was but fifty-one. The sleep into which she had retreated at the end of the war was now permanent.

Catherine Edmondston regarded the Confederacy's defeat to have taken place at its own hands, to have arisen from its failure to follow closely enough the ideals of hierarchy that she believed gave the young nation its purpose. Yet it may instead have been the behavior of southerners like Catherine and Patrick Edmondston themselves that threatened Confederate survival by insisting on privileges that weakened the South in terms of both materiel and morale.

When they resisted the use of their slaves for military labor, when they continued to live in comparative luxury, when Patrick avoided significant or dangerous military service, when Catherine ignored the prescriptions for female work and sacrifice, the Edmondstons not only failed to make substantive contributions to the Cause. Their actions encouraged growing popular resentment of a master class that seemed to have forgotten the reciprocal duties of paternalism, a class that was trying to enjoy its *noblesse* without acknowledging its *oblige*. The divisions on the homefront that recent historians have emphasized as crucial elements undermining Confederate morale and effectiveness grew out of these failures. The ideology of legitimation the southern master class embraced and practiced within the context of war proved literally self-defeating.[28]

Yet the life and thought of Catherine Edmondston suggest that perhaps she and the southern elite had little choice. Locked within a system of belief with an internal and self-serving logic that resisted the tests of reality, the South's master class was limited in its ability to recognize the truths that the moment of war presented. During the years of conflict, Catherine Edmondston used her not inconsiderable intellectual powers to articulate an ideology and to defend a social order that had granted her not just great privilege but, more fundamentally, her "own identity." Without those beliefs, without the world the slaveholders made, Catherine Edmondston was no longer truly herself.

Notes

1. Genovese, *Roll*, 98, 97; see also Drew Gilpin Faust, *The Creation of Confederate Nationalism: Ideology and Identity in the Civil War South* (Baton Rouge, La., 1988), 4.

2. Beth G. Crabtree and James W. Patton, eds., *Journal of a Secesh Lady: The Diary of Catherine Ann Devereux Edmondston, 1860–1866* (Raleigh, N.C., 1979); Eugene D. Genovese, *The World the Slaveholders Made: Two Essays in Interpretation* (New York, 1969). On women in the war, see George Rable, *Civil Wars: Women and the Crisis of Southern Nationalism* (Urbana, Ill., 1989); Catherine Clinton and Nina Silber, *Divided Houses: Gender and the Civil War* (New York, 1992); Drew Gilpin Faust, *Mothers of Invention: Women of the Slaveholding South in the American Civil War* (Chapel Hill, N.C., 1996). On women of the South's master class, see Fox-Genovese, 5.

3. *Journal*, 11, 54, 58, 50. On women and politics in the prewar years, see Elizabeth R. Varon, "'We Mean to Be Counted: White Women and Politics in Antebellum Virginia'" (Ph.D. diss., Yale University, 1993).

4. *Journal*, 342, 64, 388.

5. Ibid., 72, 331, 392.

6. Ibid., 69. See also Drew Gilpin Faust, "Altars of Sacrifice: Confederate Women and the Narratives of War," *Journal of American History* 76 (March 1990): 1200–1228.

7. *Journal,* 62.

8. Ibid., 116, 256, 270. On the draft, see Albert B. Moore, *Conscription and Conflict in the Confederacy* (New York, 1924).

9. *Journal,* 270, 315, 435.

10. Ibid., 58, 57, 60.

11. Ibid., 249.

12. Ibid., 307.

13. Ibid., 448, 593.

14. Ibid., 643, 472, 300. On the limits of household production during the war, see Faust, *Mothers of Invention,* chap. 2.

15. *Journal,* 567, 235, 634. Fox-Genovese remarks upon how often plantation mistresses simply did not see slave labor and verbally appropriated it as their own.

16. On the flight of slaves to freedom and on their wartime experience more generally, see Ira Berlin et al., eds., *Free at Last: A Documentary History of Slavery, Freedom, and the Civil War* (New York, 1992), and Leon F. Litwack, *Been in the Storm So Long: The Aftermath of Slavery* (New York, 1979).

17. *Journal,* 403, 349, 271.

18. Ibid., 349. On Job and on white southern women and religion more generally, see Faust, *Mothers of Invention,* chap. 8.

19. *Journal,* 406, 287, 552.

20. Ibid., 357, 651.

21. Ibid., 272, 166.

22. Ibid., 107, 345. On women's education in the Old South, see Christie Anne Farnham, *The Education of the Southern Belle: Higher Education and Student Socialization in the Antebellum South* (New York, 1994). On Edmondston's intellectual strivings, see James W. Patton, "Serious Reading in Halifax County, 1860–1865," *North Carolina Historical Review* 42 (April 1965): 169–79.

23. *Journal,* 345.

24. Ibid., 282.

25. Ibid., 151.

26. *The Morte d'Arthur: Its Influence on the Spirit and Manners of the Nineteenth Century* (Baltimore, 1872); on writing as a vocation for ladies, see Mary Kelley, *Private Women, Public Stage: Literary Domesticity in Nineteenth Century America* (New York, 1984); Susan Coultrap-McQuin, *Doing Literary Business: American Women Writers in the Nineteenth Century* (Chapel Hill, N.C., 1990); Anne Goodwyn Jones, *Tomorrow Is Another Day: The Woman Writer in the South, 1859–1936* (Baton Rouge, La., 1980), and Faust, *Mothers of Invention,* chap. 7.

27. *Journal,* 668, 712, 694.

28. For examples of this historiography, see Paul Escott, "The Cry of the Sufferers: The Problem of Welfare in the Confederacy," *Civil War History* 23 (Sept. 1977): 228–40; Escott, "The Moral Economy of the Crowd in Confederate North Carolina," *Maryland Historian* 13 (Spring/Summer 1982): 1–18; Escott, "Poverty and Governmental Aid for the Poor in Confederate North Carolina," *North Carolina Historical Review* 61 (Oct. 1984): 462–80; Escott, *Many Excellent People: Power—and Privilege—in North Carolina, 1850–1900* (Chapel Hill, N.C., 1985); Richard E. Beringer et al., *Why the South Lost the Civil War* (Athens, Ga., 1986).

7

African-American Women in the Literary Imagination of Mary Boykin Chesnut

THAVOLIA GLYMPH

Women who come before the public are in a bad box now.

— Mary Chesnut

"Ah," Mr. Compson said. "Years ago we in the South made our women into ladies. Then the War came and made the ladies into ghosts. So what else can we do being gentlemen, but listen to them being ghosts?"

— William Faulkner

It seems both poignant and striking how avoided and unanalyzed is the effect of racist reflection on the subject.

— Toni Morrison

O N 11 MAY 1861 Mary Boykin Chesnut recorded one of her many now famous sentiments: "This Journal is intended to be entirely *objective*. My subjective days are over."[1] Clearly, she jested. Still, the recent Ken Burns documentary *The Civil War* so importantly intones this and other sentiments expressed by Chesnut in her journal kept during the Civil War and in her manuscript based on this journal written in the 1880s that she appears to stand triumphant over the sentimental and her own self. Mary Chesnut's "diary," as Edmund Wilson concluded three decades ago, "is an extraordinary document . . . a masterpiece."[2] Yet the calm, reasoned, and even passionate voice of the Burns documentary bears in important ways little resemblance to the voice Chesnut recorded for posterity.

Born a member of the antebellum South's most powerful class, Mary Chesnut nevertheless remained throughout her life torn about her South, its values, mores, and glaring inconsistencies. But the kind of revolutionary upturning that promised to mend the tears also threatened her sense of unquestioned superiority. Mary Chesnut's wartime Journal and especially the manuscript she composed from it in the 1880s find Chesnut responding to the promise kept, attempting to restore the sense of place and identity that slavery had assured but that war and Reconstruction had dismantled. By the early 1880s, as Chesnut set herself to the task of revising and re-creating her Civil War Journal for a public audience, her agenda was clear: This manuscript, her life's work, would serve to help restitch the fabric of white women's lives torn open and left exposed by the Civil War and emancipation. It seems to have occurred to her, particularly in the aftermath of Reconstruction, that the Journal she had composed during the war was not only too subjective (despite her declaration to the contrary) but also not sufficiently supportive of women of her class and race. That she considered the work before her no small matter is evident in her devotion of hours and thousands of pages to it.

In the course of rewriting her Journal "again and again," Mary Chesnut rewrote history.[3] The book that resulted stands as a narrative of war and a narrative at war with the reality of life after the Confederacy. Chesnut submits her revised work to the public as an unfriendly brief against the gender leveling that accompanied war and emancipation, but she retains the original Journal's strong opposition to the vaunted concept of the unity of the patriarchal household. The book's focus on gender and race differs from that of the Journal, becoming a central concern in Chesnut's effort to paint, in the words of her biographer, Elisabeth Muhlenfeld, "a picture of an entire society."[4] This picture was informed principally by the Civil War and emancipation and the accompanying revolution in social relations, particularly as these affected southern women and Chesnut's own status and identity. "I think," Chesnut wrote, "*these* times make all women feel their humiliation in the affairs of the world."[5] Chesnut no more meant "all women" than she meant to be objective.

Mary Chesnut spent years cutting and culling, editing, and expanding her wartime Journal. In the result southern white women of the ruling class could take refuge. On the subject of black women—slave or free—she could find nothing to approximate an objective narrative voice. In turn, she sometimes lost her voice completely on the subject of white women, erasing from the record many of her earlier subjective criticisms of women of her own class.

Wife-beating white husbands like merchant and banker William Knox, extramarital affairs, questioned paternities, and jilted women appear regularly in the original Journal but not in the revised book.[6] Rude, ill-bred, "stupid" white women of her own class are deleted from the revision. White women who were bad mothers, whom she had earlier faulted, like the "bad tempered" Mrs. Keitt "who spanked her *baby well* several times" and Mrs. Reagan who permitted her "little negroes & her children to sleep together," also disappear from the revision.[7] Chesnut remained as shocked in the 1880s as she had been in 1861 at her mother-in-law's refusal to brand a local Camden woman a "*bad* girl" for having children out of wedlock. But in her revised manuscript the woman—the daughter of a prominent Camden merchant— identified by her last name in the 1861 entry, is given a completely fictitious name.[8] Perhaps anticipating her critics, Chesnut herself offered an explanation. The deletion of "scandalous stories," she explains, represents her desire "to not hurt any one."[9] Perhaps just as well, for as C. Vann Woodward points out, a book that included such scandals would not have been publishable.[10]

Although Woodward and Elisabeth Muhlenfeld have contributed much to the understanding and appreciation of Chesnut, they generally minimize the significance of the greater candor of Chesnut's Civil War Journal as well as the deletion of indiscretions in her revised manuscript.[11] The general pattern, they conclude, is one of consistency; only "an occasional uncharacteristic discrepancy creeps in."[12] However generally true, Chesnut's treatment of women of and not of her class and race suggests a pattern of conscious, deliberate, and more than occasional inconsistency. These and other issues demand consideration even at the risk of performing the kind of "editorial detective work" that Woodward has understandably cautioned against. Such detective work—if this essay may so be classified—leads to an enhanced appreciation of Chesnut's life and work and addresses a problem that occupied Chesnut and her contemporaries but that has interested historians little: the reconstruction of white womanhood.[13] Simply put, more than "an occasional discrepancy" exists between the Civil War Journal and the postbellum manuscript in Chesnut's narrative treatment of southern women—black and white. In the manuscript Chesnut presents a more comforting history that places African-American women distinctly outside the boundaries of womanhood. Given the clever and imaginative execution, Edmund Wilson was right. The document is indeed a "masterpiece."[14]

The aim here, in the words of Toni Morrison, is "to avert the critical gaze from the racial object to the racial subject; from the described and imagined to the describers and imaginers; from the serving to the served." As valuable as is "scholarship that looks into the mind, imagination, and behavior of slaves," Morrison writes, is the "serious intellectual effort to see what racial ideology does to the mind, imagination, and behavior of masters."[15] The describer's descriptions and images of the racial object are important, certainly, to the study of racism. Elizabeth Fox-Genovese, for example, has commented on "the manifest racism of [Chesnut's] comments on black and mulatto women."[16] Chesnut's racism is clear but is not, in and of itself, here the main concern. The goal is rather to look at the way in which the racial subject—black women—informs and frames Chesnut's understanding of the racial object—women of her race and class. Two decades of embarrassing poverty, illness, and radically changed social relations in the South separated the Chesnut of the 1860s and 1880s. The experience distorted and diminished Chesnut's sense of self. What emerges in the 1880s book constitutes, in part, a literary reconstruction of that self. The elevated white female presence and the diminished black female presence stand close to the center of that reconstruction.

Bringing to bear on her work in the 1880s literary skills honed in the years since the war, Chesnut wrote a book that when compared to the original Journal attempts to enter the sisterhood of southern women she had often previously slighted, a sisterhood that first, however, had to be reconstructed and redefined. The old world in which, Drew Faust writes, "men imparted status and meaning to social intercourse and provided Chesnut with necessary affirmation of her self-worth"[17] had disintegrated. The arrangement, in Chesnut's mind, had always been rather flimsy, but of its benefits she did not complain. The conclusion of the Civil War made the task of placing herself in the world more problematic. After all, military defeat compromised the notion of what constituted white manhood. Paul C. Cameron, formerly one of North Carolina's most prominent planters, promised his son: "We are to have a great revolution in society & social life and those who do not now go to work & make a manly effort to sustain themselves & their families will go down." Mincing no words, he added, "You will have to provide for yourself—You will have to *labor* to live either by your *head* or by your hands."[18] Chesnut also worried. Former slaves, she wrote, had practical experience in making a living, but she asked, "Do you know a young planter who can earn one hundred by the labor of his own hands?"[19]

Writing at a time when pride of white birth clearly still counted for something, but something much less than it had before the Confederacy, at a time when the idea of a white woman's place was a much murkier notion and African-American women's standing no longer unambiguously defined that of white women, Chesnut had no choice but to remove evidence of white women who personally failed to meet the standards of southern white womanhood and motherhood and of their husbands and lovers who could no longer be relied upon to uphold even the fiction of a unified patriarchal household. In turn, she had no choice but to depict black women in a way that would leave no doubt about the gulf that she needed to believe still sepa-

rated them from her. The project was a difficult one: At times it sent her reel-
ing from one language to another—sometimes switching from English to
French to Italian all in one sentence—in search of the words to sustain the
effort without betraying it.

Woodward and Muhlenfeld cite as an example of the exceptional discrepancy between the 1860s journals and the 1880s manuscript Chesnut's rendering of an anecdote told by Team, the overseer. An 1861 entry in the Civil War
Journal records Team's story about a slave woman who, "driven to despair by
the driver," protests his cruel treatment by committing suicide and homicide,
tying "her baby on her back & walking into the river," drowning herself and
her baby. In the revision Chesnut has Team explain the tragedy differently.
Team is now said to relate: "[Slavery] does not make good mothers—teaches
them to expect other people to take care of their children. Then told a story of
a woman so lazy she tied her child to her back and jumped in the river. She
said she did not mean to work—nor should her child after her."[20]

The discrepancy, Woodward and Muhlenfeld explain, indicates Chesnut's
ambition to "sketch instead a conversation about the evils of slavery—among
them the undermining of both societal 'goods' such as the work ethic and
natural maternal instincts."[21] Perhaps. But other discrepancies indicate that
Chesnut harbored other ambitions in revising Team's story and may have
been more concerned with African-American women's work ethic and maternal instincts in the post-Confederate period than with the evils of slavery.
Out of the mouth of Team comes the singsong refrain of planters and overseers, current in the postbellum South, of freedwomen who refused to work
or allow their children to do so except under conditions they deemed appropriate and consistent with their interpretation of freedom.

The determination of the slave woman to die rather than be a slave also
had noble implications that Chesnut did not care to evoke in connection with
black women, particularly in the 1880s. Like the men of her class, Chesnut
could not accord honor to a slave. The idea of honorable death resonated
deeply, even if ambivalently, in the southern code of honor and for Chesnut
especially.[22] The Civil War had made Chesnut's judgment all the more discerning because from her perch she had seen its opposite more clearly: Men
who avoided the draft, used the war to accumulate fortunes, or avoided it to
protect them earned her disdain as did the growing numbers of Confederate
soldiers who by the end of the war were "passing the *wrong way,*" away from
the front.[23] The story told by Team can be entered in the Journal as a rather
harmless anecdote of the evils of cruel overseers though not necessarily the
evils of slavery. In the 1880s the anecdote is problematic. In couching the slave

woman's resistance in the contemporary vernacular of freedwomen's "un-ruly" behavior, Chesnut rids it of dignity and honor, trivializes it.[24] As fanci-ful as it is, the revised passage is suggestive of Chesnut's struggle to revise her wartime Journal from the perspective of two decades later.

Unlike Chesnut's wartime Journal, the 1880s manuscript speaks plainly to the challenge that African-American women's freedom presented to southern white women and especially to Chesnut's discomfort with black women's ef-forts to reconstitute their own identities, as plainly as the conflicts docu-mented in the records of the Freedmen's Bureau. Although Molly and Ellen, the slave women who attended to Chesnut's personal needs during the war, remained loyal, Mary Chesnut never completely trusted their "loyalty" or their seeming lack of interest in the war. Like other women of her class, Ches-nut feared the gender-leveling influence of war and emancipation—freed-women's "disloyalty" and assertions of pride and dignity. And like them, she rebelled against freedwomen's conceptions of freedom that threatened as much as the southern military defeat to displace her. On one occasion her friends joked that one day Ellen would be a "lady driving about in [Ches-nut's] carriage."[25] The comment might have amused Chesnut in early 1865 but not in the 1880s. As Fox-Genovese writes: "The war had made mockery of the gender conventions that protected ladies, had stripped the illusion of fashion from the decay of flesh. How could such experiences not have humil-iated women? Their modesty was exposed—and even more, their artificial efforts at self-presentation. War denuded the lady of her pretenses and pro-tections and reduced her to a mere woman."[26]

Chestnut, no ordinary woman, would not be so reduced despite clinging poverty and illness. Freedwomen fare the worse for her determination. The portrait of slave and freedwomen in the manuscript as contrasted to the Jour-nal reflects a spirited determination to reorder history. The burden of women of her class, she lay at the feet of slave women.

In the original Journal, Chestnut recalls having witnessed an auction of mulatto women "in *silk dresses.*" The woman on the block as Chesnut passed looked "coy & pleased at the bidder."[27] In the revised account the young woman is rendered more disgusting to her sensibilities, appearing "magnifi-cently gotten up in silks and satins." Though Chesnut retains the description of the young woman as "coy and modest" in the revised edition, the young woman now "seemed delighted with it all—sometimes ogling the bidders," "her mouth never relaxed from its expanded grin of excitement."[28] "The orig-inal version," writes Fox-Genovese "all but sneers at the generic inappropri-ateness of mulatto women in *silk dresses.* . . . South Carolina slaveholder that she was, she might sicken at direct confrontations with slave auctions, but she also scorned a slave woman's espousal of upper-class garb and ladylike wiles." The published version, Fox-Genovese concludes, reveals "a hardening of her own always deep racism."[29] It also reveals a hardening of her contempt for black women.

In the revised book, Chestnut took aim at a slave wedding party, "all as black as the ace of spades. The bride and her bridesmaids in white swiss muslin, the gayest of sashes—and bonnets too wonderful to be described. They had on red blanket shawls, which they removed as they entered the aisle and seemed loath to put on when the time came to go out—so proud were they of their finery."[30] The extant Civil War Journal contains no corresponding passage.

Writing during the war Mary Chesnut had herself mocked southern gender conventions and exposed the pretenses of southern society and southern white women. In re-creating, she would not add to what she herself had described as the public humiliation of white women that had attended the war and Reconstruction. She could reinvent. She could make explicitly clear passages in the original Journal that might be debatable or construed in a manner different from what she now intended. Thus a brief comment in the Journal concerning a "wretched Mulatto woman who is a kept mistress" requires substantial elaboration in the book manuscript.[31] In the Journal, Martha Adamson is a woman Chesnut claims to "know"; in the book her knowledge of Adamson comes to her through Maria, one of her slaves. At any rate we learn more about the woman in the revised account and more about Chesnut. Acknowledging that the "nearly white" "Martha Adamson is a beautiful mulatress," Chesnut is quick to add: "That is, as good-looking as they ever are to me. I have never seen a mule as handsome as a horse—and I know I never will—no matter how I lament and sympathize with its undeserved mule condition." The nongendered reference to "these beastly negroes" in the original is made specific in the revised account: "Those beastly negress beauties. Animals—tout et simple—cordifiamma—no—corpifiamma."[32]

Although she railed against southern patriarchs whose sense of honor did not extend to marital fidelity, she scorned even more the slave women to whom planters turned. Mulatto women like Martha Adamson bore the brunt of her scorn. No "more impure" women existed.[33] Charles Kingsley's novel *Two Years Ago*, which featured the character of a tragic mulatto female heroine who finds her way as a runaway slave from Louisiana to the European stage as a popular actress, she derided as a "Capital work of the imagination." The notion of a black heroine was too absurd, she wrote. No doubt especially problematic for Chesnut was the author's depiction of the black heroine as a woman white men have long tried unsuccessfully to seduce — not knowing she is a slave — and as a slave who refuses the hand of the white man she does love until he commits to abolition. The slave has taken the stage name La Signora Cordifiamma, "heart of fire," to symbolize her commitment to freedom. Her seduction is not of a kind with which Chesnut claims familiarity. La Cordifiamma's beauty is renowned. But her heart, she tells the American who seeks her hand in marriage, is of fire "that I may scorch you, madden you, to do my work, and wear the heart of fire which I wear day and night." Chesnut's sensibilities recoiled from such a portrait. Cordifiamma, indeed. No, she wrote, "*corpi*fiamma." Not hearts of fire but *bodies* of fire was a more apt description of black women. Mules might not deserve their condition, but black women, hot-bodied black women did.[34]

On the question of motherhood, Chesnut, childless in a culture that little suffered childless women, continues to reveal deep-seated ambiguity. In the manuscript, though, she writes with greater certainty, and more defensively, of the superior mothering capabilities of white women relative to those of black women. In the revision she presents sassier, out-of-control slave women, the more to disassociate black women from white women like herself. There is, for example, the "yallar gal" who, according to her maid Polly, "slap[ped] a white child she was nursing"[35] — an incident not recorded in the wartime Journal. Chesnut also recounts the story (rumor) of nine black babies found abandoned in a wagon. In the original account Adam, a slave of Sally Burwell, brings his mistress three babies retrieved from a wagon where, Adam reports, "the Yankees left them." "Surely the poor black mothers were forced to leave them," Chesnut editorializes. She then reports a case of "eighteen negro women with bayonet stabs in the breast" dug up at Minnie Frierson's. "The Yankees were done with them!" Chestnut exclaims, adding, "These are not rumors but tales told me by the people who *see* it all."[36] The revised account represents the event quite differently. Here she writes: "Quantities of negro mothers running after the Yankee army left their babies by the wayside — left them — did not spring from block of ice to block — as Mrs. Stowe fondly imagines they do. So Adam came in exultant: 'Oh, Missis, I have saved a wagon load of babies for you. Dem niggers run away an' lef' dem chillun all 'long de road —' I fancy how sorely tried even Aunt Sally's Christian charity must be by such an ill-timed gift."[37]

In the revision the abandoned babies are, significantly, left not by the Yankees but rather by "quantities of negro mothers." The number abandoned increases from the nine found in a wagon in the 1860s account to additional untold numbers left scattered all along the road. The case, Chesnut is happy to report, is strong evidence that the portrait of selfless, courageous black mothers that Harriet Beecher Stowe so "fondly imagines" is but the stuff of fiction. In an entry dated three days later, 10 May 1865, Chesnut provides a conclusion to the story of the abandoned babies. The eighteen bodies dug up at the Frierson place in the original account she now presents as having also "been found along the road." Citing Frierson as an eyewitness, she writes that they were found "stabbed by the retreating army. The Yankee soldiers could not rid themselves of the pests any other way. Poor animals."[38]

There is in the Journal the suggestion that the children were taken by force from their mothers and that the women were sexually abused, when she writes, "The Yankees were done with them." In the 1880s manuscript the women flee voluntarily, "running after the Yankee army," "leaving their chillun all 'long de road." Considered unwelcome burdens by the Union soldiers—who find them, like Chesnut, to be "pests"—they are unceremoniously murdered. In her retelling the women are not even given a burial. They are, after all, "pests," "animals." There is no evidence of sympathy for them in either account. The revised version presents black mothers who selfishly abandon their babies and supports the view that the antebellum planter household—black and white—was, despite its flaws, a positive good in this respect, if only because southern mistresses were so good. Tryphena Blanche Holder Fox, for example, described her slave Susan as a "naturally lazy" mother who "would not have taken her own baby & washed & nursed it if I had not made her!"[39]

In another instance Chesnut appears to relish retelling an anecdote concerning an encounter between a mistress, a group of Yankee troops, and a slave mother. Here too, the two versions of the story are significantly at variance. In the 1860s Journal she writes:

> Sally Reynolds told me an odd anecdote. She met Mrs. Kershaw—who was all in tears the day the Yankees left here. She said in all her trials & partings from Gnl. K, she had never felt as she felt that moment. A small black boy of three years old, a great pet, had been torn from her arms by the ruthless Yanks. The child clung to her & did not wish to go even with his mother. Sally says she saw the mother running with it & whipping this screaming little dark rebel every foot of the way. Our pickets caught this party & the woman came back—but Mrs. K would not let her enter her yard. So the beloved blackamoor was banished at last for his mother's sin.[40]

The incident is presented in the revised book as follows:

Sally Reynolds told a story of a little negro pet of Mrs. Kershaw's. The little negro clung to Mrs. K and begged her to save him. The negro mother, stronger than Mrs. K, tore him away from her. Mrs. K. wept bitterly. Sally said she saw the mother chasing the child before her as she ran after the Yankees, whipping him at every step. The child yelled like mad, a small rebel blackamoor. The mother soon came back, but Mrs. K would not allow any of them to enter her yard again.[41]

This account contrasts a ruthless, even sinful slave mother to Mrs. Kershaw, the plantation mistress, who, we are told, the child prefers to his mother. In this way Chesnut creatively uses an anecdote to support the notion of mistresses' superior mothering instinct. But Chesnut is still in a quandary, still boxed in, because this account, in contradistinction to that of the African-American women who abandon their babies, shows a mother struggling to take her child with her in flight; it reveals a slave woman as caring mother. The contradiction is a small price to pay for the larger achievement of the passage. Two images stand out. The first conveys black women's lack of maternal instinct. Their actions leave their children, in today's parlance, "homeless." In the original account the party of runaway slaves is captured by Confederate pickets, and when Mrs. Kershaw refuses to take them back, Chesnut pointedly relates, "the beloved blackamoor was banished at last for his mother's sin." In the revision she suggests that the mother returns voluntarily, but the consequences for the child are the same.

Chesnut's literary achievement is no conundrum, as the second of the two images makes clear. In this seemingly insignificant passage, she weaves an image of the dangerous black woman: big, strong, and mean. In the revised version the slave mother, "stronger than Mrs. K, *tore* him away from her," while "Mrs. K wept bitterly." In the original version it is the "ruthless" Yanks who tear the boy away from his owner's arms.[42] To be feared and denied are black women's "pretending to be ladies" and black women's being ladies, that is, mothers of children that white "mothers" see as "pets." In the literary imagination of Mary Chesnut, black mothers are a tiresome, lazy, and comical lot despite the contrary evidence before her.

Evidence of African-American women's sense of self was manipulated to meet Chesnut's revised needs. In the 1880s manuscript Chesnut records an entry for 1861—one of many for which she is now famous—suggestive of the varied uses to which she put her literary imagination in the effort to present herself anew and present black women as sensible only when serving. In 1861, at the outset of the war, when the slaves around her appeared indifferent both to the conflict raging at nearby Fort Sumter and the conversations of whites who "talk before them as if they were chairs and tables," she wrote: "And they make no sign. Are they stolidly stupid or wiser than we are, silent and strong, biding their time?"[43] This oft-cited passage does not appear in the wartime Journal.

By the time Chesnut sat down to revise her wartime Journal, she knew that the black women had indeed been biding their time. Even Myrtilla, the old African, had become a fugitive from slavery. Myrtilla's story is much enhanced in the revised account. In the original Journal, "Old Myrtilla, so old that a servant was given her by her master to cook & wash for her, left with the Yankees—has sent word she wants to be *sent for*. She got tired in two days' journey. Ellen said, 'All Aunt Myrtilla wanted was a little good religion to die with.'"[44] Chesnut's revised account offers more about Myrtilla's background. She was formerly James Chesnut Sr.'s head nurse at his "summer resort for his invalid negroes and especially for the women with ailing babies" and was "very good, very sensible, very efficient." The reconstructed Myrtilla of the 1880s manuscript regains her senses: "After the first natural frenzy of freedom subsided, [she] knew too well on which side her bread was buttered." She whom Chesnut's father-in-law had treated "like a lady," meaning she "had a woman to wash and cook for her," remembered "where her real friends were" and was too soon back "on our hands to support once more."[45] In the original version Myrtilla is said to return simply because the journey proved too much for an old woman.

By the time of Myrtilla's departure, such stories no longer shocked Chesnut. It is in the 1880s manuscript that Chesnut most forcefully acknowledges black people's desire for freedom, their support for the Union, and their "disloyalty." In her wartime Journal, with the exception of her response to the murder of Betsy Witherspoon by her slaves, she noted but generally brushed aside such matters.[46] In the entry dated 16 February 1865 in the 1880s manuscript, she wrote of learning that the Martins had left Columbia without "their mammy, the negro woman who had nursed them." She had "refused to go with them. That daunted me."[47] This passage has no counterpart in the original diary. Neither the discourse that promoted the notion of an archetypal "Confederate Woman" nor the postwar monuments constructed to honor her were sufficient ballast against the storm that followed the loss of mastery for mistresses.[48]

From the vantage point of the 1880s, Chestnut could take some comfort in her maid Ellen who accompanied her in flight from Sherman's approach to North Carolina and who in the revised version receives expanded treatment.

Ellen's enhanced standing, Muhlenfeld suggests, evidences Chesnut's in-creased concern for the humorous potential of her work and provides a means for Chestnut to leave herself out of the work, to shift the focus of the work to the world around her.[49] Ellen, Muhlenfeld writes, provides in the re-vised account "comic relief and a very human tone." She "is having the time of her life," delighting in the elevated standing among the slaves at the Hotel Lincolnton that the "prominence of her mistress" gives her.[50] Ridiculing the hotel proprietor's contention that she and Laurence were brought to North Carolina to prevent their escaping to the Yankees, Ellen replies: "Name o' God ole Missis! If dats it—what she bring Laurence and me for—She's got plenty more—Laurence and me's nothing—to our white people."[51] The revised characterization of Ellen may be just as profitably understood as a literary de-vice that allows Chesnut to center herself squarely as the focus of the passage, rather than shift attention away from herself. The main focus is not on Ellen, except as she represents the proper kind of subservient black woman. Rather, it is on "the prominence of her mistress." Although by February 1865 the southern bid for independence has been reduced to ashes and the prominent Chesnut to living quarters without carpets and feather beds, an exile living with bare floors and a pine table for a bed, she still has "plenty more" ser-vants.[52] At a time when citizens at the home front, like soldiers at the war front, are barefooted and starving, Ellen, the slave, protests against having to eat a "a piece of meat—and a whole plateful of raw ingins": "I never did eat raw ingins, and I won't begin now."[53] Yet even the loyal Ellen does not com-pletely escape Chesnut's biting pen.

In the original Journal, Ellen tells Chesnut that Miss Johnson, the landlady, has banished her from the kitchen. Her presence is distracting. Miss Johnson is quoted as saying: "My niggers won't work for looking at you." Ellen is de-lighted, telling her mistress, "Ain't I *a show*. I never knew it before—but I am *somfin* for folks to look at."[54] In the Journal, Chesnut makes no comment on Ellen's new self-image. In the revision she prefaces Ellen's declaration of her beauty with a description of Ellen's physiognomy that declares the opposite.[55] Chesnut does render Ellen comical, but for Chesnut the point seems to have little to do with a desire to experiment with literary devices. Ellen and Molly, Muhlenfeld argues, remain loyal during and after the war and "by their loy-alty to and love for their mistress, earned the right [in the revised book] to fully realized portraits in her writing."[56] It also seems that Ellen and Molly represent for Chesnut good black women as opposed to those who had al-ways made her uncomfortable and even ill. Chesnut characterizes Ellen's de-votion and love as steadfast even after she has become a free woman. In slavery and freedom Ellen places her mistress above her family. When her husband demands that Chesnut pay Ellen a wage, Ellen takes her mistress's position that he "is an old fool."[57] Ultimately though, Chesnut recognizes the limits of her maids' devotion. "Ellen is a maid—comme il y en a peu—and if I do a little work it is quite enough to show me how dreadful it would be without her *if I should have to do it all.*"[58] And Molly, still attending Chesnut's personal cows, continues to make and sell butter for Chesnut but now does so on shares.[59]

By 1865 Mary Chesnut knew, as did others of her class, that the "old reb times" were done and gone. Tryphena Fox, a northern schoolteacher who marries to her constant dismay not quite into Chesnut's class, recognized the new order, though loath to do so. Finding herself once again in 1868 without a servant and "her own cook," she was at once blessed and disgraced by the decision of Old Aunt Sally to help her out for a few days. She wrote: "Old Aunt Sally—the *elite* of the next plantation, and of the old Virginny stock, hearing of my inability to get any one volunteered her services & came & cooked dinner & washed for me & the next day cooked & ironed & yesterday cooked the breakfast & dinner & picked & cleaned my turkey. . . . She is a mighty wise old body and it seems like 'old reb times' to have her in the kitchen calling me 'Miss Blanche' & Dr R—'Mas'r Ramon.'"[60]

"Miss Blanche" knew, however, that she had no control over Aunt Sally, who did not show up on the day she was scheduled to cook the turkey. A hard rain on that day, Fox supposed, accounted for her absence. But Aunt Sally had made it quite clear on the first day that she did not have to work for anyone because her son could "sport" her; she was merely rendering Fox a favor, not a service. "That is the way," Fox concluded, "she apologized to her *pride,* & freedom when she came down the first morning."[61] Whether or not Aunt Sally actually had a son who could "sport" her is unknown and in some ways immaterial. Clearly she recognized that it was not her pride on the line but Fox's. After all, she told Fox, "You knows Miss Blanche—I wouldn'nt cook for every body . . . but you knows I *would* come seein twas you & Mas'r Ramon."[62]

When African-American women took to wearing veils, dressing up on days other than church day, playing the lady, "dressing themselves in their mistresses' gowns and walking off" before their mistresses' very faces, white women found themselves indeed under the gun.[63] Mary Boykin Chesnut fired back, reminding her potential readers that the war was not really over. In this respect the title Woodward gave to the edited 1981 version of her postwar manuscript is both appropriate and ironic. The book may be seen quite literally as Mary Chesnut's Civil War. The revised book more powerfully than the original would remind southerners of how the South had been done in before it ever became the Confederacy and how southern women were done in before, during, and after the Confederacy.

If there was ever any doubt that the family stood at the center of life in the nineteenth-century South, as "the essential foundation of southern public life and values,"[64] Chesnut's revisions drive home that point and another. This essential foundation had proved to be just as porous and unreliable as the cornerstone of slavery upon which Alexander Stephens placed the hope of southern independence in 1861. As Chesnut saw it, the family, "bulwark of the Southern social order," had been severely compromised from the outset by slavery, the very institution that had made the family so central. As Eugene Genovese argues, although the ubiquitous expression "our family, white and black," cannot be dismissed as facile mythmaking or apologetics and must be taken seriously "notwithstanding its ideological rationalizations, its gaping contradictions, and its dose of hypocrisy,"[65] Chesnut's lambaste against black women highlighted the hypocrisy and the reduced sense of self it created for white women.

Mary Chesnut was like most women of her class both comfortable with the system of slavery and discomfited by elements of its basic nature. She could and did defend the system, yet she also could be more clearheaded than the menfolk in discerning its internal weaknesses, which to her mind included the men. And the men frequently appeared to her variously as vapid, stupid, cowardly, silly, affected, and generally incompetent like the "troopless generals"[66] who rate her sneers as they parade around in the early months of 1865 as if the Confederacy were not on its deathbed. Next to her husband, few Confederate men had stood the test in her opinion. And at the end, even the most revered of this group had failed her. When she heard that Jefferson Davis had been "taken in woman's clothes," she knew the end had come for the Confederacy and the Old South way of life: "Never! If Jeff Davis is not pluck—I give up. What can one believe in hereafter—if he is not game."[67] To Chesnut, the men of her race and class were most vapid on the question of family and played too loosely with its importance. The consequences for white men and women, she recognized, differed substantially.

The conclusion of the war dispersed "our family, white and black." Although whites bemoaned this end even as they shouted "good riddance," freedpeople celebrated it amidst painful efforts to reconstitute families not black and white. In this light Chesnut's critique of slave and freedwomen can be understood on several levels. She recoiled at the emancipation of the defining terms *woman* and *lady* from their moorings to white females. Neither was she impressed with the notion that there could be something called "our family" that included masters and their slaves, dependent white women and dependent slave mistresses — some of whom were bright, white, intelligent, and beautiful; some of whom were beastly mulatto beauties — and children, some of whom were bright and white with futures to consider and some of whom were pets. In the revision Chesnut attributes to the overseer Team a statement that effectively sums up the task she had before her and, perhaps, the logic behind this monumental work that is the 1880s book. Team says, "Yes. That Miss Stowe don't know nothing. The way a man's wife and chillen stops things or suffers — when men are so bad, that's where the trouble comes in."[68] Still, Chesnut was unwilling to go as far as she had gone in her 1860s journals in criticizing the master class. Perhaps nothing better states the case for this interpretation than her decision to delete her most strongly worded indictment. The most widely cited and celebrated passage from Chesnut's writings, the one upon which her abolitionist credentials most famously rest, is the one she chose not to include in the revised manuscript:

> I wonder if it be a sin to think slavery a curse to any land. Sumner said not one word of this hated institution which is not true. Men & women are punished when their master & mistresses are brutes & not when they do wrong — & then we live surrounded by prostitutes. An abandoned woman is sent out of any decent house elsewhere. Who thinks any worse of a Negro or Mulatto woman for being a thing we can't name. God forgive *us,* but ours is a *monstrous* system & wrong & iniquity. Perhaps the rest of the world is as bad. This *only* I see: like the patriarchs of old our men live all in one house with their wives & their concubines, & the Mulattoes one sees in every family exactly resemble the white children — & every lady tells you who the is father of all the Mulatto children in every body's household, but those in her own, she seems to think drop from the clouds or pretends so to think — Good women we have, *but* they talk of all *nastiness* — tho they never do wrong, they talk day and night of [*six unrecoverable words, apparently a quote*]. My disgust sometimes is boiling over — but they are, I believe, in conduct the purest women God ever made. Thank God for my country women — alas for the men! No worse than men every where, but the lower their mistresses, the more degraded they must be. . . . So it is — flocks & herds & slaves — & wife Leah does not suffice. Rachel must be *added,* if not *married.* & all the time they seem to think themselves patterns — models of husbands & fathers.[69]

In Mary Chesnut's Journal and posthumously published manuscript and in the diaries and correspondence of other southern white women, the "painful and spiteful past" of southern history is a central theme. Attempting to come to terms with the failure of her husband to achieve his and her political ambitions, Chesnut declared, "I am trying to look *defeat* of my personal ambition in the face."[70] The statement applies with equal force to her sense of her own reduced status out of the Confederacy. That too challenged other former mistresses. "The black ball is in motion," Chesnut wrote on 4 June 1865. "Mrs. DeSaussure's cook shook the dust off her feet and departed from her kitchen today, free, she said. The washerwoman is packing to go."[71] What she had always predicted had come true. The slaves would leave.

In the end she concluded the revised manuscript with a quite simple acknowledgment of the pain and the spite that even her creatively expanded book could not dissipate: "And the weight that hangs upon our eyelids—is of lead."[72] This last line is absent from the original diary. In the words of Drew Faust, "Mary Chestnut was compelled by Confederate defeat to lead a new sort of life, an existence in which survival demanded that she become a different sort of person."[73] Yet the problem remained, for Chesnut was not convinced. A different sort of person in the sense of more forthrightly claiming a past that was in part fiction, yes. A different sort of person in the sense of relinquishing her claim to membership in a distinctly superior community of women, no.

It is impossible to know whether Chesnut died certain of her literary achievement, bedeviled as her efforts were by all of the contradiction that was the South. She did achieve a literary victory for the women of her class and race. The monumental task she had set before herself, when done, reclaimed the purity of white women—even when their men could not do so except through violent action against black people or the threat of it. She gave voice to a reduced status that neither force of their men nor Confederate memorializing to them seemed capable of uplifting. She reinvented and reproduced a history of the impurity of African-American women, slave and free—a history that struck at their struggle to be free.

In a recent small but important book, *Playing in the Dark: Whiteness in the Literary Imagination,* Toni Morrison refers to *Uncle Tom's Cabin:* "As a writer reading, I came to realize the obvious: the subject of the dream is the dreamer. The fabrication of an Africanist persona is reflexive; an extraordinary meditation on the self; a powerful exploration of the fears and desires that reside in the writerly conscious. It is an astonishing revelation of longing, of terror, of perplexity, of shame, of magnanimity. It requires hard work *not* to see this."[74]

Mary Chesnut's meditations on the self set in the context of the changed world of the New South were precisely those. In the end these meditations may have had less to do with race and black women, per se, than with the literary uses race and gender served in the reinvention of Mary Chesnut. It has been said of the African Hall in New York City's American Museum of Natural History that "the recomposition produces a story that is reticent, even mute, about Africa."[75] In a similar way Mary Chesnut's recomposition produces a story about "a white woman's battle for coherence"[76]—a story mute about black women. African-American women do not exist in the literary imagination of Mary Boykin Chesnut, only her images of them, and these only as they serve her battle for coherence.

Notes

This essay was originally prepared for and presented at the 1993 meeting of the Southern Association of Women Historians. I am especially indebted the close and critical readings provided by Elizabeth Fox-Genovese and Eugene D. Genovese. Elisabeth Muhlenfeld also kindly read and commented on a draft of this essay presented at the 1994 meeting of the Southern Intellectual History Circle, and though I am sure I have not met her objections, I hope I have benefited some from her insight. John G. Sproat and the late George C. Rogers of the University of South Carolina also provided valuable comments as did audiences at the University of Richmond, Pennsylvania State University, and the University of Illinois.

1. C. Vann Woodward and Elisabeth Muhlenfeld, eds., *The Private Mary Chesnut: The Unpublished Civil War Diaries* (New York, 1984), 11 March 1861, 33.

2. Edmund Wilson, *Patriotic Gore: Studies in the Literature of the American Civil War* (New York, 1962), 279. In this essay the terms *book* and *manuscript* are used interchangeably to refer to the manuscript Chesnut composed during the 1880s based on her wartime journals, the most complete edition of which is *Mary Chesnut's Civil War*, ed. C. Vann Woodward (New Haven, 1981). Following the usage established by Woodward, "Journal" refers to the diary Chesnut kept during the Civil War.

3. Elisabeth Muhlenfeld, *Mary Boykin Chesnut: A Biography* (Baton Rouge, La., 1981), 197.

4. Ibid., 197.

5. Woodward, *Mary Chesnut's Civil War*, 29 Aug. 1861, 172.

6. Ibid., 2, 3 , 6 , 7 March 1861, 12 June 1865, 18, 20, 24, 25–27, 828.

7. Woodward and Muhlenfeld, *Private Mary Chesnut*, 12 March, 27 June, 24 July, 26 Aug., 15 Oct. 1861, 37, 85, 105, 140, 178. Even Harriet Grant, a relative for whom Chesnut had little patience and even less respect, is portrayed a bit less reprehensibly in the 1880s manuscript.

8. Woodward and Muhlenfeld, *Private Mary Chestnut*, 30 Sept. 1861, 165; Woodward, *Mary Chesnut's Civil War*, 24 Sept. 1861, 200–201.

9. Woodward, *Mary Chesnut's Civil War*, 10 March 1862, 301; see also Muhlenfeld, *Mary Boykin Chesnut*, 201–202.

10. Woodward, *Mary Chesnut's Civil War*, xxi. The point is also made by Daniel Aaron in his *Unwritten War: American Writers and the Civil War* (London, 1973), 259.

11. Woodward, *Mary Chesnut's Civil War*, xix–xxvii; in Muhlenfeld, *Mary Boykin Chesnut*, see, for example, 202.

12. Woodward and Muhlenfeld, *Private Mary Chesnut*, xvi.

13. Other scholars have charted inconsistencies between the Civil War journals and the 1880s manuscript, and Elizabeth Fox-Genovese and Drew Gilpin Faust have argued persuasively for a reconsideration of the view that positions Chesnut as an abolitionist and feminist. See, for example, Faust, "In Search of the Real Mary Chesnut," *Reviews in American History* 20 (March 1982): 55–56, and Fox-Genovese, 339–65. For a different perspective on Chesnut's narrative strategies, see Melissa Mentzer, "Rewriting Herself: Mary Chesnut's Narrative Strategies," *Connecticut Review* 14 (Spring 1992): 49–55.

14. Wilson, *Patriotic Gore*, 279.

15. Toni Morrison, *Playing in the Dark: Whiteness and the Literary Imagination* (Cambridge, Mass., 1992), quotations on 90, 11–12.

16. Fox-Genovese, 356.

17. Faust, "In Search of the Real Mary Chesnut," 55–56.

18. Paul C. Cameron to [Duncan Cameron], 17 Feb. 1865, Cameron Family Papers, SHC.

19. Woodward, *Mary Chesnut's Civil War*, 12 March 1865, 761. Chesnut saw that a reappraisal of many of the class and caste biases of the planter class—no longer able to rule from a position of "insolent prosperity"—was in order. Shopkeepers, engineers, architects might now be "the best investment" for women (ibid., 19 April, 12 June 1865, 788, 826).

20. The first quote is from Woodward and Muhlenfeld, *Private Mary Chesnut*, 8 Dec. 1861, 214; the second, Woodward, *Mary Chesnut's Civil War*, 6 Dec. 1861, 256.

21. Woodward and Muhlenfeld, *Private Mary Chesnut*, xvi.

22. On southern honor, see Bertram Wyatt-Brown, *Southern Honor: Ethics and Behavior in the Old South* (New York, 1982), and Kenneth S. Greenberg, *Honor and Slavery* (Princeton, N.J., 1996).

23. Quotation from Woodward, *Mary Chesnut's Civil War*, 30 March 1865, 773.

24. I am indebted to Elizabeth Fox-Genovese for this insight.

25. Woodward, *Mary Chesnut's Civil War*, 26 Feb. 1865, 737.

26. Fox-Genovese, 354; see also Leeann Whites, "The Civil War as a Crisis in Gender," in *Divided Houses: Gender and the Civil War*, ed. Catherine Clinton and Nina Silber (New York, 1992).

27. Woodward and Muhlenfeld, *Private Mary Chesnut*, 4 March 1861, 21.

28. Woodward, *Mary Chesnut's Civil War*, 4 March 1861, 15.

29. Fox-Genovese, 348–49 (quotations on 349).

30. Woodward, *Mary Chesnut's Civil War*, 8 Dec. 1861, 259.

31. Woodward and Muhlenfeld, *Private Mary Chesnut*, 26 Nov. 1861, 207.

32. Woodward, *Mary Chesnut's Civil War*, 25 Nov. 1861, 243.

33. Woodward and Muhlenfeld, *Private Mary Chesnut*, 26 Nov. 1861, 207.

34. Charles Kingsley, *Two Years Ago*, 2 vols. (1857; New York, 1899), quotation on 1:225–26; Woodward, *Mary Chesnut's Civil War*, 25 Nov. 1861, 243. My thanks to Philip Baldi and Guido Rugierro of Pennsylvania State University for their assistance with the Italian translations.

35. Woodward, *Mary Chesnut's Civil War*, 4 June 1861, 69. Chesnut made numerous references to her own childlessness and to the social disgrace that childlessness attached to other white women. See, for example, ibid., 28, 32, and Woodward and Muhlenfeld, *Private*

Mary Chesnut, 40–41, 44. She tended, however, to erase such references to herself from the 1880s manuscript.

36. Woodward and Muhlenfeld, *Private Mary Chesnut,* 11 May 1865, 241–42.

37. Woodward, *Mary Chesnut's Civil War,* 7 May 1865, 806.

38. Ibid., 10 May 1865, 809–10.

39. Wilma King, ed., *A Northern Woman in the Plantation South: Letters of Tryphena Blanche Holder Fox, 1856–1876* (Columbia, S.C., 1993), 87.

40. Woodward and Muhlenfeld, *Private Mary Chesnut,* 15 May 1865, 246.

41. Woodward, *Mary Chesnut's Civil War,* 10 May 1865, 812–13.

42. For the original version, see Woodward and Muhlenfeld, *Private Mary Chesnut,* 15 May 1865, 246; for the revision, see Woodward, *Mary Chesnut's Civil War,* 10 May 1865, 813.

43. Woodward, *Mary Chesnut's Civil War,* 13 April 1861, 48.

44. Woodward and Muhlenfeld, *Private Mary Chesnut,* 7 May 1865, 237.

45. Woodward, *Mary Chesnut's Civil War,* 7 May 1865, 805–6.

46. See, for example, the following entries in the wartime journal: Woodward and Muhlenfeld, *Private Mary Chesnut,* 27 Sept., 27 Oct., 12, 28 Nov. 1861, 164, 190, 199–200, 208.

47. Woodward, *Mary Chesnut's Civil War,* 16 Feb. 1865, 715.

48. Drew Gilpin Faust discusses the failed discourse in "Altars of Sacrifice: Confederate Women and the Narratives of War," in Clinton and Silber, *Divided Houses,* see esp. 172–73, 191.

49. Muhlenfeld, *Mary Boykin Chesnut,* 198–99.

50. Ibid., 199.

51. Woodward, *Mary Chesnut's Civil War,* 16 Feb. 1865, 718.

52. Ibid., 717–18.

53. Ibid., 717.

54. Woodward and Muhlenfeld, *Private Mary Chesnut,* 16 Feb. 1865, 230.

55. Woodward, *Mary Chesnut's Civil War,* 16 Feb. 1865, 717.

56. Muhlenfeld, *Mary Boykin Chesnut,* 203.

57. Woodward, *Mary Chesnut's Civil War,* 12 June 1865, 830.

58. Ibid., 26 Feb. 1865, 733.

59. Ibid., 7 May 1865, 805.

60. King, *Northern Woman,* 2 Oct. 1868, 226.

61. Ibid.

62. Ibid.

63. Woodward, *Mary Chesnut's Civil War,* 12 June 1865, 833; Thavolia Glymph, "I'se Mrs. Tatum Now: Freedom and Black Women's Reconstruction," paper presented at Southern Historical Association Meeting, 1992.

64. Drew Gilpin Faust, "Epilogue," in *In Joy and in Sorrow: Women, Family, and Marriage in the Victorian South,* ed. Carol Bleser (New York, 1991), 253.

65. Eugene Genovese, "'Our Family, White and Black': Family and Household in the Southern Slaveholders' World View," in Bleser, *In Joy and in Sorrow,* 69–87 (quotation on 87); see also Genovese, *Roll,* 70–74.

66. Woodward, *Mary Chesnut's Civil War,* 17 Jan., 16 Feb. 1865, 707, 716.

67. Woodward and Muhlenfeld, *Private Mary Chesnut,* 25 May 1865, 252; Woodward, *Mary Chesnut's Civil War,* 21 May 1865, 819.

68. Woodward, *Mary Chesnut's Civil War,* 6 Dec. 1861, 256.

69. Woodward and Muhlenfeld, *Private Mary Chesnut,* 18 March 1861, 42–43.

70. Woodward and Muhlenfeld, *Private Mary Chesnut*, 3 Aug. 1861, 124.

71. Woodward, *Mary Chesnut's Civil War*, 4 June 1865, 823.

72. Ibid., 26 June 1865, 636.

73. Faust, "Real Mary Chesnut," 57.

74. Morrison, *Playing in the Dark*, 17.

75. Donna Haraway, *Primate Visions: Gender, Race, and Nature in the World of Modern Science* (New York, 1989), 27.

76. Morrison, *Playing in the Dark*, 20.

PART III

SOUTHERN HISTORY

8

Measuring the South:
Health, Height, and Literary Myths

LOUIS A. FERLEGER AND RICHARD H. STECKEL

The praise given to William Styron's current prize-winning, best-selling novel, *The Confessions of Nat Turner,* has been followed by strong dissent and hostility. . . . The burden of the attack on Styron's book is the charge of historical falsification. . . . The novel is historically sound. Styron takes liberties with fact, as every novelist does, but he does not do violence to the historical record.

—Eugene D. Genovese, *In Red and Black* (1988)

LITERATURE undoubtedly influences perceptions of history. Students bring to teachers powerful images of the past gleaned directly from novels or indirectly from movies, newspaper articles, or television commentary that have been shaped by novels. Teachers regularly confront these images in the classroom and quickly discover that they cannot easily convey to students the "truth" about the past as learned from standard historical sources until they first understand what students know, or what they believe they know, from literary sources.

The line between fact and fiction is no longer just an issue addressed in the classroom by teachers or literary scholars; it has also entered more public debates in newspapers about the extent to which a novel is considered "literature" or something else. In a recent editorial in the *New York Times* entitled "Is it Literature-or Merely an Entertainment?" Verlyn Klinkenborg discusses Tom Wolfe's new book *A Man in Full* and remarks that "ironically, like many writers, he has overvalued the novel by abandoning nonfiction, and, ironically, he has underestimated the extent to which all fiction, not just his own, is based on fact."[1]

To be sure, a novel's descriptions of a region, society, or culture can strikingly illuminate a historical period and create stark images of people and places. Debate invariably arises, however, over the extent to which fiction is based on fact and is useful to historians as a factual description of the past.

No novelist has had a greater impact on historians of the South than William Faulkner. His rich, layered depictions of numerous aspects of southern life in the late nineteenth and early twentieth centuries have provoked volumes of commentary. His discussions of race relations, merchant-landlord interactions, and the Civil War have opened an extensive menu of important historical questions that many historians have addressed. In *The Social Origins of the New South*, for example, Jonathan Wiener begins his discussion of post–Civil War merchant-landlord relations by quoting Will Varner, one of the main characters from Faulkner's novel *The Hamlet*. In his Pulitzer Prize–winning book *Voyagers to the West*, Bernard Bailyn draws upon Faulkner's historically inspired imagination in comparing one of the South's immigrants to Colonel Sutpen of *Absalom, Absalom!*[2] Joel Williamson in *The Crucible of Race* quotes Faulkner several times to support his argument about the nature of postbellum race relations. At one point Williamson observes, "William Faulkner, with his usual unflagging instinct for truth about the South, caught the image perfectly in the lynching of Joe Christmas in his novel *Light in August* (1932)." At other times when Williamson discusses Faulkner's work, he notes approvingly that Faulkner was "right again." In 1993 Williamson underscored Faulkner's powerful impact on historians in a book entitled *William Faulkner and Southern History*.[3]

Historians have quoted Faulkner again and again because his work provides a succession of unforgettable southern characters. In one striking passage in *The Sound and the Fury*, Faulkner focuses on the physical characteristics of one of his southerners, remarking: "She had been a big woman once but now her skeleton rose, draped loosely in unpaddled skin that tightened again upon a paunch almost dropsical, as though muscle and tissue had been courage or fortitude which the days or the years had consumed until only the indomitable skeleton was left rising like a ruin or a landmark above that the collapsed face that gave the impression of the bones themselves being outside the flesh."[4] Faulkner's stark images of southerners' physical characteristics have left a lasting impression of an impoverished population yearning for health as well as happiness.

Faulkner does not dwell in his novels on the physical and health conditions of southerners per se. Yet by his descriptions he strongly suggests that southerners were unhealthy. Historians have tended to agree. Jack Temple Kirby, for example, writes: "One generalization seems unassailable. Because of their climate and their poverty, southerners were less healthy than other

Americans, and they looked it."[5] The words "they looked it" could have been elicited from Faulkner's images. For it is Faulkner who constructed in his novels indelible images of southern physical traits, eating habits, and stature. His characters, whether they be men or women, black or white, young or old, rich or poor, tend to look rather frail, declining, and deficient. Their complicated social and emotional lives spring from rather unhealthy bodies. Faulkner's characters struggle with some of the central questions of our time or the human condition, but when they are described in physical terms, they appear weak and physically vulnerable. They frequently swill alcohol, chain-smoke, and are either underweight or overweight. Even when Faulkner portrays a tall character, that person usually has prominent physical debilities.

Faulkner's seeming predilection for diminishing his character's stature and health surfaces throughout the corpus of his work.[6] Most of Faulkner's physical descriptions convey an image of a frail, weak, sallow population. Even when he uses positive adjectives to describe tall, strong, or lean characters, they tend to be accompanied by negatives. It is indeed hard to imagine one of Faulkner's characters reaching the average lifespan of the typical southerner in the twentieth century. Nor does one sense from Faulkner that southerners had a history of height advantage over northerners, for his physical descriptions of southerners leave the impression of lesser stature.

Nutrition, of course, influences height and average length of life. A well-nourished population will fare better than poorly nourished ones. In this regard Faulkner's novels contain detailed descriptions of the food and drink consumed by his characters. They eat meat and flour products, various starches, garden vegetables, and fruits. His descriptions of southern food cover a wide range of nutritious produce that was readily available to southerners. These descriptions are puzzling, for if Faulkner recognized in his descriptions the kinds of good food even poor southerners had at their disposal except during the war years, why did he usually craft his characters as either obese or gaunt?[7]

Although Faulkner describes his characters as drinking various liquids, alcohol consumption is ubiquitous. The same is true for tobacco use. Habitual consumption of alcohol and smoking can, of course, seriously compromise a person's health and longevity.[8] Yet in Faulkner's South people drank and smoked heavily and ate either too much or too little. His descriptions of characters as "gaunt," "fat," "plump," "anemic," "mountainous," "small," "thin," and "drunk" comport nicely with their apparent drinking and smoking habits. Many of Faulkner's characters are addicted to alcohol and are chronically trying to recover from its effects. In *Absalom, Absalom!* for example, Faulkner writes: "And Grandfather (he was young then too) brought some champagne and some of the others brought whiskey. . . . They just sat around the fire with the champagne and the whiskey . . . filling the room with alcohol snoring . . . holding out the bottle of whiskey already uncorked."[9]

But were southerners that unhealthy? During Faulkner's lifetime the South was poor relative to other regions of the United States. Although the South's income did fall below that of other regions, the region did not lag behind the rest of the nation or comparable national economies in terms of health and height, two critical measures of living standards.[10] Before the end of World War II, social scientists such as Howard Odum and Gunnar Myrdal had defined the South's standard of living in terms of income alone. Though influential, their depiction of life in the South is incomplete and misleading. A more comprehensive portrait of well-being would also recognize health as a critical component. Like Faulkner's fiction, Odum's and Myrdal's work inaccurately portrays certain dimensions of southern history.[11]

Economists, demographers, and auxologists (students of human growth) have long sought to define and measure living standards or the quality of life. The standard approaches in these fields focus on different but important aspects of well-being. Living standards as measured by economists rest on national income accounting techniques that were developed over the past three centuries.[12] In the highly competitive mercantilistic environment of newly formed nation-states in the seventeenth century, political leaders who wondered about the military and economic capacity of their countries sought measures of their performance. In 1665 Sir William Petty, a British philosopher who pioneered methods of accounting for what economists now call human capital, suggested that a country's annual income could be measured as the sum of the annual value of labor and the annual proceeds of property. Shortly thereafter the French judge Pierre Boisguillebert, a precursor of the Physiocrats, formulated a similar approach, defining national income in terms of a flow of goods and services and money incomes. In his view national income consisted of two nearly equal parts: income from labor, which was derived from peasants, artisans, factory workers, petty tradesmen, and professionals, and income from property, which consisted of land, houses, mills, tollhouses, revenue-producing public offices, and money capital. Although the French Physiocrats defined national income in terms of consumable commodities alone and treated agriculture as the only productive occupation, Adam Smith took a broader view, including agriculture, manufacturing, and trade in his accounting but excluding services as not productive.[13] Comprehensive production and income concepts were not firmly established in the literature until economist Alfred Marshall set forth his ideas in the late nineteenth century.

In the twentieth century national income accounting changed from the casual and sporadic activities of individual researchers to become a nearly universal preoccupation of nation-states. The greatest boost to progress in the United States occurred in the Great Depression when the Senate instructed the Department of Commerce to prepare national income estimates, which were delivered in 1934 under the guidance of the Russian-born economist Simon Kuznets, whose methods earned him in 1971 the Nobel Prize in economic science. By 1939 nine countries were preparing estimates on a continuing basis, but after World War II international organizations such as the United Nations made possible a rapid diffusion of accounting methods to the point that within three decades 130 nations were systematically publishing income accounts.

Economists who designed the system of national accounts in the 1930s were aware of the historical debates about the form and content of the accounts yet were pressed by the exigencies of the Great Depression to produce results that would depict the extent of economic decline and lead to expedient remedies. Led by practical considerations, they followed a narrow approach, defining national income based on the market value of the output of final goods and services produced by a nation's economy. Though useful for investigating macroeconomic matters such as savings, investment, and unemployment, the measure omits nonmarket activity (such as preparation of meals at home) and is conspicuously silent on welfare considerations involving pollution, crime, congestion, safety in the workplace, and the hours and rigors of work required to produce a given income. Though it had recognized shortcomings, per capita national income soon emerged as a widely used measure of living standards.

Demographers, in contrast, use longevity as their centerpiece for living standards. Several developments in the late 1700s led to growing interest in measuring the average length of life, including the need for accurate mortality data by the newly emerging life insurance industry, the ongoing debate between Europeans and Americans over the health consequences of the New World environment, and the rise of scientific societies.[14] Useful results awaited advances in the conceptual framework and in the collection of appropriate evidence. Experts in this new field of demography soon realized that reliable estimates could not be obtained by a simple procedure such as tabulating the average age at death recorded from tombstones. Evidence from graveyards can be distorted by migration and by births, both of which influence the age distribution of a population. For example, the average age at death tabulated today from tombstones in Florida is biased upwards by in-migration of retirees because the cemeteries do not contain members of their cohort who died elsewhere at younger ages. Similarly, a state such as Utah, which has a high birthrate, contains a disproportionate share of young children, who tend to have high death rates and thus bias downward the average age at death as tabulated from a graveyard. Demographers soon devised the model life table as a conceptual device that standardizes or adjusts for variations in the age distribution. Based on death rates by age (the number of deaths in a particular age group divided by the number of people in that age group), the life table compensates for variations in the age distribution and expresses health status by life expectancy at birth.

The empirical problem of reliably calculating death rates, which are the raw materials for the life table, took much longer to resolve. By the late 1700s some cities and towns used bills of mortality to report deaths as they occurred, but most of these sources were sporadic or omitted some deaths. The federal census of 1850 was the first of several censuses to ask household heads about deaths within the previous twelve months, but analysis of this source shows that people often failed to report deaths, particularly those that occurred early in the reporting period. As early as the middle of the nineteenth century, some states, such as Massachusetts, passed laws providing for certificates to record deaths as they occurred, and by the end of the century ten states were following these procedures. In 1900 the Bureau of the Census encouraged the practice of collecting death statistics on an annual basis and served as the advocate and coordinator for expanding the Death Registration Area, a collection of states whose death registration systems were virtually comprehensive. The Death Registration Area was completed when the last state joined in 1933.

The histories of national income accounting, demography, and auxology have two things in common: The first substantial studies occurred in the seventeenth and eighteenth centuries, and they were all sporadic, imprecise efforts made by individuals. Unlike national income accounting and demography, however, useful measurements of height and related attributes could be made on a small scale. Systematic national income data and model life tables awaited government involvement and support in the twentieth century, although important progress in auxology had been made before the end of the nineteenth century. Although desires to monitor social conditions or to engage in the therapeutic treatment of children have led to many growth studies in the past, interest in anthropometry, or measurement of the human body, did not originate with science or medicine but with the arts, for painters and sculptors needed human measurements to create lifelike images.[15] Such artists were interested primarily in relative proportions rather than in absolute size, however, and the data they gathered during the Renaissance had little value for the scientific understanding of human growth.

The first person to use measurements for medical purposes may have been Johann Sigismund Elsholtz, a German physician, who tried to relate body proportions to health in the mid-seventeenth century. In the next century early attempts at systematic anthropometry appeared in the form of measurements of orphans by Christian Friedrich Jampert, a German physician; a study of newborns by Johann Georg Roederer, also a German physician; and a table of measurements taken by Filibert Gueneau de Montbeillard, a French nobleman, of his son's growth from birth (in 1759) to maturity. When scholars realized in the 1820s and 1830s that environmental conditions systematically influenced human growth, studies multiplied. The rise of auxological epidemiology can be traced to France, where the French economist Louis-René Villermé studied the stature of soldiers; to Belgium, where the brilliant mathematician and astronomer Adolphe Quetelet measured children and formulated mathematical representations of the human growth curve; and especially to England, where the public health reformer Edwin Chadwick inquired into the health of factory children. After examining the height of soldiers in France and Holland and studying the economic conditions in their places of origin, Villermé concluded in 1829 that poverty was much more important than climate in influencing growth. The idea that human growth reflected health was put into political action in reports on the stature of factory children that were submitted to Parliament in 1833. Legislation in that year incorporated stature as a criterion in evaluating minimum standards of health for child employment.

A major impetus for collaboration between economic historians and auxologists in the study of living standards occurred in the mid-1970s when height data were analyzed for insights into contentious historical questions. Specifically, slave height profiles obtained from coastwise manifests, surviving children listed on probate records, and evidence from other growth studies showed that menarche occurred early among slave women compared with their age at first birth. The general controversy over the diet, disease, and workload of American slaves was investigated using height-by-age profiles, gender differences, regional patterns, time trends, and ethnic contrasts in stature.[16] Thereafter economic historians and others invested in auxology as a field of study, assembling and analyzing evidence on stature from military and other sources for insights into health, nutrition, and labor productivity. Height studies soon appeared for Sweden, England, colonial America, black recruits in the Union army, and Trinidadian slaves.[17]

Researchers determined that the process of postpartum growth is organized into two periods of intense activity.[18] The change in height, or velocity, is greatest during infancy, falls sharply, and then declines irregularly into the preadolescent years. During adolescence velocity rises sharply to a peak that equals approximately one-half of the velocity during infancy, then declines rapidly, and reaches zero at maturity. In girls the adolescent growth spurt begins about two years earlier than for boys, but the magnitude of the spurt is slightly smaller. Girls and boys reach about the same height at a given age prior to adolescence in girls, but girls temporarily overtake boys in average height during their spurt. Males eventually grow taller than females primarily because they have approximately two additional years of growth prior to their spurt.

The height of an individual reflects the interaction of genetic and environmental influences during the period of growth. Although genes are important determinants of individual height, studies of genetically similar and dissimilar populations under various environmental conditions suggest that differences in average height across most populations are largely attributable to environmental factors. In a 1974 review of studies covering populations in Europe, New Guinea, and Mexico, L. A. Malcolm concluded that differences in average height between populations are almost entirely the product of the environment.[19] Subsequent investigators, using data from well-nourished populations in several developed and developing countries, have reported that children from Europe or of European descent, from Africa or of African descent, and from India or the Middle East have similar growth profiles. Differences between European and Far Eastern children or adults suggest a possible genetic basis, but recent gains in height by the Japanese cast doubt on the importance of the genetic component. More relevant for interpreting stature in the United States is that during the eighteenth and nineteenth centuries Europeans and people of European descent and Africans and people of African descent who grew under good nutritional circumstances had nearly identical stature.[20]

Scientists now know that height at a particular age reflects an individual's history of net nutrition. The body devotes a substantial share of food received to maintenance. Work or physical activity, disease, and basal metabolism make other claims on diet. The nutrition left over for growth may be further reduced by a synergistic effect of malnutrition and illness. Exposure to infectious disease may make extraordinary claims on the diet. Poorly nourished children prove more susceptible to infection, and infection reduces the body's absorption of nutrients. The character of stature as a net measure implies that explanations for temporal or geographic patterns must recognize not only inputs to health such as diet and medical care but also the implications for growth of work effort and related phenomena such as methods of labor organization.

The sensitivity of growth to deprivation depends on the age at which it occurs. For a given degree of deprivation, the adverse effects are approximately in proportion to the velocity of growth under optimal conditions at that age. Young children and adolescents are particularly susceptible to environmental insults. At the end of a period of slow growth, normal height may be restored by catch-up growth if nutritional conditions are adequate. If conditions are inadequate for catch-up, normal adult height may be approached by an extension of the growing period. Prolonged and severe deprivation results in stunting, or a reduction in adult size.

Although a well-known correlation has been established between income and life expectancy, less work has been done on the relation between stature and concepts of living standards as devised by economists. One would expect average height to be a function of per capita income and positively related to the degree of equality in the distribution of income. At the individual level extreme poverty results in malnutrition, retarded growth, and stunting. Higher incomes enable individuals to purchase a better diet, more housing, and health care that improves growth, but once income is high enough to satisfy most basic needs, little further increase in stature occurs with additional income. Given this relation between per capita income and height, one would expect that redistribution of income from rich to poor would increase average height because the nutrition of the rich would not be lessened by loss of some income whereas the poor would allocate much of the additional income to diet and other inputs to health. Data on average height and per capita income for many countries in the mid- to late twentieth century confirm a high correlation between per capita income and average height.[21]

Average height changes little as income increases from high to higher levels, but the average heights of the poor are sensitive to increases in income, a feature that places average height nicely within the basic needs approach to living standards. Although the basic needs approach has drawn fire for its conception of what is indeed basic, average height in many ways finesses this problem because it is a measure of net nutrition that incorporates greater nutritional needs imposed by high workloads or a harsh disease environment. Average height also meets satisfactorily the criteria set forth by the economic historian Morris D. Morris for an international standard of the physical quality of life: it is adaptable to diverse societies; "avoids standards that reflect the values of specific societies; measures results not inputs; reflects the distribution of social results; is simple to construct and easy to comprehend; and lends itself to international comparison."[22]

These alternative approaches to assessing human welfare—national income accounting, life expectancy, and anthropometric measure—have long, distinguished intellectual traditions that emanated from humanitarian considerations. Yet until recently there has been little overlap of personnel or cross-fertilization of ideas. Why these movements unfolded in isolation requires explanation. Perhaps the demands of understanding and making important contributions to economics and national income accounting precluded forays into other, seemingly distant areas. Perhaps the perversion of human measurements and study of human form that occurred in Hitler's Germany repelled the national income accountants and the demographers of the 1930s and 1940s. Whatever the explanation, auxology permits the testing of certain images in Faulkner's South.

Over the span of Faulkner's life, the southern economy was growing relatively rapidly, and southerners were remarkably healthy by global standards. The most comprehensive historical study of regional income patterns, published in 1961 by Richard Easterlin, used census data on productive activity and market prices to approximate income by region in earlier years.[23] He found that per capita income in the South was 51 percent of the national average in 1880 and in 1900. Yet in 1920 the South's position had risen to 62 percent, and by 1950 it was 73 percent of the national average. Despite low incomes in the South of Faulkner's formative years (he was born in 1897), the region prospered in that income grew faster in the South than in the North or West. Though poor by national standards, the southern economy actually showed noteworthy growth compared to other regions of the United States. These data suggest that southerners were generally industrious and hardworking.

The South's economic performance can be put into perspective by noting that average per capita income for the entire country in the first half of the twentieth century was growing at approximately 1.68 percent per year, or doubling every forty-one years. In moving from 51 percent of the average in 1900 to 62 percent of the average in 1920, the South grew at 2.65 percent per year, which amounts to a doubling every twenty-six years. Few nations with populations as large as the South's attained this level of economic growth over a period as long as twenty years until the Asian economic miracles after World War II. Little changes in this analysis if the period is extended from 1900 to 1950. In the first half of the century, southern per capita income grew at an annual rate of 2.40 percent and doubled every twenty-nine years.

The South of the early twentieth century also performed well by the standards of life expectancy at birth. The earliest period for which life tables are available for the entire country is the 1930s. In 1939–41 life expectancy at birth in the country as a whole was 62.77 years for white males and 67.23 years for white females.[24] Only slightly behind in this category, the South attained 61.91 years for white males and 66.76 years for white females. Most of the difference between North and South is attributable to higher mortality in childhood. Once southerners reached the age of fifteen, their life spans nearly equaled those of their northern counterparts. Interestingly enough, the situation within the South was slightly better in Faulkner's home state of Mississippi, where life expectancy at birth was 62.26 years for white males and 67.17 years for white females.

Southerners have a history of height advantage over northerners that appeared as early as the mid-eighteenth century. Among troops who fought in the French and Indian War, those from the South averaged 67.9 inches in height; those from the Middle Atlantic states averaged 67.7 inches. In the American Revolution the average heights for soldiers was 68.3 inches for the South, 68.0 inches for the Middle Atlantic states, and 67.8 inches for New England.[25] Troops aged twenty-four and above who served in the Union army during the Civil War from New England were 68.3 inches; from New York, Pennsylvania, and New Jersey, 68.0 inches; from Ohio or Indiana, 68.8 inches; from Kentucky and Tennessee, 69.2 inches; and from slave states other than Kentucky and Tennessee, 68.8 inches.[26] Evidence from the twentieth century also shows that southerners were relatively tall. According to data compiled by the biologist Bernard Karpinos, average heights among United States troops who fought in World War I were 66.7 inches for those from the Northeast, 67.9 for those from the Southeast, and 68.2 for those from the South

Central states. In World War II the corresponding figures were 67.6, 68.1, and 68.6 inches, respectively.[27]

The quantitative evidence on living standards in Faulkner's South is compelling. Incomes were low compared to the North but growing rapidly, and depending on the measure used, the health of southerners was as good or better than the national average. Reasonably good health in the face of poverty is not a puzzle; it is something observed in other societies that have low population density but abundant arable land remote from commercial centers. Ireland before the famine of the 1840s is a good example consistent with this point.[28] The abundant arable land supported a wholesome diet by providing garden produce, game, fish, and low-priced foodstuffs. Perhaps more important, the low population density and lack of commercial activity limited the spread of communicable diseases such as cholera, which diffused along trade and migration routes. The South did suffer during the early twentieth century from hookworm and pellagra.[29] Yet by the measurable standards of height and life expectancy, the South performed respectably, even better than many writers have recognized. Though many southerners, especially blacks, had relatively poor incomes, most southern whites and blacks were healthy and robust by the standards of the era.[30]

Faulkner's character portrayals notwithstanding, the typical southerner from the eighteenth to the twentieth century bettered the national average in health and nutrition. This point in no way denies the plausibility of Faulkner's individual characters because matters of health and nutrition vary widely within large populations. We are not saying that Faulkner's characters could not have existed. Real southerners resembled his characters, but readers should not interpret them as a representative sample. Yet for many the South will continue to be Faulkner's South, for as Cleanth Brooks, perhaps the greatest of Faulkner scholars, puts it, "Most of us identify Faulkner with the South, and it is natural that we should do so, for his fiction is filled with references to its history, its geography, its customs; and his prose often employs its special idiom."[31] As Brooks and others have made clear, if you study the South, you begin with Faulkner's South. His novels have been a catalyst or inspiration for generations of historians and social scientists, who often excerpt Faulkner's novels to justify an interest in a particular topic and even cite Faulkner's novels as accurate portrayals of particular problems in southern history.[32]

Literature has the power to inspire historical scholarship, primarily by forcing historians to consider issues and questions raised by literary sources and impressed on the popular mind. But historians should be cautious in using characters and circumstances presented in literature as hard evidence depicting life in the past. It is unlikely that all, or even most, of the characterizations in historical fiction are false or widely distanced from the truth. Otherwise the work would too easily be dismissed. Instead, the challenge in using literature as a historical source is to separate the truth from the fiction. In doing this, readers should be aware that writers often use literary devices for dramatic effect to hold reader interest. For the novelist, stature can be a measure of character. Sometimes, "form" is juxtaposed with character, as in *The Hunchback of Notre Dame*. It is also possible that some writers of historical fiction are poor historians in the sense that they do not understand the facts as learned from standard historical sources. Instead, they build characters and create circumstances based upon misunderstandings of the past. Moreover, writers may have axes to grind—personal, social, or political objectives that distort their perceptions of the past. Nevertheless, many celebrated authors are sufficiently well informed about history to create memorable characters who not only awaken or heighten public interest in the past but force historians to seek evidence and methods that will prove or disprove the validity of fictional images.

Notes

1. *New York Times,* 14 Dec. 1998.

2. Jonathan M. Wiener, *Social Origins of the New South* (Baton Rouge, La., 1978), 109; Bernard Bailyn, *Voyagers to the West* (New York, 1986), 488.

3. Joel Williamson, *The Crucible of Race* (New York, 1984), 309, 316, 438, 454–55, and *William Faulkner and Southern History* (New York, 1993).

4. William Faulkner, *The Sound and the Fury* (New York, 1956), 331.

5. See Jack Kirby, *Rural Worlds Lost: The American South, 1920–1960* (Baton Rouge, La., 1987), 186. See also the discussion of health conditions in the South in Charles Reagan Wilson and William Ferris, eds., *Encyclopedia of Southern Culture* (Chapel Hill, N.C., 1989), 165, 1354.

6. For examples of Faulkner's tendency to describe his characters as frail, short, fat, or diminished, see Louis Ferleger and Richard H. Steckel, "Faulkner's South: Is There Truth in Fiction?" *Journal of Mississippi History* 2 (1998): 107–110.

7. In a biography of Faulkner, Robert Karl observes that "in the process of retelling, Faulkner had also discovered a historical method, a means by which history could be revealed. It does not matter whether history is 'true' or not. As he mentioned later in his life, there were facts, and there was the truth. Faulkner did not ignore facts; they were useful as pawns on a larger chessboard to which he sought the truth of things. This is not so different from any other novelist, except that his material was deeply historical and therefore, connected to verifiable truth—that is, to facts. Yet Faulkner was concerned not only with

writing history, but with rewriting it" (*William Faulkner, American Writer: A Biography* [New York, 1989], 23).

8. Harry G. Levine, "The Discovery of Addiction: Changing Conceptions of Habitual Drunkenness in America," *Journal of Substance Abuse Treatment* 2:1 (1985): 43–57.

9. Faulkner, *Absalom, Absalom!* 219, 237, 257. For other examples of alcohol and tobacco consumption, see Ferleger and Steckel, "Faulkner's South," 111 n. 19.

10. For additional discussion and references on living standards and health and height, see Richard H. Steckel and Roderick Floud, eds., *Health and Welfare during Industrialization* (Chicago, 1997).

11. See Howard Washington Odum, *Report on Economic Conditions in the South* (Chapel Hill, N.C., 1934); Gunnar Myrdal, *An American Dilemma: The Negro Problem and Modern Democracy*, 2 vols. (New York, 1944).

12. See James W. Kendrick, "The Historical Development of National-Income Accounts," *History of Political Economy* 2 (1970): 284–315; Paul Studenski, *The Income of Nations: Theory, Measurement, and Analysis: Past and Present* (New York, 1958).

13. Elizabeth Fox-Genovese, *The Origins of Physiocracy* (Ithaca, N.Y., 1976), 272.

14. See James H. Cassedy, *Demography in Early America: Beginnings of the Statistical Mind* (Cambridge, Mass., 1969); Louis I. Dublin, Alfred J. Lotka, and Mortimer Spiegelman, *Length of Life: A Study of the Life Table* (New York, 1949); Maris A. Vinovskis, "The 1789 Life Table of Edward Wigglesworth," *Journal of Economic History* 31 (1971): 570–90.

15. For additional discussion and references, see J. M. Tanner, *A History of the Study of Human Growth* (Cambridge, 1981).

16. See James Trussell and Richard H. Steckel, "The Age of Slaves at Menarche and Their First Birth," *Journal of Interdisciplinary History* 8 (1978): 477–506; Richard H. Steckel, "A Peculiar Population: The Nutrition, Health, and Mortality of American Slaves from Childhood to Maturity," *Journal of Economic History* 46 (1986): 721–41; Steckel, "Slave Height Profiles from Coastwise Manifests," *Explorations in Economic History* 16 (1979): 363–80.

17. See Robert Fogel et al., "Secular Changes in American and British Stature and Nutrition," *Journal of Interdisciplinary History* 14 (1983): 445–81; Lars G. Sandberg and Richard H. Steckel, "Soldier, Soldier, What Made You Grow So Tall? A Study of Height, Health, and Nutrition in Sweden, 1720–1881," *Economy and History* 23 (1980): 91–105; Roderick Floud and Kenneth W. Wachter, "Poverty and Physical Stature: Evidence on the Standard of Living of London Boys, 1770–1870," *Social Science History* 6 (1982): 422–52; Kenneth L. Sokoloff and Georgia C. Villaflor, "The Early Achievement of Modern Stature in America," ibid., 453–81; Gerald C. Friedman, "The Heights of Slaves in Trinidad," ibid., 482–515; Robert A. Margo and Richard H. Steckel, "The Heights of American Slaves: New Evidence on Slave Nutrition and Health," ibid., 516–38; Richard H. Steckel, "Strategic Ideas in the Rise of New Anthropometric History and Their Implications for Interdisciplinary Research," *Journal of Economic History* 58 (1998): 803–21.

18. See J. M. Tanner, *Fetus into Man: Physical Growth from Conception to Maturity* (Cambridge, Mass., 1978).

19. See "Ecological Factors Relating to Child Growth and Nutritional Status," in *Nutrition and Malnutrition: Identification and Measurement*, ed. Alexander F. Roche and Frank Falkner (New York, 1974), 329–52.

20. See Reynaldo Martorell and Jean-Pierre Habicht, "Growth in Early Childhood in Developing Countries," in *Human Growth: A Comprehensive Treatise*, ed. Frank Falkner and J. M. Tanner (New York, 1986), 241–62, and Tanner, *History.* For additional discussion

and references on the growth process and heights as a measure of living standards, see Richard H. Steckel, "Stature and Living Standards in the United States," in *American Economic Growth and Standards of Living before the Civil War,* ed. Robert E. Gallman and John Joseph Wallis (Chicago, 1992), 265–310; Steckel, "Stature and the Standard of Living," *Journal of Economic Literature* 33:4 (1995): 1903–40; Steckel, "New Perspectives on the Standard of Living," *Challenge* 38:5 (1995): 12–18.

21. See Richard H. Steckel, "Height and Per Capita Income," *Historical Methods* 16 (1983): 1–7. Technically, a strong correlation (0.8 to 0.9) holds between average height and the log of per capita income at the national level. The relationship between average height and per capita income is nonlinear, which is another way of observing that children of the rich are healthy but not physical giants.

22. See Morris D. Morris, *Measuring the Condition of the World's Poor: The Physical Quality of Life Index* (New York, 1979), 21.

23. See Richard Easterlin, "Regional Income Trends, 1840–1950," in *American Economic History,* ed. Seymour Harris (New York, 1961), 525–47.

24. Metropolitan Life Insurance Company, Statistical Bureau, *State and Regional Life Tables, 1939–41* (Washington, D.C., 1948).

25. Sokoloff and Villaflor, "The Early Achievement of Modern Stature in America."

26. Benjamin Apthorp Gould, *Investigations in the Military and Anthropological Statistics of American Soldiers* (New York, 1869), 123.

27. Bernard D. Karpinos, "Height and Weight of Selective Service Registrants Processed for Military Service during World War II," *Human Biology* 30 (1958): 311.

28. See Stephen Nicholas and Richard H. Steckel, "Tall but Poor: Nutrition, Health, and Living Standards in Pre-Famine Ireland," *Journal of European Economic History* 26 (1997): 105–34.

29. See Charles E. Rosenberg, *The Cholera Years* (Chicago, 1962); Elizabeth W. Etheridge, *The Butterfly Caste: A Social History of Pellagra in the South* (Westport, Conn., 1972).

30. See Louis Ferleger, "Sharecropping Contracts in the Late Nineteenth Century South," *Agricultural History* 67 (1993): 31–46; Jay R. Mandle, *Not Slave, Not Free: The African American Economic Experience since the Civil War* (Durham, N.C., 1992).

31. Cleanth Brooks, *William Faulkner, First Encounters* (New Haven, 1983), 1.

32. For some examples, see Wiener, *Social Origins,* 49ff., 197ff.; Kirby, *Rural Worlds Lost,* 216; Steven Hahn, *The Roots of Southern Populism* (New York, 1983), 170–71; Pete Daniel, *Standing at the Crossroads* (New York, 1986), 53, 119; Neil McMillen, *Dark Journey* (Urbana, Ill., 1989), 19, 22.

9

"No Second Troy": *The Fathers* and the Failure of Southern History

MARK G. MALVASI

> Struck in the wet mire
> Four thousand leagues from the ninth burned city
> I thought of Troy, what we had built her for.
>
> — Allen Tate, "Aeneas at Washington," *Collected Poems*

I T WOULD HAVE all happened some other way," says Lacy Gore Buchan, the narrator of Allen Tate's novel *The Fathers*.[1] If the South had not separated from the Union, if southerners had not fought a war for independence, civilization in the antebellum South would still have fallen. For Tate, the South was doomed without secession and civil war.

The action of *The Fathers,* which takes place during 1860–61, revolves around the Buchans of Pleasant Hill, located in Fairfax County, Virginia. Major Lewis Buchan, the patriarch, is generous, kind, dignified, and courteous. But he is also guileless. He inherited Pleasant Hill from his mother's family, the Lewises of Spotsylvania. His wife, Sarah Semmes Gore, comes from people who settled in the Valley of Virginia around 1800. Lacy is their third son and youngest child.

The Buchan household embodies all the simplicity of the old order. The family maintains decorum in the present by appealing to the past. Each member lives within the confines of ritual and tradition. They need not formulate some abstract principle to determine appropriate conduct. They have only to refer to the customs of their ancestors. But their unthinking reliance on ritual and tradition, custom and taste, leaves them vulnerable. They cannot imagine that life at Pleasant Hill will ever differ from what they have known. They have lived as their forebears lived for longer than anyone can remember, believing that their world was inviolate and immutable.

Change comes to this peaceful and contented world in the person of George Posey, a charming, intelligent, unprincipled, and rootless young man who seeks the hand of Susan Buchan, the major's daughter and Lacy's sister. Posey takes the Buchans by storm. Late in the novel Lacy, delirious with hunger, fatigue, and grief, imagines a conversation with his dead grandfather who tells him that George is "like a tornado. His one purpose is to whirl and he brushes aside the obstacles in his way."[2]

George woos, courts, and marries Susan, thus systematically realizing his designs, despite the major's objections. The Buchans can neither delay nor withstand Posey's onslaught. They are dazzled by George's commanding personality and his consummate skill at manipulating any situation to his advantage.

Susan, although not in love with George, is deeply attracted to him. He is boisterous, reckless, and exciting—everything that the men in her world are not. He craves wealth and power, not merely as ends in themselves but as symbols of his ability to possess and control the people and the world around him—always, of course, with good intentions in mind. Susan, in turn, wishes to tame George, to have him to herself on her own terms. She and George are governed by the same impulse. They are two of a kind. But Susan cannot compel George to submit to her will and, failing, goes mad.

George, however, will never lose his sense of reality, for he remakes it constantly to suit his needs. Although he cannot live in the world of custom and tradition, although he is alone and unprotected, receiving the "shock of the world at the end of his nerves," George always appears confident, relaxed, and secure. He invents and reinvents his world to satisfy his immediate desires or to fulfill his immediate purposes. He carries nothing extraneous that will hinder him in the pursuit of his objectives, whatever those might be at the moment.

George's actions are often unpredictable and astonishing, even to him. However much he may regret the consequences, George cannot restrain himself because action is the source of his being. Whenever he encounters something that he cannot use, he simply discards or ignores it. Whenever he experiences some event that shakes his composure and assurance, he simply mounts his big bay mare and rides away.

The central tension in *The Fathers* arises between George Posey and Major Buchan, and the worldviews that each embodies. The major is perhaps the last of his kind. He is certainly a dying breed. His world is perfectly ordered and integrated. Everyone, from the master of the plantation to the lowliest field hand, occupies a place, enjoying the privileges and performing the duties appropriate to it. All human experience is governed by a common respect for the customs and manners authenticated by time and trial. The old man has an abiding sense of community. He lives faithfully according to a code of honor. Outside of community and code, he does not exist.

Posey, on the contrary, spurns the traditions that Major Buchan holds dear. He refuses to behave like a gentleman or to conduct himself according to any code. His behavior is self-serving, but not always intentionally or maliciously so. He usually means well, but he cannot distinguish between right and wrong or good and evil. Isolated from the human community, devoted to no people, he can only cultivate an intensely personal vision of the world. He is calculating and pragmatic, recognizing only what will work and what will not.

The major, formidable as he seems to Lacy, cannot resist Posey. Lacy overhears his father saying that "George could make anybody do anything."[3] Like his children, the major is bewildered by Posey's frighteningly seductive power. His subtle withdrawal of courtesy when George reveals his intention to marry Susan, which would have embarrassed, humiliated, or insulted another man, is utterly lost on Posey, who senses no discourtesy. Major Buchan refuses to do more than express his disapproval of the marriage with a polite and formal rebuke, which Posey does not even understand. He will not engage Posey in terms that the latter would appreciate. To do so would tarnish his honor.

Major Buchan can either violate his code by adopting his enemy's tactics and thereby sacrifice everything that he is and everything that he stands for, or he can protect his code and suffer a decisive beating. He cannot uphold his tradition by mounting a practical defense of it because in doing so he would undermine and destroy what he ardently cherishes and desperately wishes to preserve. Having exhausted his options and his arsenal, the major, stunned and defeated, withdraws from the field.

Lacy, too, admires and loves George. For his part, George sincerely returns Lacy's affection to the extent that he can. "You're my friend, Lacy boy," George reassures him throughout the novel. Lacy is torn between his loyalty to his father and the way of life that his father represents and his desire to become like "Brother George."

But Lacy comes to see that he really has no choice. Neither alternative is viable for him. As much as he wishes to emulate George Posey, he knows that he will never permit himself to do so.

Nor can he accommodate to his father's world. Manners and tradition are not grace. However necessary they might be to sustain civilized life, they do not bring salvation. The events of the fateful year 1860–61 have taught Lacy that men and women must face the accidents, contingencies, and vicissitudes of life while holding tightly to immutable truth. No people, not even those who complacently lived out their days at Pleasant Hill, have a right to conceive of their world as timeless and eternal. During the course of the novel, Lacy develops what his clan lacked: a historical consciousness. He loves his family. He loves Pleasant Hill. He loves Virginia. But for him the South is a world immersed wholly and inescapably in the past.

The Fathers is Tate's most complex and complete judgment of the antebellum South. In it, he testified to the mortality of southern civilization. The novel is not a fable, an epic, or a tragedy. Tate offered no moral. Nor does the violence and suffering that the characters endure lead to a complete illumination of the human condition. Lacy does not fully understand the story that he tells. He knows only that he must tell it. His tale may inspire feelings of pity and awe, but neither Lacy nor the reader experiences a cleansing or purging. There is no catharsis, only the promise of a bleak future.[4]

The history of the South, Tate declared, was, indeed, the history of failure and defeat. Southerners had put their faith in history, and in 1865 history disappointed them. Before the war antebellum southerners had been virtually indifferent to time and change. Unlike northerners, for whom, Tate thought, time and change were almost sensuous facts of experience, southerners could contemplate only a static and permanent existence.

In another kind of civilization, such as the settled, stable, harmonious world of the Middle Ages or even of eighteenth-century Virginia, this quality would have been a virtue. But in modern civilization, which thrived on change, southerners operated at a distinct disadvantage. Haughty and complacent, they could not imagine the death of their world. When the end came, Tate wrote, they were only "shocked by events into a sort of dumb resistance."[5]

The theme of failure and defeat captivated Tate, who identified intimately with the collapse of southern civilization. He took the failure of the South personally, equating the meaning of his life with the defeat, humiliation, and subjugation of his ancestors. Tate was most frustrated, though, by his inability as a man of letters to formulate for the defeated South an authoritative spiritual order through the disciplined use of language. Why had southerners not realized their historical destiny and carried out a spiritual, not merely a political, secession from the North? Why had the South not become at last a redemptive community that would save humanity? How could the values that Tate associated with the southern way of life be preserved in defeat? Were they worth preserving at all? How could he discover any meaning in southern history beyond failure and defeat? What significance could he find in the only image available to him: the cursed and benighted South? In June 1931, seven years before he published *The Fathers,* Tate wrote of his distress to his friend John Peale Bishop:

> The older I get the more I realize that I set out about ten years ago to live a life of failure, to imitate, in my own life, the history of my people. For it was only in this fashion, considering the circumstances, that I could completely identify myself with them. We all have an instinct — if we are artists partic- ularly — to live at the center of some way of life and to be borne up by its in- nermost significance. The significance of the Southern way of life, in my time, is failure. . . . What else is there for me but a complete acceptance of the idea of failure? There is no other "culture" that I can enter into, even if I had the desire.[6]

When the novel opens, Lacy Buchan is an elderly gentleman in his mid- sixties living in Georgetown, across the Potomac River from his ancestral home in Virginia. He practiced medicine for many years and is now retired. The year is 1910. The incidents that he recounts occurred fifty years earlier. But that moment, and the men and women who peopled it, are still very much alive in Lacy's mind. He witnessed the destruction of his family and the death of his civilization, and even after fifty years he has not pieced together from the fragments of memory an explanation of those disasters. He still can- not discern the meaning of these events or say with assurance that they had any meaning at all.

Lacy's memory is faulty and random. As he walks down Fayette Street to- ward the Potomac River, he catches the aroma of salt fish that takes him back to the day of his mother's funeral in late April 1860. He recalls the salty taste of the roe herring that his aunt Myra Parrish served to the kinfolk and friends who had traveled from Washington and Alexandria to pay their respects.

Pungent as the smell of salt fish is, Lacy gets only a "whiff" of it. The aroma, like the past of which it reminds him, is remote and fleeting. The salt fish itself, however, is an apt symbol for the antebellum southern society that Lacy knew as a boy. Salt applied as a preservative deprives the fish of its natu- ral juices. The fish remains intact, but desiccated and lifeless.

In the opening scene Tate established the mood and tone of the entire novel. Death pervades Lacy's world. He cannot recover the past and breathe life into it. He can only try to remember what happened and try to relate the narrative coherently. But he understands the limitations, inconsistencies, and peculiarities of memory. He cannot escape the present in his thinking about the past. What he knows and feels now about that time structures and focuses what he remembers. His memories are, at best, subjective and incomplete. The aromas, sounds, voices, and objects that recollect the past yield woefully meager images. The rest is a mystery. Lacy reveals: "In my feelings of that time there is a new element—my feelings now about that time: there is not an old man living who can recover the emotions of the past: he can only bring back objects around which, secretly, the emotions have ordered themselves in memory, and that memory is not what happened in the year 1860 but is rather a few symbols, a voice, a tree, a gun shining on the wall—symbols that will preserve only so much of the old life as they may, in their own mysterious history, consent to bear."[7]

Even under these circumstances, Lacy is compelled to tell his story. He remembers how, on the day of his mother's funeral, he went outside after breakfast and stood beneath the blossoming dogwood tree. The delicate white flowers tinted with red shooting into "the air like spray" contrast starkly with the dead woman laid out in the front parlor and with the pall cast over the inhabitants of Pleasant Hill. As Lacy wanders aimlessly about the lawn, his brother-in-law, George Posey, approaches him.

Handsome and strong, Posey appears to Lacy the epitome of manhood. He informs Lacy that he cannot stay for the funeral. Lacy does not understand the significance of George's sudden wish to depart but obeys the command to bring his horse.

"I knowed he'd do it," says the old slave Coriolanus when Lacy tells him to saddle Queen Susie. Lacy doubts that the old man knew what George would do, but it comforts him to think that someone actually imagines he could have predicted Posey's actions. To Lacy, George's impulse is unprecedented, shocking, mysterious, and exciting. But George has also violated Lacy's sense of propriety. Although he defends George against the criticisms of Coriolanus and the overseer Mr. Higgins, Lacy suspects that he has witnessed an event "extraordinary and violent, more violent even than the death which had not happened to me till now but which could always happen in the world in which I lived." Lacy understands death, but he does not understand George. He knows only that "George Posey could never have anything to do with death."[8]

Despite his confusion the respect and esteem that Lacy feels for George are undiminished. George is the most splendid and affable, the most cheerful and careless, man he has ever met. Lacy shares George's desire for the freedom to

be his own person, unrestricted by tiresome rules and customs. He delights at
the prospect of riding off with George on some bold adventure that would
capture his boyish fancy. Lacy knows, though, that his wish is inconceivable.
He cannot accompany his brother-in-law but must remain behind with his
father and the rest of his family.

Although Lacy is not aware of it, his attachment to George is qualified and
limited. Time will erode it. As Lacy nears manhood, accepting the discipline
and responsibility of being an adult, George's personality will grow less attractive to him. Like St. Paul, he will put away a child's things. George's conduct is indecent and appalling to any mature person. Even Mr. Higgins, the
overseer, and Coriolanus, the slave, know better. Only a child would find it al-
luring. Lacy the boy could not fully comprehend this distinction. But as an
old man, remembering, he concludes: "I admired George Posey even when I
did not understand him, for I shared his impatience with the world, as indeed
every child must whose discipline is incomplete. He could do the things that
I should lose the desire to do by the time I was grown and my own master."9

George is not a scoundrel, a rogue, or a villain. He is neither malevolent
nor evil. If he were a sinister figure, the Buchans would not have fallen so
completely under his influence. George confounds, entrances, and dominates
them with kindness, generosity, courage, and intelligence. "Ain't I told you
you can't do nothing about hit?" Coriolanus tells Lacy. "Ain't nobody kin stop
that young gentleman, nobody. The major can't stop him. Old Mistis can't
stop him. How you stop him?"10

Coriolanus is right. George not only marries Susan Buchan over her father's objections. He also assumes control of the Buchans' estate without
Major Buchan's consent, not in an effort to satisfy his greed but from a disinterested concern for the family's welfare. George believes that he is protecting
the Buchans from insolvency. The major's ineptitude at business and his fas-
tidious indulgence of his slaves will no doubt ruin him and cost his children
their legacy. To prevent this unhappy occurrence, Charles and Semmes
Buchan, Lacy's older brothers, sign over to George their portions of the family property in return for a cash settlement. Semmes goes further, conspiring
with George to sell slaves whom Major Buchan thinks he has freed in order to
dispose of some outstanding debts.

The sons are not worthy of their father. Unlike him, they envision the land
as a commodity that they can dispose of when it becomes burdensome. To
them, the slaves are no longer members of the family. "Twenty negroes are
too many for this place," Semmes tells Lacy. Worse, Charles and Semmes do

not even acknowledge the slaves' humanity. They are things to be bought and sold as economic necessity dictates. Or, as George puts it, they are "liquid capital."

With the best intentions George Posey intrudes on the comfortable and dignified world of Pleasant Hill and destroys it. He scorns the manners, customs, ceremonies, and traditions by which Major Buchan and his family live. Yet his actions were so devastating, Tate suggested, because the southern social order was already fragile. "Our lives," Lacy remembers, "were eternally balanced upon a pedestal below which lay an abyss that I could not name."[11]

Southern civilization, which for Tate the closed world of Pleasant Hill represented, was static and ossified. Major Buchan, the archetypical southern gentleman, cannot function outside the accepted forms and established traditions of his society. "Within that invisible tension," Lacy recalls, "my father knew the moves of an intricate game that he expected everybody to play. That, I think, was because everything he was and felt was in the game itself; he had no life apart from it and he was baffled . . . by the threat of some untamed force that did not recognize the rules of his game."[12] The major moves through life with a simple nobility and a disinterested innocence that, in the end, proves to be his undoing.

He has only one standard of conduct. Benevolent but impersonal, he operates at a clear disadvantage against a man like George Posey who modifies his behavior to conform to the exigencies of the moment. The major's life is rigid and disciplined, his world austere and artificial. George, on the contrary, lives spontaneously. His world is chaotic and violent. He often finds himself at the mercy of his impulses. In the tournament scene Tate dramatized the terrible and irreconcilable opposition between these conflicting worldviews and ways of life.

Critics of *The Fathers* have not appreciated Tate's description of the jousting tournament for its humor. But it is comedy with serious implications. A formal notice signed by the tournament committee, of which Lacy's brother Semmes is a member and his cousin Will Lewis is chairman, announces the upcoming event to the Gentleman's Tournament Association of Fairfax County. With great propriety, fanfare, and vanity, the young men of Fairfax County thus prepare to compete for the right to crown the Queen of Love and Beauty.

Ironically, the man who has won the annual event for as long as Lacy can remember is anything but a gentleman. John Langdon is a perpetual drunkard whose range of knowledge is limited to foxhounds, horses, and whiskey.

The locals whisper that he has never read a book and can barely write a letter or sign his name. His vocabulary consists principally of the colloquial idiom spiced with oaths and curses. But he can outride anyone in Fairfax County and yearly leads the Parade of Chivalry with which the tournament commences.

This year promises to be no different, except for the remarkable rider clad in orange and black, his face concealed from the spectators by a hood, mounted on a stately bay mare. The rider, of course, is George Posey. Langdon performs superbly. George excites and stuns the crowd with a display of equestrian skill more brilliant than any they have ever witnessed. The outcome is close, but Posey defeats Langdon because of his more elegant and flamboyant horsemanship.

Before he announces the judges' decision, Mr. Henry Broadacre, Esq., who has sponsored the tournament, proclaims the wonders of the chivalric tradition and the glories of Fairfax County, Virginia. Tate used Mr. Broadacre's remarks to caricature the pretensions that Virginia society represented the magnificent culmination of Western civilization:

> It is beyond disputation that the chivalry of this County is unsurpassed in our State, which in turn is unsurpassed in the world for cultivation of the manly arts of Nimrod and Mars—the hunting field and the field of war— those great and ancient preoccupations of manhood handed on by our English sires as eminently befitting the notice of janetlemen. But if this is true of you, young janetlemen, where shall I find the eloquence to praise the ladies, without whom your efforts here today in this contest were in vain? It is the ladies alone who are the repositories, nay the gyuardians of our virtues, it is they, it is for them that you have achieved this brilliant performance. The ladies! God bless the ladies![13]

Throughout his oration Mr. Broadacre is troubled by a rather unfortunate blunder. He has forgotten to remove his chewing tobacco before rising to speak. As he expounds the virtues of Fairfax County, as he confirms the courage and gallantry of its young men and the beauty and purity of its young ladies, Mr. Broadacre swallows his tobacco, with the predictable results.

Mr. Broadacre's demeanor contrasts vividly with the image of the South that he presents in his declamation. His manner reveals that the South is not the majestic civilization that he portrays it to be. The irony, of course, is lost on the spectators and the participants. That was precisely Tate's point. Mr. Broadacre's audience cannot distinguish the contradiction between his eloquent language and his coarse demeanor, for they sense no contradiction. They cannot imagine that an outsider like George Posey might find them stupid, graceless, and vulgar and might consider their traditions quaint or absurd.

In his description of the jousting tournament, Tate intended to show the folly of life predicated on a reverence of tradition for its own sake. Archaic revivals of the past, however splendid, only reaffirmed the goodness of tradition as an end in itself. The conclusion toward which such reasoning pointed, Tate argued, was the notion that tradition was good because it was tradition, not because it reflected a transcendent vision of reality superior to any that the vagaries of history could provide.

For Tate the historical consciousness and the religious imagination were intimately connected. Antebellum southerners lacked both. They forgot that they lived in a fallen world of sinful men and women. Or, alternately, if they had not forgotten this truth, then they had come to believe that their manners, customs, rituals, and traditions, originally intended to remind them of it, were, in fact, sufficient in themselves to restrain the evil in human nature. From their point of view, the society that they cherished was blessed; as its citizens they were not subject to the same wickedness or misery as the rest of the world's peoples. They had made the perfect world for themselves, and it would last forever. Later in the novel Lacy makes plain the nature of the delusion that Tate thought infected the southern way of life: "People living in formal societies, lacking the historical imagination, can imagine for themselves only a timeless existence: they themselves never had any origin anywhere and they can have no end, but will go on forever."[14]

If the people of Fairfax County are pompous and complacent, George Posey is disdainful and contemptuous. When Langdon protests the judges' decision to award Posey the prize and attempts to block his way to the podium, George knocks him down and reduces him to a drunken heap. Although Langdon's actions do not accord with the strictures of chivalry, Posey's are an affront to civility. John Langdon, too, disdains the ceremonies. But everyone knows that Langdon is not a gentleman. They expected more of George Posey, whom they had welcomed as a guest of one of the oldest and most distinguished families in the county.

Disposing of Langdon is the least serious and embarrassing of George's offenses. He names Susan the Queen of Love and Beauty. Instead of crowning her with the laurel wreath as is the immemorial custom, he drops the wreath in her lap and bellows with laughter. The judges and the spectators are astonished and appalled. Never before has anyone thwarted the ritual that surrounded the event. His antagonist may be ungentlemanly, but George is uncivilized. He is a renegade.

Langdon challenges Posey to a duel for insulting him. George accepts the challenge but, in the end, refuses to fight. After firing a practice shot, which incidentally demonstrates that he is an expert marksman, he tosses the pistol aside and knocks Langdon senseless with one punch.

"Mr. Posey agreed to come out here and there was only one thing to come for," complains Jim Mason, whom Langdon had engaged as his second. "Not for this."[15] Although a buffoon and a rogue, John Langdon still operates within the accepted southern code of conduct. When he feels that Posey has ridiculed and humiliated him, he does not retaliate by beating him, ambushing him, or shooting him on sight. Instead, he presents his grievances and demands satisfaction. As uncouth as he is, Langdon can imagine no other solution.

Posey's options are not limited by any code. He acts according to the impulses of the moment, which even he cannot predict. He does not know what he is going to do until he does it. No doubt as he walks up the hill to the pavilion where Langdon awaits him, he believes that he is about to fight a duel, either to kill or be killed—although he can scarcely credit the latter possibility. Up to the moment when Langdon and Posey must face each other, a duel seems imminent, until George changes his mind. Unlike Langdon, George does not channel and circumscribe his personal feelings by adhering to a recognized code. George's feelings—and actions—are utterly personal. No one, not even George himself, understands them. He simply acts, oblivious to the consequences.[16]

In the version of *The Fathers* reissued in 1977, almost forty years after it first appeared, Tate declared in a brief preface that George Posey was not the villain of the novel but rather a "modern romantic hero."[17] To understand Tate's meaning we must discover what he thought of modern romantic heroes. "Caveat Lector," he wrote. Tate never gave more sensible advice.

Posey opposes his ego to all forms of order. He has embarked on a quest to defy the world, subdue it, and impose his will upon it. But George's will is boundless, and his potential series of conquests is infinite. He is, therefore, destined to remain eternally frustrated. New objectives will forever present themselves. Posey's very success in attaining them will reveal the aimlessness of his undertaking. He succeeds as a wheel turns; he is in perpetual motion and can only conquer again and again without purpose or end.

George lives blindly, ignoring whatever contradicts or undermines his illusion of power. When he is deprived of the means of affirming the will, which he inevitably is, he instinctively rejects the authority of civilization, the agreement at which men and women arrived through struggle over a long period of time. He constantly flirts with the abyss while simultaneously denying its existence. Lacy envisions him as a horseman, perpetually riding off over a precipice. "But," Lacy asks, "is not civilization the agreement, slowly arrived at, to let the abyss alone?"[18] Posey is like a badly spoiled child, all appetite without sensibility, all will without reflection, all desire without satisfaction. For Tate, Posey, the modern romantic hero, is a monster.[19]

Lacy's dead grandfather, whom he conjures up in the final section of the novel, retells the story of Jason and his quest for the Golden Fleece more clearly to explicate George's character and dilemma. George and Jason are both admirable men who sacrifice their loyalty to family and community in order to pursue the objects of their desire. Like his mythical counterpart George is left with only the raw facts of existence and experience. He cannot escape the confines of his own fierce personality. He cannot appeal to any idea, cause, tradition, or faith by which he could extinguish his personality and become a part of something larger than himself. He shares no expectancy with the rest of humanity except the rotting corpse and the ravenous grave, which makes success in this world all the more imperative.

Capable of passionate feelings, even love, George is at the same time driven by an inexhaustible ambition, and without an appropriate release, he destroys whatever and whomever he encounters. His sincerity is beyond question—as Lacy recognizes, he is "appallingly too sincere"—but sincerity cannot restrain the destructive aspects of his nature. Having abandoned his land, his family, and his faith, he has little choice but to act on impulse, without deliberation. Only by such means can he authenticate his being. "People have got to get life where they can," Susan explains to Lacy, "that's all there is to it."[20]

In his solipsism Posey offers a frightening anticipation of the spiritual tumult of the twentieth century. His existence has become so rarefied that he has lost all connection with nature and humanity. Attempting to cheat the human condition, he sets himself up as his own god, a surrogate divinity who worships himself. George does not cast his lot with the rest of humanity. At crucial moments he withdraws from life and isolates himself from his fellow human beings. Despite the immense prowess of his intellect and the savage determination of his will, George is bound to fail because he cannot define the object of his striving. He is the quintessential modern man: rootless, isolated, alienated, and destructive. In the end George Posey as god sits alone and silent in the dark, trapped in an abyss that yawns not beneath him but within him and that emanates outward to swallow the whole universe.

Curiously, Posey's vision of reality in some ways remains superior to that of Major Buchan. Although Tate mentions it only in passing, George Posey is Roman Catholic. Walter Sullivan, one of the few critics to discuss Posey's Catholicism at length, has written that "some moral advantages accrue to those who are the ecclesiastical descendants of the Borgias. They are perhaps more likely than others to see life whole."[21]

George's Catholic heritage precludes his worship of society, tradition, or the past. He is not enticed by the myth of southern virtue and invincibility. No social arrangement however elaborate, no tradition however grand, no past however glorious can shelter human beings from their folly and sinfulness. Posey's derision of southern society arises, in part, from his recognition that the southern way of life is incomplete and imperfect. He does not feel the same obligations, nor is he subject to the same misconceptions that trouble most of the southern characters in the novel.

But George is not pious. He follows the teachings of the Catholic Church only in a desultory way, if at all. He is an apostate, a Protestant in all but name—or, perhaps, an infidel who has pressed the individualist logic of Protestantism to its nihilistic conclusions. He can offer no alternative to Major Buchan's idolatrous veneration of the South.

The traditional civilization of eighteenth-century Virginia would have restrained George Posey because the inherited code was still adequate to accommodate and control a wide range of human emotions and behavior. That society would have found an acceptable and safe outlet for his zeal and ambition. As the South became more deeply entangled in the social relations of the modern world, however, the old morality no longer served.

Posey senses that Major Buchan's vision of the past is nostalgic, picturesque, and sentimental. For the major Virginia society—or, more specifically, Pleasant Hill—is the source and end of being. That world is all he knows and all he needs to know. Perfect and immutable, it is a place upon which no one can improve, a veritable Eden set in Virginia's "green and pleasant land." He thus mistakes the partial, particular, and temporal for the absolute, universal, and eternal, viewing as the literal incarnation of paradise a society that is, at best, only a metaphoric and incomplete image of it.

Major Buchan is damned not so much because he reveres tradition, but because the tradition has become deficient. His devotion to family and community notwithstanding, he is preoccupied with maintaining some personal arrangement that no longer bears any relation to what is happening in the real world. The collapse of this private order anticipates and reflects the general failure of southern history that arrested Tate's imagination.

In *The Fathers*, Tate was not vindicating the social order of the antebellum South. He was, rather, exposing the infirmities that he detected in southern civilization and assessing the consequences of its collapse. On 19 November 1938 he wrote to John Peale Bishop that although he was disappointed with the quality of men the South had produced, he thought they were far superior to either their New England or modern counterparts. Tate cautioned that his awareness of the defects in the southern way of life should not be misconstrued as a concession to northern preeminence, an assumption that his critics have made repeatedly since the 1930s.[22]

Tate criticized the South, comparing it to the great civilizations of the past to find it wanting. He could never bring himself to abandon it. The antebellum South still represented "the good society," its many imperfections notwithstanding. In that world of aristocracy and hierarchy, discipline and order, violence and chaos may have raged just below the surface, but southerners had done their best to inhibit them. Besides, Tate complained to Bishop, corruption and depravity were not exclusively characteristic of the South; the modern world, with its utopian fantasies, had not displayed any great facility for eliminating evil from human life.

The most compelling recommendation that Tate could offer in behalf of the South was that men and women in the modern world no longer seemed capable or desirous of remedying their plight. Indeed, they seemed to welcome its coming. "At present we live in a world where the disorder is at the surface," he declared to Bishop. "So all honor to Major Buchan."[23]

Unfortunately, Major Buchan, who depended on an elaborate social order to give his life meaning, was an anachronism. George Posey was no longer exceptional. All men and women, Tate concluded, now resembled him. In the novel Lacy laments this turn of events:

> How many of us know that there are times when we passionately desire to hear the night? . . . Nobody today, fifty years after these incidents, can hear the night; nobody wishes to hear it. To hear the night, and to welcome its coming, one must have deep inside one's secret being a vast metaphor controlling all the rest: a belief in the innate evil of man's nature, and the need to face that evil, of which the symbol is darkness, of which again the living image is man alone. Now that men cannot be alone, they cannot bear the

dark, and they see themselves as innately good but betrayed by circumstances that render them pathetic. Perhaps some of the people in this story
are to be pitied, but I cannot pity them; none of them was innately good.
They were all, I think, capable of great good, but that is not the same thing
as *being* good.[24]

George Posey and Major Buchan are both Lacy's "fathers," and both abdi-
cate their patriarchal responsibilities. Lacy is thus left to live alone in the
modern world in search of whatever meaning he might find in the past. He
knows that he is not an "elegant gentleman" like his grandfather. He realizes
also that his worldview is now merely a private fiction that makes bearable his
present circumstances.

Lacy Buchan, nevertheless, is Tate's analogue to the classical hero. He resembles Aeneas, and *The Fathers* is Tate's extended and ironic commentary
on *The Aeneid*. For Lacy is a failed Aeneas. He cannot sail for the *litora Italiae*.
There is no Rome for him to found. Unmarried and childless, he cannot even
reproduce the family or perpetuate his race. Lillian Feder has written that
"Vergil . . . provided for Allen Tate a means of extending his view of history
and, as the 'story of Aeneas' was for Vergil 'a statement of relatedness between
two great cultures,' so it became for Tate a symbol of both the 'relatedness'
and the tragic separation between the past and the present."[25] Lacy cannot
preserve the old ways any more than he can vindicate and avenge his ancestors or venerate their God. The life that he knew has passed from the earth
and exists only in memory.

But Lacy does remember. In remembering, he can at least measure the
present against the past. If he cannot re-create a world in which people can
live heroically, Lacy still enjoys certain advantages over most of his contemporaries in the modern world. Modern men have squandered their inheritance and disavowed their heritage, unwittingly sacrificing their dignity and
their humanity in the process. Lacy can still recall that men once lived by a
formal code of honor that made heroic action possible.

Aeneas asked the gods of Ilium for respite from the anguish that he
endured in creating a new nation for his defeated brethren. Even in defeat,
Aeneas was a "whole man." Inspired by a deep love for his people, he set aside
personal desires in pursuit of a larger objective. Only at the end of the novel,
after Major Buchan has committed suicide and Federal troops have reduced
Pleasant Hill to ashes, does Lacy understand that the same opportunity is unavailable to him. His world is already gone, lost before either army fired a
shot. The war was only a denouement.

Nevertheless, Lacy returns to fight. In the enigmatic closing scene, which has generated much controversy among students of the novel, Lacy rejoins the Army of Northern Virginia to defend what remains of his world.[26] In so doing, he subtly rebukes George Posey, who again mounts his bay mare and canters away into the darkness. Until this moment, Lacy has always wished to accompany George. He wanted to ride with him away from his mother's funeral. Later, on the eve of war, after a tense meeting between George, Semmes, and Major Buchan during which Semmes declares his fidelity to the Confederacy, Lacy resolves at last to give in to his impulse. "I decided that this time I would go with him, because it was so simple to go and leave behind all the things that I would have to think about if I stayed. Then I thought how easy it would have been if I could have gone off with George away from the funeral, . . . how easy it would have been to have had all my feelings simplified, to have felt the exaltation of loyalty not to myself or to all the life around me, but to one person who to my dying day will be a man always riding off somewhere.[27]

When the occasion at last presents itself, however, Lacy refuses to go with George. "I'll go back and finish it," he says after the hoofbeats of George's horse have died away. "I'll have to finish it because he could not finish it."[28] Lacy cannot bring himself to discard his old sentiments and allegiances. Life for him can never be that simple. He resolves to see the destruction of his world through to the end.

Yet, in defying George, Lacy discovers the depth of his love for him. The love he feels for George has driven him back to face death, something that Posey himself could never do. Lacy's willingness to take a last stand in defense of a lost cause is a dramatic attempt to pay homage to what is best about southern civilization. But Lacy has no illusions. He cannot, after all that has happened, entertain romantic dreams of heroism and glory. He knows that his gesture is futile and will change nothing. It has come too late. Lacy resigns himself to the inevitable: an unheroic death in battle or a sordid life in the modern world. It no longer matters. "It won't make any difference if I am killed. If I am killed it will be because I love him more than I love any man."[29]

Lacy is not alone in his expression of love for George. The other members of his family have all, in one way or another, fallen under George Posey's spell, and their devotion to him effected their demise. They have forsaken the verities, principles, and traditions by which they have always lived. But even had George not married Susan or assumed control of Major Buchan's property, the Buchan family and their world would have disintegrated. Their inability to withstand Posey's advances indicates how feeble they had already become.

Lacy will forever wonder whether, had it all happened differently, some aspect of that world might have been preserved. He will never know. Mystified by much that has occurred, Lacy does come to understand that he and his family have loved George not wisely but too well. Their love was inordinate, a violation of the balance and restraint that once characterized their way of life.

In the *Nicomachean Ethics* Aristotle emphasized the "just sentiments" and the "ordinate affections" as the prerequisites for an education in virtue. Augustine, in *The City of God,* similarly defined virtue as *ordo amoris,* according to every object and person the kind and degree of love appropriate to it. The Buchans ignored these strictures and gave themselves to George without reservation. Their ardor cost them dearly.

Lacy's vision was more prophetic than he realized. Looking back on these events after fifty years, he catches some of the irony that surrounds them, which he could not have divined as a boy. Generous and amiable, George wished only to protect the Buchan household from misfortune. His efforts worked to the opposite effect. He could not keep catastrophe from striking the Buchans.

Moreover, he unintentionally encouraged their malevolent tendencies, which their manners and their tradition had for so long kept at bay, to come to the surface. George Posey thus helped to transform Pleasant Hill into a world so wretched that exploitation, brutality, and despair were the only bonds remaining between human beings. Lacy Buchan learned from hard experience that in such a world no man can keep his soul, and all human acts become evil, even love.[30]

Notes

The author wishes to acknowledge generous grants from the Rashkind Fund of Randolph-Macon College and the Earhart Foundation that aided in the completion of this essay.

1. *The Fathers* (Chicago, 1938), 5.
2. Ibid., 268.
3. Ibid., 10.
4. The critical literature on *The Fathers* is vast. Especially helpful are Arthur Mizener, "*The Fathers* and Realistic Fiction," *Sewanee Review* 67 (Autumn 1959): 604–13; Walter Sullivan, "Southern Novelists and the Civil War," in *Death by Melancholy: Essays on Modern Southern Fiction* (Baton Rouge, La., 1972), 66–84; Sullivan, "*The Fathers* and the Failures of Tradition," *Southern Review* 12 (Autumn 1976): 758–66; Sullivan, *A Requiem for the Renaissance: The State of Fiction in the Modern South* (Athens, Ga., 1976), 31–36; Frank Kermode,

"Old Orders Changing," *Encounter* 15 (Aug. 1960): 72–76; Cleanth Brooks, "Allen Tate and the Nature of Modernism," *Southern Review* (Autumn 1976): 685–97; Brooks, "The Past Alive in the Present," in *American Letters and the Historical Consciousness: Essays in Honor of Lewis P. Simpson,* ed. J. Gerald Kennedy and Daniel Mark Fogel (Baton Rouge, La., 1987), 216–25.

5. Thomas Daniel Young and Thomas Hindle, eds., *The Republic of Letters in America: The Correspondence of John Peale Bishop and Allen Tate* (Lexington, Ky., 1981), 33; see also Allen Tate, *Collected Essays* (Denver, 1959), 554–68; Tate, *Memoirs and Opinions, 1926–1974* (Chicago, 1975), 35–38, 144–54.

6. *Republic of Letters,* 34.

7. *The Fathers,* 22.

8. Ibid., 14.

9. Ibid., 44.

10. Ibid., 52.

11. Ibid., 43–44.

12. Ibid., 44.

13. Ibid., 66. I have omitted Lacy's commentary without indicating such with ellipses, since to do so would have been distracting.

14. Ibid., 183.

15. Ibid., 76.

16. For a different interpretation of the tournament scene, see Richard Gray, *The Literature of Memory: Modern Writers of the American South* (Baltimore, 1977), 88–90. Gray argues that the tournament scene shows the benefits of living in a traditional society where even ordinary persons can behave "with a grace and flexibility that reflects real credit on the code to which they subscribe, the accepted forms that have given their every step a certain shapeliness. And this, Tate seems to be saying, is the ultimate achievement of traditionalism."

17. *The Fathers and Other Fiction* (Baton Rouge, La., 1977), xxi.

18. *The Fathers* (1938, 1960), 186.

19. Cf. Allen Tate, "The Symbolic Imagination: The Mirrors of Dante," 32–55, "The Angelic Imagination: Poe as God," 56–78, and "Our Cousin, Mr. Poe," 79–85, in *The Forlorn Demon: Didactic and Critical Essays* (Chicago, 1953), and "Three Types of Poetry" (1937), in *Collected Essays,* 91–114.

20. *The Fathers,* 172–75.

21. Sullivan, "*The Fathers* and the Failures of Tradition," 765. Thomas Daniel Young, "Introduction," to *The Fathers and Other Fiction,* ix–xx, and Louis D. Rubin Jr., *The Wary Fugitives: Four Poets and the South* (Baton Rouge, La., 1978), 310–25, have also noted Posey's Catholicism.

22. See, for example, Lionel Trilling's review of *The Fathers* in the *Partisan Review* 6 (Fall 1938): 111–13, and Daniel Joseph Singal, *The War Within: From Victorian to Modernist Thought in the South, 1919–1945* (Chapel Hill, N.C., 1982), 254–59.

23. *Republic of Letters,* 146.

24. *The Fathers,* 218–19.

25. Lillian Feder, "Allen Tate's Use of Classical Literature," *Centennial Review* 4 (Winter 1960): 89–114 (quotation on 89). See also George Core, "A Metaphysical Athlete: Allen Tate as Critic," *Southern Literary Journal* 2 (Autumn 1969): 138–47; Cleanth Brooks, *Modern Poetry and the Tradition* (New York, 1965), 95–109.

26. See especially Brooks, "The Past Alive in the Present," 220–25.

27. *The Fathers*, 149–50.

28. Ibid., 306.

29. Ibid.

30. To maintain the copyright to the novel, Tate altered the conclusion of the version reissued in 1977. Instead of having Lacy say in the final sentence, "If I am killed it will be because I love him more than I love any man," he had him say, "I venerate his memory more than the memory of any man." This altered conclusion is less powerful than that of the original, to which I have returned in my analysis. Except for the conclusion, the body of the novel remained unchanged.

Cleanth Brooks also suggested that Tate change the ending of the novel, substituting "loved" for "love" in the final sentence. In a letter to Tate dated 9 June 1975, Brooks wrote: "Lacy is writing his account of the events many years later, and he has come to understand so much of what is essentially wrong with George—has isolated so clearly George's part in the family disaster—that the reader, unless he is very discerning indeed, may find it hard to believe that Lacy now, a half-century later, can still say 'I love him more than I love any man.' Your version 'I loved him more than I could love any man' has proved accordingly very helpful to this admiring, almost persuaded, but still fumbling and puzzled reader." That the recommendation for this change came from Brooks is suggested by an earlier letter to Brooks dated 28 May 1975 in which Tate declared, "What you said about the ending of *The Fathers* inspired me to revise it at once." For both letters, see Alphonse Vinh, ed., *Cleanth Brooks and Allen Tate: Collected Letters, 1933–1976* (Columbia, No., 1998), 259–60. Neither Brooks nor Tate explained why Tate did not in the end heed Brooks's advice.

Appendix A

Eugene D. Genovese and History: An Interview

Eugene D. Genovese responded to these questions during several interviews conducted by the editors from July 1995 to December 1998.

Q. What historian(s) have had the greatest influence on your work?

A. "Influence" is hard to define, identify, or characterize and harder to measure. I suppose I must begin with Marx, the author of the great historical sections of *Capital,* the *Grundrisse, Theories of Surplus Value,* and some extraordinary historical essays on France and Germany. I do not think I ever paid much attention to the vaunted Preface to the *Critique of Political Economy,* in which Marx comes close to engaging in the kind of suprahistorical generalization he scorned in his own historical writing. Nor did I pay much attention to his writing on the United States, a country about which he knew and understood little. Thus, even as an undergraduate, I found virtually useless his interpretation of the South but found priceless the contributions in his theoretical work and in his writing on the history of countries he knew well.

Among Marxist historians I must mention Maurice Dobb, the economist who gave us *Studies in the Development of Capitalism,* a seminal contribution to the Marxist interpretation of capitalist development, which I read before I studied *Capital* and which had a powerful impact on my own work. By the way, although I decided early that I could not swallow Lenin's *State and Revolution* and was appalled by his *Materialism and Empirio-Criticism,* I profited much from his work on Russian agriculture. I have not reread his little-known study of American agriculture and have no idea what I would think of it now. But it did have a big impact on my thinking about the South when, as an undergraduate, I began to formulate my own interpretation of southern slave society. I cannot begin to measure the impact of Eric Hobsbawm's work, but it surely looms larger than that of any other historian. Hobsbawm has provided a model for those who are prepared to build upon what Marx had to offer without becoming imprisoned in formulas and dogmas.

Among my teachers at Brooklyn College, I would single out Hans Rosenberg, who taught me and many others what being a historian is all about. In particular, Rosenberg introduced us to the work of Max Weber, which shaped my own work from the beginning. I have always been accused of reading Marx through Weberian eyes, and that charge may well be true. Daniel Bell once quipped, "Genovese thinks he is a Marxist historian, but he is in fact a left-Weberian sociologist." If so, so be it. I see no need to apologize. Certainly, before I read Gramsci, Weber taught me to see social classes as much broader categories than an exclusive focus on economic relations would suggest.

I also had the privilege of studying with Arthur C. Cole, among other fine professors at Brooklyn College. I still think that Cole's "two civilizations" thesis, which he placed at the center of his admirable book *The Irrepressible Conflict,* was on the money. And there is where Marx, Dobb, and the Japanese Marxist Takahashi proved especially valuable, for they provided the necessary insights into the nature of social relations that Cole never did master. As an undergraduate and long after, I probably read more European than American history, and in later years especially I came to admire the work of the great Marc Bloch.

As a graduate student at Columbia, I also had some exceptional teachers from whom I learned a great deal. I cannot say that I thought I was learning much from Dumas Malone, my thesis adviser, whose laid-back style of teaching was easy for an arrogant young-man-in-a-hurry to slight. But over the years, reading his work, especially his great six-volume biography of Jefferson, and recalling the insights he casually dropped on us, I came to recognize that I had in fact learned a great deal more from him than I appreciated at the time. David Donald, then a stripling as graduate professors go, was unquestionably the toughest and best classroom teacher at Columbia. Like Rosenberg, he was a slave driver who instilled professionalism, albeit largely with a whip.

Frank Tannenbaum was special. With the possible exception of Rosenberg, he taught me more than any other professor. He was the wisest man I ever met in academia. He understood human relations, notably relations of superordination and subordination, better than any other historian or professor I have ever known, and I am sure he had an incalculable influence on my own work, especially on *Roll, Jordan, Roll*—a book he literally demanded that I write. He also introduced me to the work of the Brazilian sociologist Gilberto Freyre, which helped to shape my understanding of slavery.

Who knows what I learned from others? I do know that I regarded Charles Beard and Frederick Jackson Turner as big men with whom one had to come to terms, whether positively or negatively. I do not want to pick and choose among the many American historians whom I have admired and found challenging, but none made a deeper impression on me in graduate school than Perry Miller, whose *New England Mind* I continue to regard as a genuinely great work. And like all others who study the history and doctrines of Christianity, I cannot say enough about Jaroslav Pelikan's work, most notably his multivolume *History of Christian Doctrine*. Among my contemporaries in American history, I consider Forrest McDonald our most learned and penetrating historian and the one from whom I probably have learned the most, albeit often kicking and screaming.

Ulrich Bonnell Phillips was for me, as for other southern historians of my generation, the man you had to take on, and I have retained high regard for his accomplishments. And for all my quarrels with Herbert Aptheker, Kenneth Stampp, Stanley Elkins, and Robert Fogel and Stanley Engerman, I have found their work indispensable and inspiring. For an understanding of slavery in world history, my debt to David Brion Davis and Sir Moses Finley is immense, as is everyone else's. Among southern historians I have been most deeply influenced, at least since about 1970, by Lewis P. Simpson, who sooner or later will be recognized for what he is — our greatest historian of the high culture of the South. But I must pay tribute to a list of largely forgotten men and women whose work proved indispensable to my generation and will prove indispensable to a future generation not encumbered by current ignorance and claptrap. Off the top of my head, and at the risk of omitting some good people, I would mention Richard Beale Davis, Lewis C. Gray, Thomas Wertenbaker, James Bonner, Minnie C. Boyd, Weymouth Jordan, John Hebron Moore, and Bennett Wall.

Since 1970 or so, the most important and direct influence on my understanding of the Old South has been, along with Simpson, Elizabeth Fox-Genovese. She came to southern history late, having begun as a historian of eighteenth-century France, but she saw the weaknesses in my interpretation of the Old South right at the start. She compelled me to rethink and reformulate, and our collaboration has been at the center of my work during the last quarter century.

Q. What tradition do you consider yourself part of; what authors, scholars, etc., are representative of that tradition?

A. I began squarely in a Marxist tradition — that is, the kind of Marxism shaped by Antonio Gramsci. I first read Gramsci while doing a stint in the army after I left college. Being married, I used my free time to learn to read Italian instead of hitting the nightspots, and I cut my teeth on Gramsci's *Materialismo storico* and other works. By that time I had already roughed out a crude version of my interpretation of the Old South in a 100-page paper for Arthur Cole. Gramsci, as it were, authenticated my departure from Marx's own interpretation and that of the "orthodox" American Marxists of the time.

From the beginning I understood and acknowledged that my own views were closer to those of some southern conservative historians than to orthodox Marxist or liberal historians. My response to Phillips suggests as much. But, curiously,

I did not systematically study southern conservative thought until the beginning of the 1970s, when Lewis Simpson's literary studies shook me up. Although I discussed the Agrarians and others briefly in *The World the Slaveholders Made* (1969), I had not yet immersed myself. M. E. Bradford saw that in a penetrating review in *National Review,* which led me to write him and which launched a warm friendship that lasted until his untimely death in 1994.

Where does all this leave us? I have no idea beyond what I suggested in *The Southern Tradition.* I have developed a strong appreciation of the strength of that tradition but, for the reasons outlined in that book, continue to believe that the short shrift given Marx by southern conservatives has led them into a cul-de-sac. Future historians will, I believe, draw upon both traditions to formulate a better interpretation than we now have. If I have contributed something toward that end, I shall be satisfied.

Q. You grew up in a working-class family. Did this experience influence your scholarship? If so, how?

A. Undoubtedly it did and in a big way. The specifics, however, are hard to come by. To take a direct example, my discussion of the driver in *Roll, Jordan, Roll* drew upon the stories that my father, a wood caulker, told me of the contradictory roles of foremen on the docks in the port of New York. More broadly, growing up with workers and in a working-class neighborhood provided a strong antidote to the romanticism that characterizes a good deal of the "new labor history." I entered the Communist movement in 1945 at age fifteen and spent summers working in shops as an organizer for Communist-led unions. It was a valuable experience, which reinforced my hard class attitudes but also my resistance to romanticism.

I was born in 1930 and spent my first eight or nine years in the worst depression in American history. My father knew nothing of left-wing ideology and, like so many other workers, was a New Deal Democrat. Roosevelt was his god. Those were rough years, especially 1938, when my father was out of work for six months or so and too proud to go on "relief," as welfare was then called. It is not enjoyable to watch your parents stint themselves on food so that you and your brother can get a proper meal. Take my word for it, it is bad for the digestion. In any case, I grew up in a class-conscious home—class-conscious but by no means ideologically driven. I hated the bourgeoisie with the terrible passion that perhaps only a child can muster. When I came across some Communists at age fifteen and read the *Communist Manifesto* and some other pamphlets, I suddenly had a precise focus for my hatred. I would have happily sent the bastards to firing squads in large numbers, and their wives and children along with them.

Yet something always bothered me about my father. No one could have hated "the bosses" more intensely than he. But unlike his son, he was selective in his hatred. He admired old Mr. Cadell, who had begun as a worker and built the small shipyard in which Dad worked. He regarded Mr. Cadell as a decent man who had worked hard for what he had and tried to treat his workers decently. It was Cadell Jr., who took over the business, who incurred Dad's wrath and whom he would have shot. (I cannot imagine my father, who was a hard man, ever agreeing to shoot anyone's wife and children.) In particular, he was enraged by the sight of Jr.'s flunkies throwing his dogs steaks while his unemployed workers were begging for a day's work. I know that Dad did not make up that story or the story of the foreman who was even worse than his employer and wound up with his head crushed by a caulker's mallet. The workers, including my father, told the police that they had seen nothing and knew nothing. They did know, but they were not about to pass judgment on him.

My biggest problem as a historian has always been, I suppose, the conscious effort to rein in that hatred and not let it distort my reading of the historical record. I am sure that it has taken a toll, but I hope I have kept that toll to a minimum. Beyond that, my boyhood experiences gave me at least some sense of the humiliation and impotence felt by people who, through no fault of their own, have to watch their children suffer at the hands of those who presume to run their lives. My father was eaten alive by his bitterness. What must slaves have felt? In later years—but while I remained an atheist and long before I returned to the Church—I came to glimpse the meaning of the Crucifixion and the Atonement. For while Jesus suffered bodily torments, they were hardly the worst anyone had or has ever suffered. But his humiliation, abasement, and momentary sense of having been abandoned encapsulated the worst a man might suffer. The slaves, I believe, grasped the depth of his sacrifice better than all others.

Q. You have written extensively about race, slavery, and southern history. How did your ideas about these topics develop over time?

A. Nothing makes me laugh more than the charge that I substitute "class" for "race" or underestimate American racism. People who read me that way are simply being dense. From the beginning I understood—can anyone read American history and fail to understand?—the depths of American racism and its terrible consequences. And is nothing clearer than that racism has cast a longer shadow over our country's history than slavery has? What I saw as a student and insist upon now is that the determination of whites to keep the South (and America) under white racial dictatorship—Phillips's "Central Theme"—can explain only so much, if for no other reason than that racial dictatorship did not require slavery.

I have argued that slavery, understood as a social system, constituted the basis of antebellum southern civilization. The social relations of slavery (the master-slave relation) had its own imperatives, which shaped the region. Carl Degler has been right to remind us that, with marginal exceptions, masters were white and slaves black and that American slavery was a system of racial control, whatever else it may have been. I have never dissented from that view. But I insist that the southern slaveholders cannot be understood wholly in such terms and that the development of a master class had vast consequences on the economy, polity, and all aspects of the culture.

I am not aware of having shifted ground on that matter, which has constituted the heart of my life's work. Where I have shifted ground, largely under the influence of Gramsci, Simpson, and Fox-Genovese, has been in my understanding of the cultural consequences. Even as a youth I parted company with "orthodox" Marxism on the "base-superstructure" problem, which, frankly, I thought a nuisance and a bore, but I nonetheless began with a much too one-sided understanding of the relation of social relations to culture and politics. My difficulty is apparent in *The Political Economy of Slavery,* which is really a collection of essays written over a decade when I was in my twenties and early thirties. Stan Engerman and Betsey were the first to chide me about the tension in that book between a residual "economism" and the cultural interpretation that I was struggling to formulate. I had seen the tension before they chided me, as *The World the Slaveholders Made* should make clear, but I still had a long way to go. Certainly, I consider the formulations in *Fruits of Merchant Capital,* which I coauthored with Elizabeth Fox-Genovese, who wrote the larger part of it, much superior to those in *The Political Economy of Slavery.* My failure to take seriously the religious dimension of the southern experience cost me dearly in my early work—an error that I now find inexcusable since, after all, I should have pondered the wider implications of Perry Miller's work on New England. I tried to correct that error with reference to southern blacks in *Roll, Jordan, Roll* and have continued with reference to southern whites in the recent papers I have written singly and in collaboration with Betsey. Here too, Tannenbaum's influence helped considerably.

As for postbellum southern history, I have of course been influenced by C. Vann Woodward's *Origins of the New South* and his emphasis on discontinuity—a discontinuity that does not dispense with respect for the vitality of continuity. Everything, as Woodward succinctly demonstrated in *Thinking Back,* depends on the nature of the problem you are exploring. But I would have thought, as he gently suggested, that everyone knew that all history exhibits continuity and discontinuity and that the historian's job is to analyze the one in relation to the other, not to engage in pigeonholing and suprahistorical generalization.

Q. For the last fifteen years you have increasingly attempted to address many nonacademic audiences. Why?

A. My first reaction to your question was to wonder what you were talking about since I thought I had been addressing nonacademic audiences from the beginning. But you did put your finger on a problem. I am afraid that I wasted a good part of my life in trying to influence a left-wing audience most of which wanted no part of me. To take a single illustration: In 1967 I advanced a thesis about the black experience, which I presented at the Socialist Scholars Conference and which was published in *Studies on the Left* and republished in *In Red and Black*. Briefly, I argued that from the beginning the black experience combined integrationism and black nationalism; that notwithstanding the assorted irrationalities that generally accompany nationalism, black nationalism has reflected an authentic and unique experience and cannot be dismissed as a pathological response to oppression; and that the expression "a nation within a nation," which, by the way, dates from the seventeenth century, deserves to be taken seriously.

The reaction from the white Left: Zero. Now emphatically, I was not trying to tell black people how to be black. I may be, as often charged, an arrogant man, but I try not to behave like an idiot—and only an idiot would have tried that gambit in the 1960s. Rather, I was trying to help develop a left-wing orientation toward the reemerging problem of black nationalism so that the white Left could prepare itself to contribute constructively to emerging struggles.

Now, after a quarter century that thesis has been trotted out and made the center of discussion in certain black communities, most notably the Dorchester community in Boston, where the Reverend Eugene Rivers has introduced it into the Freedom Summer Projects for black youth. The black people in Dorchester asked me to explain the failure of the white Left even to discuss it all these years. What was I supposed to say? I am not the one to whom that question should be addressed.

I am afraid, however, that the Left, or the faction that speaks in its name, has been ducking most of the big questions of our time. The reasons will have to be left to another day, but a few words are in order on another question that is not being discussed seriously: the collapse of socialism. For socialism has in fact collapsed. That grim truth will not be gainsaid by theoretical gyrations. We spent three-quarters of a century in building socialism(s) that cost tens of millions of lives, created hideous political regimes, and could not even deliver a decent standard of living. The essential ingredient in a proper evaluation would have to be a frank assessment of the extent to which the assumptions that underlay the whole Left (the Social Democratic and left-liberal groups, as well as the Stalinist Left) have proven untenable, not to invoke a harsher word.

And here let me return to my boyhood hatreds. One thing I have learned, however long it has taken me, is that class hatred, like other hatreds, will eat you alive, send your soul to damnation, and lead your political movement to a well-earned defeat. If Martin Luther King had accomplished nothing more, we would still be deep in his debt for having taught that lesson as powerfully and eloquently as it could be taught.

In *The Southern Tradition* and *The Southern Front* I said my piece on the moral decadence and social catastrophe of our time. Here I shall only stress that I am convinced of the need for a new political movement that can draw upon the best elements of the Right, Center, and Left—categories that have become worthless. I now speak to those audiences that will hear me, including those of the black Left. As for the white Left, my wife and I have been declared persona non grata, and the matter is done. But I stand by what I have said about there being good and healthy elements on the Left. What should be noticed is that those elements are steadily being driven out of the official Left and are, consequently, at sea. To take one illustration: The Left contains countless people who oppose abortion. Many if not most of the women in Feminists for Life whom I know are firmly left-wing on most if not all other issues. Yet if you believe the media, anyone who opposes abortion must be a right-winger—and an extreme right-winger at that.

I had to laugh at the response from much—by no means all—of the Left to *The Southern Tradition*. The most widespread response was to see evidence that I had become a southern conservative. Yet southern conservatives do not claim me as one of their own, nor do stalwarts of any other section of the Right. To the contrary, almost every conservative who reviewed *The Southern Tradition* warned readers that my criticisms of the southern conservative traditions came decidedly from a left-wing position. Make of that what you will. The pigeonholing does not interest me one way or the other.

Q. What is your historical method? Are there contemporary examples of historians or others whose historical work is examining a set of issues similar to your work?

A. The second part of your question puzzles me. In antebellum southern history there are many fine historians who are examining the issues I consider central. But then, I doubt that they needed me to discover the centrality of those issues. After all, we are all heirs of Beard and Turner, of Phillips and Stampp, of Aptheker and Gray, of Du Bois and Woodson, and more recently of C. Vann Woodward and Richard Weaver. The points of view that are being brought forward differ widely, but the quality of the best scholarship remains admirable and may be seen in the fine work that is being done by historians who are now just starting out.

Those of my generation—I must especially mention Harold Woodman—who have worked in a Marxist tradition take pride in our collective effort to sharpen the profession's awareness of the class dimension and the centrality of the master-slave relation. A younger generation of Marxist and marxisant scholars has turned out such seminal works as Mark Tushnet's study of slave law and Barbara Fields's study of the social transformation of the border states. Scholars now in their thirties and forties and younger ones who are coming up behind them are building on our work but assimilating it to alternate viewpoints that draw on other than Marxist traditions. Whatever our errors and inadequacies, I think we can claim to have accomplished what we set out to do: to reorient the study of southern slave society and to compel a confrontation with a new set of questions. In view of the fine work that is being done by younger scholars, we have reason to believe that the best is yet to come.

On method: J. D. Bernal, the great scientist and Marxist historian of science, wrote somewhere that when social scientists run out of things to say, they talk about method. You cannot write serious history today without drawing heavily on econometrics and the methods contributed by folklorists. Extend the list as you will. The great historians have always drawn on the methods of economics, psychology, literature, and much else. It should be enough to mention Gibbon or Bloch. But in the end, history remains an art. We know damned well that we cannot really reconstruct the past as it was lived, but we also know that we have a responsibility to come as close as we can. And that requires every relevant method that the sciences, natural and social, can offer. In our own day Bloch and Hobsbawm have come as close as anyone to offering an integrated history of society. And an integrated history of society is precisely what is at issue.

Q. What elements of conservative thought do you find most important in your interpretation of history?

A. That depends on the historical problem at hand. For an understanding of the Old South, my central subject, I have learned much from conservative historians and perhaps even more from conservative poets and literary critics. We could begin with the sense of a "tradition," as I tried to describe it in *The Southern Tradition,* for it leads directly to an appreciation of the nature of the many discrete communities that, in a meaningful historical sense, forged what may be called a southern community. From the beginning of my work at Brooklyn College, I sensed that the South was indeed different, or maybe that the North was. In any case, I have never been among those who treat the South as just another regional variant on the American experience. Rather, I have seen it as a historical phenomenon that once generated a people apart and had the germs of a separate nationality. Curiously, it was my—perhaps idiosyncratic—understanding of Marxism that conditioned my early views, but a growing awareness of conservative contributions deepened it.

More generally, I have certainly learned much from Edmund Burke and George Santayana, from T. S. Eliot and Allen Tate, from Vilfredo Pareto and Eric Voegelin, from Richard Weaver and Wilmoore Kendall, from M. E. Bradford and John Lukacs, and from any number of other conservatives. How much and how specifically? Those who read my work will have to tell me. I am too close to sort it out.

There is, however, one matter that comes to mind. I never could take seriously Marx's utopian view of human nature, although I suppose I paid it lip service as a youth. Almost instinctively, I saw the darker side and only half-joking described

myself as an atheist who believed in original sin and human depravity. I think that
that attitude contributed a good deal to my early Stalinism and post-Stalinist pen-
chant for social engineering. If anything, I have tended to err on the side of a pes-
simistic view of man. Secular conservatives sharpened my insights into the limits
of social engineering and man's aspirations to be like the gods. And Christian
conservatives and, more generally, Christian theologians have helped me to strike
a better balance. Pope John Paul II's *Crossing the Threshold of Hope,* which I read
well before my decision to reenter the Church, to take a recent and especially
powerful example, has provided a needed antidote.

Q. What elements of Marxist thought do you find of continuing importance in
your interpretation of history?

A. Marx seemed to think that he made his great contributions through his theory
of surplus value and his claim of a scientific validity for an interpretation of history as the unfolding of class struggles that would lead to Communism. His theory of surplus value, and the theory of commodity value on which it was based,
proved scientifically weak as economics and has had no constructive impact
upon the development of socialist economies in practice. And what is there left to
say about history as the story of class struggles that must end in Communism?

Yet Marx's focus of social struggles, primarily but not entirely class-based, has
proven salutary to historians of the Right as well as the Left, at least when shorn
of an implicit Hegelian teleology. Here Marx was his own severest critic, for he
pointed out that many before him had seen that much. I continue to find much
that is rich in his historical interpretations, particularly in his understanding of
the extent to which social relations shape culture. His originality, then, must be
sought in the specifics of his historical analyses, rather than in his more flamboyant generalizations. Consider, for example, the high tribute paid him by Joseph
Schumpeter, one of the intellectual giants of our century, who rejected much of
Marx's framework and yet chided his fellow conservatives and fellow economists
for stupidly ignoring Marx's insights into the process of capitalist development.
In my view nothing has so badly disoriented southern conservative thought as its
flippant disregard of Marx's analyses of the development, structure, and logic of
the world market and of the problem of human atomization. Adam Smith, not
Marx, deserves primary credit for having raised the problem of "alienation"
under capitalism, but has anything been written as powerful and incisive as the
section on "The Fetishism of Commodities" in *Capital?*

I have settled my own accounts with Marx. I developed my interpretation of
the slave South from a self-consciously Marxist point of view, and I have found
no reason to discard the essential of that interpretation, which, if anything, I have
strengthened over time. I know that my assailants on the Left sneer that my con-

sistency in that matter only proves that I was never a real Marxist at all. Maybe. But I remain content with the essentials of the interpretation and am grateful to Marx and to Marxists like Gramsci, Dobb, and Hobsbawm for whatever may remain of value in it.

Q. Much of your recent work on slavery and southern history has led you into searching discussions of religious and theological questions. How has your view of the role of religion in southern history changed since *Roll, Jordan, Roll*?

A. When I began work on *Roll, Jordan, Roll* I did not expect to make religion the centerpiece of my account of slave life. To the contrary, I brought to my work all the biases of an atheist, a materialist, a smart-assed New York intellectual, and for good measure, an ex-Catholic who was probably trying to root out every last element of what, if anything, I had learned in a not-very-committed Catholic boyhood. Still, my reading of history had instilled in me a grudging respect for the Christian churches, including and especially the Catholic Church. Tannenbaum's influence undoubtedly sharpened that respect. In any case, even in those days I was growing impatient with the "sociologization" of religion — that is, with interpretations of religious experience that betrayed a contempt for the spiritual dimension of life. When I came to study the slaves, that impatience exploded, and I knew I had to step back and try to take religious experience on its own terms.

Roll, Jordan, Roll was a detour for me. Stanley Elkins's book and the controversy it engendered forced me to acknowledge that I could not pursue my lifelong ambition of writing a comprehensive book on the slaveholders without being able to weigh the slaveholders' view of the slaves against the realities of slavery and the perceptions of the slaves themselves. What started out as a projected two-year detour and was supposed to be a short interpretive essay turned out to take ten years and result in the longest book by far that I have written. Here I must pay tribute to Vincent Harding, Sterling Stuckey, and other young — we were all still young then — black scholars who raised hell with me about my inattention to black culture.

Beyond acquiring a heightened awareness of the cultural dimension of the black experience in slavery, I had to do two things. First, I had to read the Bible and extend widely my reading in religious history. And second, I saw immediately that if Christianity, however understood, was central to the lives of the slaves, it was also central to the lives of their masters. I knew that when I returned to write on the masters, I would have to reread everything, especially the diaries and letters and other primary sources, with a fresh eye. By that time Betsey had moved into American history, fallen in love with the South, and agreed to join me in the writing of *The Mind of the Master Class*. Since she is a trained intellectual historian and a literary critic with a foundation in the ancient classics, who for good measure has had professional training in psychoanalysis, her agreement to collaborate has proven a windfall. At the outset she knew much more religious history and theology than I did. That is no longer true since, until recently, she was devoting more and more time to her literary studies and work in Women's Studies, while I was spending years in reading religious history and especially theology.

(By the way, to return to your question about my working-class background: I am proud of it and value it highly, but it had its drawbacks. I attended a good elementary and high school back in the Bensonhurst section of Brooklyn, and I got a fine education at Brooklyn College. But none of it could substitute for the elite education that she got at private schools in America and Europe. Believe me, it makes a huge and permanent difference, at least in the few cases in which the beneficiaries of an elite education do not take their privileges for granted and have been raised by a Calvinistic father who demands that they work their butts off and recognize their social duty to make the most of their opportunities.)

If I were to rewrite my early books today, I would have to spend a great deal more time on the religious influences on the slaveholders and the southern people generally. Religion will have a prominent place in our forthcoming book, as it has had in the articles we have been publishing. But you will have to wait for the comprehensive results. Here, I would only suggest, as I have in *The Southern Front,* that the class nature of the slaveholders, to reinvoke a central Marxist category, cannot be fully understood without due attention to their religious life, understood to include the spiritual, the institutional, the social, the political, and the intellectual.

Among other considerations, the slaveholders' commitment to slavery rested on scriptural foundations that deserve much more careful and extended attention than they have been getting. The genuinely tragic aspect of the war cannot be understood without that due attention. As a final observation, or rather a piece of the preaching old men are allowed, I hope that the rising generation of southern historians will pay attention not only to religious history but to theology. To try to write religious history without a solid knowledge of theology is to risk a plunge into the trivial. That, too, is a big subject for another day, but at the least I shall say confidently that historians who read the theology of Thornwell, Dabney, Girardeau, and the other luminaries of the southern churches are in for a pleasant surprise. They were learned men with first-rate brains, and what they had to say deeply influenced southern political and social life. After all, they and their fellow divines controlled the educational system and trained the leaders of society. But more than that, any good theologian must face all the great questions of politics, political economy, social relations, and much more, and those men met their responsibilities. I find remarkable how much they still have to teach about life in this world. I say nothing of the next.

Q. How has your recent return to the Catholic Church affected your work as a historian?

A. With malice aforethought, I shall do my best to deflect your question, if only because I am not sure of the answer. Permit me, instead, to share some random thoughts.

When I published *The Southern Front* in 1995, I was still a materialist and an atheist, but I was doing a lot of private soul-searching. (Stop worrying: I shall not try your patience with a review of my *crise de conscience,* which is none of your business anyway.) As soon as *The Southern Front* came off the press, and I reread my essays on the theology and politics of Martin Luther King and Cornel West, I knew I could no longer sustain my atheism and materialism. For in those essays I had forcefully dissociated myself from their belief—so forcefully, in fact, that one reviewer later asked if I were not protesting too much. I asked myself a question: If the Reverend Dr. King or Dr. West challenged me to defend my atheism, could I do so in a manner convincing at least to myself. I found that I could not. I recognized that I had long been gagging and had finally started to choke. I had to go back to first principles, especially since I never took seriously the droll notion that Christianity and Marxism were compatible. I found no way to defend my philosophical commitment to atheism, but intellectual conversion is one thing and faith another. Meanwhile, Betsey, a lifelong nonbeliever, converted to Christianity and entered the Catholic Church. I resisted the impulse to follow her, but to no avail. Within a year I made my own decision.

Here, I shall restrict myself to an observation on the history I have written. If I had any interest in rewriting my historical studies of the Old South, I suppose that I would have to recast some important matters—but not the essentials of the interpretation I laid out in my earliest efforts. During the last twenty years, while still consciously a Marxist, I made many revisions and tried to clean out assorted rigidities and dogmatic assertions. My current work continues along that line. As for my present position, my recent book, *A Consuming Fire: The Fall of the Confederacy in the Mind of the White Christian South,* will have to speak for me. Discerning readers will have no trouble in recognizing a shift in sensibility and concerns. Certainly, I wrote it as a committed Christian. But consider my critique of the failure of the slaveholders to reform their society and transform slavery in accordance with their own criteria into the Christian institution they professed to want to make it. Readers should have no trouble in recognizing that my critique of their failure proceeds in a straight line from *The Political Economy of Slavery,* as modified by *Fruits of Merchant Capital.* If my analysis has merit, it should at least contribute to an understanding of the limits that social relations impose upon the practical efforts of those who seek to spread the Gospel.

The implications of my course will remain open to interpretation by any friend or foe who wishes to trouble himself over the question that has always bored me: Is Genovese (was he ever) really a Marxist after all? A well-known ex-Marxist historian, an intellectually first-rate woman who defected to the Right, remarked twenty or so years ago that anyone who knew me well and studied my work carefully had to see that I was a left-wing closet Catholic and not a Marxist at all. A nonbeliever herself, she intended no compliment—quite the contrary— but I was neither pleased nor offended. Rather, I wondered how much truth there might be in her caustic remark. One way or the other, the only thing I have ever cared about is the extent to which my interpretation of the slave society of the Old South will prove as accurate and useful as one can reasonably hope for.

Appendix B

The Principal Writings of Eugene D. Genovese

Books and Pamphlets

The Political Economy of Slavery: Studies in the Economy and Society of the Slave South. New York, 1965; rev. ed., Middletown, Conn., 1989; French ed., Paris, 1968, 1979; Spanish ed., Barcelona, 1970; Italian ed., Torino, 1972; Portuguese ed., Rio de Janeiro, 1976.

The World the Slaveholders Made: Two Essays in Interpretation. New York, 1969; rev. ed., Middletown, Conn., 1988; Spanish ed., Barcelona, 1971; Portuguese ed., Rio de Janeiro, 1979.

In Red and Black: Marxian Explorations in Southern and Afro-American History. New York, 1971; rev. ed., Knoxville, 1984; Italian ed., Rome, 1977.

Roll, Jordan, Roll: The World the Slaves Made. New York, 1974.

From Rebellion to Revolution: Afro-American Slave Revolts in the Making of the Modern World. Baton Rouge, La., 1979; Portuguese ed., Sao Paulo, 1983.

The American People (with David Burner and Forrest McDonald). St. James, N.Y., 1980.

Fruits of Merchant Capital: Slavery and Bourgeois Property in the Rise and Expansion of Capitalism (with Elizabeth Fox-Genovese). New York, 1983.

"Slavery Ordained of God": The Southern Slaveholders' View of Biblical History and Modern Politics. Gettysburg, Pa., 1985.

Western Civilization through Slaveholding Eyes: The Social and Historical Thought of Thomas Roderick Dew. New Orleans, 1986.

Firsthand America: A History of the United States (with Virginia Bernhard, David Burner, Elizabeth Fox-Genovese, and Forrest McDonald). St. James, N.Y., 1991.

The Slaveholders' Dilemma: Freedom and Progress in Southern Conservative Thought, 1820–1860. Columbia, S.C., 1991.

The Southern Tradition: The Achievement and Limitations of an American Conservatism. Cambridge, Mass., 1994.

Debates on American History (with Forrest McDonald). St. James, N.Y., 1995.

The Southern Front: History and Politics in the Cultural War. Columbia, Mo., 1995.

A Consuming Fire: The Fall of the Confederacy in the Mind of the White Christian South. Athens, Ga., 1998.

Edited Works

The Slave Economy of the Old South: The Selected Social and Economic Essays of Ulrich Bonnell Phillips. Baton Rouge, La., 1969.
Slavery in the New World: A Reader in Comparative History (with Laura Foner). Englewood Cliffs, N.J., 1969.
"Black History and the History of Slavery." Special edition, *Journal of Social History* 3 (1970).
The Slave Economies. 2 vols. New York, 1973.
Plantation, Town, and County: Essays on the Local History of American Slave Society (with Elinor Miller). Urbana, Ill., 1974.
Race and Slavery in the Western Hemisphere: Quantitative Studies (with Stanley L. Engerman). Princeton, N.J., 1975.
Geographic Perspectives in History (with Leonard Hochberg). Oxford, 1989.

Articles and Essays

"The Medical and Insurance Costs of Slaveholding in the Cotton Belt," *Journal of Negro History* 45 (1960): 141–55.
"The Negro Laborer in Africa and the Slave South," *Phylon* 21 (1960): 343–50.
"The Civil War Era," *Science and Society* 25 (1961): 379–82.
"Cotton, Slavery, and Soil Exhaustion in the Old South," *Cotton History Review* 2 (1961): 3–17.
"Problems in the Study of Nineteenth-Century American History," *Science and Society* 25 (1961): 38–53.
"The Slave South: An Interpretation," *Science and Society* 25 (1961): 320–37.
"The Significance of the Slave Plantation for Southern Economic Development," *Journal of Southern History* 28 (1962): 422–37.
"Dr. Herbert Aptheker's Retreat from Marxism," *Science and Society* 27 (1963): 212–26.
"Livestock in the Slave Economy of the Old South—A Revised View," *Agricultural History* 36 (1963): 365–82.
"The Low Productivity of Southern Slave Labor: Causes and Effects," *Civil War History* 9 (1963): 365–82.
"Genovese Looks at American Left—New and Old," *National Guardian* 19 Feb. 1966.
"The Legacy of Slavery and the Roots of Black Nationalism," *Studies on the Left* 6 (1966): 3–26.
"Rejoinder," *Studies on the Left* 6 (1966): 55–65.
"A Georgia Slaveholder Looks at Africa," *Georgia Historical Quarterly* 51 (1967): 189–93.

"Race and Class in Southern History: An Appraisal of the Work of Ulrich Bonnell Phillips," *Agricultural History* 41 (1967): 345–59.

"Rebelliousness and Docility in the Negro Slave: A Critique of the Elkins Thesis," *Civil War History* 13 (1967): 293–314.

"An Exchange on Nat Turner." *New York Review of Books,* 7 Nov. 1968.

"Letter to the Editor," *American Historical Review* 73 (1968): 993–95.

"Marxian Interpretations of the Slave South," In *Towards a New Past: Dissenting Essays in American History,* ed. Barton J. Bernstein, 90–125. New York, 1968.

"Materialism and Idealism in the History of Negro Slavery in the Americas," *Journal of Social History* 1 (1968): 371–94.

"The Nat Turner Case," *New York Review of Book,* 7 Sept. 1968.

Preface to *Les bourgeois gentilshommes de la Nouvelle France, 1729–1748,* by Cameron Nish. Montreal, 1968.

"Black Culture and St. Gronlesex Paternalism," *Artforum* 7 (1969): 34–37.

"Black Studies: Trouble Ahead," *Atlantic* 223 (1969): 37–41.

"The Education and the University We Need Now," *New York Review of Books,* 9 Oct. 1969 (with Christopher Lasch).

Foreword to *American Negro Slavery: A Survey of the Supply, Employment, and Control of Negro Labor as Determined by the Plantation Regime,* by Ulrich Bonnell Phillips. Baton Rouge, La., 1969.

"The Treatment of Slaves in Different Countries: Problems in the Application of the Comparative Method," in *Slavery in the New World: A Reader in Comparative History,* ed. Laura Foner and Eugene D. Genovese, 202–10. Englewood Cliffs, N.J., 1969.

"War on Two Fronts," *Canadian Dimension* 6 (1969): 25–29.

"American Slaves and Their History," *New York Review of Books,* 3 Dec. 1970.

"Commentary: An Historian's View," *Agricultural History* 44 (1970): 143–47.

"The Comparative Focus in Latin American History," *Journal of Inter-American Studies and World Affairs* 12 (1970): 317–27.

"The Fortunes of the Left," *National Review* 22 (1970): 1266–70.

"The Influence of the Black Power Movement on Historical Scholarship: Reflections of a White Historian," *Daedalus* 1 (1970): 473–94.

"Black Plantation Preachers in the Slave South," *Louisiana Studies* 11 (1972): 182–214.

"The Slave States of North America," in *Neither Slave nor Free: The Freedmen of African Descent in the Slave Societies of the New World,* ed. David W. Cohen and Jack P. Greene, 258–77. Baltimore, 1972.

"The Language of Class and Nation," *Urban Review* 8 (1975): 84–100.

"When the Slaves Left Old Master," *Civil Liberties Review* 2 (1975): 67–76.

"Yeoman Farmers in a Slaveholders' Democracy," *Agricultural History* 49 (1975): 331–42.

"Charles A. Beard and the Economic Interpretation of History," in *Charles A. Beard: An Observance of the Centennial of His Birth,* ed. Marvin C. Swanson, 25–44. Greencastle, Ind., 1976.

"Is History Dead?" *American Heritage* 28 (1976): 87, 90.

"The Political Crisis of Social History: A Marxian Perspective," *Journal of Social History* 10 (1976): 205–20.

"Slavery—The World's Burden," in *Perspectives and Irony in American Slavery,* ed. Harry P. Owens, 27–50. Jackson, Miss., 1976.

"What Is a Liberal—Who Is a Conservative?" *Commentary* 62 (1976): 58–59.

"Blacks in the United States: From Slavery to the Present Crisis," *New Review* 4 (1977): 3–11.

"'Rather Be a Nigger than a Poor White Man': Black Perceptions of Southern Yeomen and Poor Whites," in *Toward a New View of America: Essays in Honor of Arthur C. Cole,* ed. Hans Trefousse, 79–96. New York, 1977.

"A Reply to Criticism," *Radical History Review* 4 (1977): 94–110.

"Capitalism, Socialism, and Democracy," *Commentary* 65 (1978): 41–43.

"Reflections on the 1960s," *Socialist Review* 38 (1978): 59–71.

"Toward a Psychology of Slavery: An Assessment of the Contribution of *The Slave Community,*" in *Revisiting Blassingame's* The Slave Community: *The Scholars Respond,* ed. Al-Tony Gilmore, 27–42. Westport, Conn., 1978.

Prolegomena to *Australia and America, 1788–1972: An Alternative History,* by Lloyd Gordon Churchward. Chippendale, Australia, 1979.

"The Slave Economies in Political Perspective," *Journal of American History* 66 (1979): 7–23 (with Elizabeth Fox-Genovese.)

"Academic Freedom Today," *South Atlantic Quarterly* 79 (1980): 125–40.

"The Politics of Class Struggle in the History of Society: An Appraisal of the Work of Eric Hobsbawm," in *The Power of the Past: Essays for Eric Hobsbawm,* ed. Pat Thane, Geoffrey Crossick, and Roderick Floud, 13–36. Cambridge, Mass., 1984.

"Slavery, Economic Development, and the Law: The Dilemma of Southern Political Economists, 1800–1860," *Crossroads: A Journal of Southern Culture* 2 (1984): 83.

"Illusions of Liberation: The Psychology of Colonialism in the Work of Octave Mannoni and Frantz Fanon," in *Rethinking Marxism: Struggles in Marxist Theory; Essays for Harry Magdoff and Paul Sweezy,* ed. Stephen Resnick and Richard Wolff, 127–50. Brooklyn, 1985 (with Elizabeth Fox-Genovese).

"Comment," in *The State of Afro-American History: Past, Present, and Future,* ed. Darlene Clark Hine, 37–41. Baton Rouge, La., 1986 (with Elizabeth Fox-Genovese).

"Herbert Aptheker's Achievement and Our Responsibility," in *In Resistance: Studies in African, Caribbean, and Afro-American History,* ed. Gary G. Okihiro, 21–31. Amherst, Mass., 1986.

"The Religious Ideals of Southern Slave Society," *Georgia Historical Quarterly* 70 (1986): 1–16 (with Elizabeth Fox-Genovese).

"The Cultural History of Southern Slave Society: Reflections on the Work of Lewis P. Simpson," in *American Letters and the Historical Consciousness:*

Essays in Honor of Lewis P. Simpson, ed. J. Gerald Kennedy and Daniel Mark
    Fogel, 15–41. Baton Rouge, La., 1987 (with Elizabeth Fox-Genovese).
"The Divine Sanction of Social Order: Religious Foundations of the Southern
    Slaveholders' World View," *Journal of the American Academy of Religion* 55
    (1987): 211–12 (with Elizabeth Fox-Genovese).
"James Henley Thornwell and Southern Religion," *Southern Partisan* 7 (1987):
    16–21.
"Master-Slave Relations," in *Dictionary of Afro-American Slavery,* ed. Randall M.
    Miller and John David Smith, 449–54. Westport, Conn., 1988.
Foreword to *If You Took the Grand Tour: Traveling to Europe in the Eighteen-
    Fifties and Nineteen-Nineties,* by William Smyth. Manassas, Va., 1989.
"George Fitzhugh," in *Encyclopedia of Southern Culture,* ed. Charles Reagan
    Wilson and William Ferris, 1132–33. Chapel Hill, N.C., 1989.
"Social Classes and Class Struggles in Geographic Perspective," in *Geographic
    Perspectives in History,* ed. Eugene Genovese and Leonard Hochberg, 235–55.
    Oxford, 1989 (with Elizabeth Fox-Genovese).
"The Social Thought of the Antebellum Southern Theologians," in *Looking
    South: Chapters in the Story of an American Region,* ed. Winifred B. Moore
    Jr. and Joseph F. Tripp, 34–40. Westport, Conn., 1989 (with Elizabeth
    Fox-Genovese).
"The Southern Slaveholders' View of the Middle Ages," in *Medievalism in
    American Culture,* ed. Bernard Rosenthal and Paul E. Szarmach, 31–52.
    Binghamton, N.Y., 1989.
"The 80s: Disaster or Triumph?" *Commentary* 90 (1990): 48–50.
Foreword to *Whistling Dixie: Dispatches from the South,* by John Shelton Reed.
    Columbia, Mo., 1990.
Foreword to *Witness to Sorrow: The Autobiography of William J. Grayson,* ed.
    Richard J. Calhoun. Columbia, S.C., 1990.
"The South in the History of the Transatlantic World," in *What Made the South
    Different?* ed. Kees Gispen, 3–18. Jackson, Miss., 1990.
"Ulrich Bonnell Phillips as an Economic Historian," *Ulrich Bonnell Phillips:
    A Southern Historian and His Critics,* ed. John David Smith and John C.
    Inscoe, 203–6. Westport, Conn., 1990.
"Hans Rosenberg at Brooklyn College: A Communist Student's Recollections of
    the Classroom as War Zone," *Central European History* 24 (1991): 51–57.
"'Our Family, White and Black': Family and Household in the Southern Slave-
    holders' World View," in *In Joy and in Sorrow: Women, Family, and Marriage
    in the Victorian South, 1830–1900,* ed. Carol Bleser, 69–87. New York, 1991.
"South Carolina's Contribution to the Doctrine of Slavery in the Abstract," in
    *The Meaning of South Carolina History: Essays in Honor of George C. Rogers,
    Jr.,* ed. David R. Chesnut and Clyde N. Wilson, 141–60. Columbia, S.C., 1991.
"Toward a Kinder and Gentler America: The Southern Lady in the Greening of
    the Politics of the Old South," in *In Joy and in Sorrow: Women, Family, and*

Marriage in the Victorian South, 1830–1900, ed. Carol Bleser, 1125–34. New
    York, 1991.

"Town and Village in the Consolidation of Southern Slave Society," in *Dialectical
    Anthropology: Essays in Honor of Stanley Diamond,* ed. Christine Ward Gai-
    ley, 207–25. Gainesville, Fla., 1992.

"Eugene Rivers' Challenge: A Response," *Boston Review* 18 (1993): 34–38.

"Is There a Cure for Anti-Semitism?" *Partisan Review* 61 (1994): 368–445.

"Living with Inequality," *National Review* 46 (1994): 44–45.

"Political Virtue and the Lessons of the French Revolution: The View from the
    Slaveholding South," in *Virtue, Corruption, and Self-Interest: Political Values
    in the Eighteenth Century,* ed. Richard K. Matthews, 202–17. Lehigh, Pa., 1994
    (with Elizabeth Fox-Genovese).

"The Question," *Dissent* 41 (1994): 371–76.

"The Riposte," *Dissent* 41 (1994): 386–88.

"Robert W. Fogel, Historian," *Newsletter of the Cliometric Society* 9 (1994): 16–18.

"The Southern Tradition and the Black Experience," *Chronicles* 18 (1994): 20–22.

"The National Prospect," *Commentary* 100 (1995): 59–61.

"A Retrospective on the Moynihan Report," *Commentary* 100 (1995): 59–61.

"Sex, Families, Race, Poverty, Welfare: A Symposium Revisiting the Moynihan
    Report at Its Thirtieth Anniversary," *American Enterprise* 6 (1995): 37.

"Black Studies as Academic Discipline and Political Struggle," in *The Liberal
    Persuasion: Arthur Schlesinger, Jr., and the Challenge of the American Past,* ed.
    John Diggins, 251–60. Princeton, N.J., 1997.

"Marxism, Christianity, and Bias in the Study of Southern Slave Society," in
    Religious Advocacy and American History, ed. Bruce Kuklick and D. G. Hart,
    83–95. Grand Rapids, Mich., 1997.

"Religious and Economic Thought in the Proslavery Argument," *Essays in
    Economic and Business History* 15 (1997): 1–9.

"Secularism in the General Crisis of Capitalism," *American Journal of Jurispru-
    dence* 42 (1997): 196–210.

"Olmsted's Cracker Preacher," *Southern Cultures* 4 (1998): 54–62.

"Religion in the Collapse of the Union," in *Religion and the American Civil War,*
    ed. Randall M. Miller, Harry S. Stout, Charles Reagan Wilson, 74–88. New
    York, 1998.

Foreword to *The Metaphysical Confederacy: James Henley Thornwell and the Syn-
    thesis of Southern Values,* by James Oscar Farmer Jr. 2d ed. Macon, Ga., 1999.

"M. E. Bradford's Historical Vision," in *A Defender of Southern Conservatism:
    M. E. Bradford and His Achievements,* ed. Clyde N. Wilson, 78–91. Columbia,
    Mo., 1999.

Foreword to *Balancing Evils Judiciously: The Proslavery Writings of Zephaniah
    Kingsley,* ed. Daniel W. Stowell. Gainesville, Fla., 2000.

Book Reviews and Review Essays

Labor, Free and Slave: Workingmen and the Anti-Slavery Movement in the United States, by Bernard Mandel. *Science and Society* 19 (1955): 360–61 [as Vittorio della Chiesa].

The Battle Cry of Freedom, by Samuel A. Johnson. *Science and Society* 20 (1956): 87–89 [as Vittorio della Chiesa].

The Peculiar Institution: Slavery in the Ante-Bellum South, by Kenneth Stampp. *Science and Society* 21 (1957): 259–63 [as Vittorio della Chiesa].

Agricultural Developments in North Carolina, 1783–1860, by Cornelius Oliver Cathey; *Economic Readjustment of an Old Cotton State: South Carolina, 1820–1860,* by Alfred Glaze Smith Jr.; *Ante-Bellum Alabama: Town and Country,* by Weymouth T. Jordan; and *J. D. B. DeBow: Magazinist of the Old South,* by Ottis Clark Skipper. *Science and Society* 24 (1960): 53–60.

American Foreign Policy and the Cold War, by Herbert Aptheker. *Science and Society* 27 (1963): 212–26.

Economic Co-operation between the USSR and Underdeveloped Countries, by V. Rimalov. *Science and Society* 27 (1963): 494–95.

The Farmer's Age: Agriculture, 1815–1860, by Paul Gates; *The Economic History of the United States,* vol. 3, ed. Henry David et al.; *The Economic Growth of the United States, 1790–1860,* by Douglass C. North. *Studies on the Left* 3 (1963): 116–27.

Revolution, by Hannah Arendt. *National Guardian,* 12 Sept. 1963.

Slavery and Jeffersonian Virginia, by Robert McColley. *American Historical Review* 71 (1965): 301–2.

Slavery in the Cities: The South, 1820–1860, by Richard Wade. *Nation,* 11 Jan. 1965.

David Walker's Appeal, ed. Charles M. Wiltse; *One Continual Cry: David Walker's Appeal to the Colored Citizens of the World, 1829–1830, Its Setting and Its Meaning,* by Herbert Aptheker. *Science and Society* 30 (1966): 363–65.

The Great Evasion: An Essay on the Contemporary Relevance of Karl Marx and on the Wisdom of Admitting the Heretic into the Dialogue about America's Future, by William Appleman Williams. *Studies on the Left* 6 (1966): 70–86.

Southern Wealth and Northern Profits, by Thomas P. Kettell. *Labor History* 17 (1966): 361–65.

The Burden of Race: A Documentary History of Negro-White Relations in America, ed. Gilbert Osofsky. *Chicago Tribune Book World,* 22 Oct. 1967.

A History of Negro Slavery in New York, by Edgar J. McManus. *Science and Society* 31 (1967): 117–19.

Jacob N. Cardozo: Economic Thought in the Antebellum South, by Melvin M. Leiman. *American Historical Review* 72 (1967): 1495–96.

The Problem of Slavery in Western Culture, by David Brion Davis. *Journal of Southern History* 53 (1967): 111–12.

Storia della guerra civile americana, by Raimondo Luraghi. *Journal of American History* 54 (1967): 669–70.

Writing Southern History: Essays in Historiography in Honor of Fletcher M. Green, ed. Arthur S. Link and Rembert W. Patrick. *Civil War History* 13 (1967): 170–82.

Class Conflict, Slavery, and the United States Constitution; Intellectual Origins of American Radicalism, by Staughton Lynd. *New York Review of Books,* 26 Sept. 1968.

Dahomey and the Slave Trade: An Analysis of an Archaic Economy, by Karl Polanyi. *Journal of Economic History* 28 (1968): 149–50.

Sins of the Fathers: A Study of the Atlantic Slave Traders, 1441–1807, by James Pope-Hennessy. *American Historical Review* 74 (1968): 542.

William Styron's Nat Turner: *Ten Black Writers Respond,* ed. John Henrik Clarke et al. *New York Review of Books,* 12 Sept. 1968.

The South and the Sectional Conflict, by David M. Potter; *The Burden of Southern History,* rev. ed., ed. C. Vann Woodward. *New York Review of Books,* 13 Sept. 1969.

The Atlantic Slave-Trade: A Census, by Philip D. Curtin, *American Historical Review* 75 (1970): 2011.

The Children of Pride: A True Story of Georgia and the Civil War, ed. Robert M. Myers; *The Diary of Edmund Ruffin,* vol. 1, ed. William K. Scarborough; *The American Slave: A Composite Biography,* vols. 1–19, ed. George Rawick. *New York Review of Books,* 21 Sept. 1972.

The Blacks in Canada: A History, by Robin Wink. *Canadian Journal of Political Science* 6 (1973): 159–60.

Booker T. Washington: The Making of a Black Leader, 1856–1901, by Louis R. Harlan. *National Review* 25 (1973): 375–76.

Caribbean Transformations, by Sidney W. Mintz. *Dialectical Anthropology* 1 (1975): 71–79.

Money: Whence It Came, Where It Went, by John Kenneth Galbraith. *New York Times Book Review,* 8 Sept. 1975.

Slaves without Masters: The Free Negro in the Antebellum South, by Ira Berlin. *New Republic,* 1 Feb. 1975.

Justice Accused: The Political Foundations of Justice, by Robert M. Cover, *Yale Law Journal* 85 (1976): 582–90.

The Black Family in Slavery and Freedom, 1750–1925, by Herbert Gutman. *Times Literary Supplement,* 25 Feb. 1977.

In the Matter of Color: The Colonial Period, by A. Leon Higginbotham. *New York Times Book Review,* 18 June 1978.

The Transformation of American Law, 1780–1860, by Morton J. Horwitz. *Harvard Law Review* 91 (1978): 726–36.

Slave Religion: The "Invisible Institution" in the Antebellum South, by Albert J. Raboteau, and *Deep like the Rivers: Education in the Slave Quarter Community, 1831–1865,* by Thomas L. Webber. *New Republic,* 10 Feb. 1979.

Authority, by Richard Sennett. *New York Times Book Review*, 13 July 1980.

New Masters during the Civil War and Reconstruction, by Lawrence N. Powell; *Retreat from Reconstruction, 1869–1879*, by William Gillette. *New York Times Book Review*, 4 May 1980.

The American Law of Slavery: Slavery in the Legal History of the South and the Nation, 1810–1860, by Mark V. Tushnet; *Prison and Plantation: Crime, Justice, and Authority in Massachusetts and South Carolina, 1767–1878*, by Michael Steven Hindus; *An Imperfect Union: Slavery, Federalism, and Comity*, by Paul Finkelman. *Texas Law Review* 59 (1981): 969–98.

James Henry Hammond and the Old South: A Design for Mastery, by Drew Faust. *New York Review of Books*, 31 March 1983.

Slavery and Human Progress, by David Brion Davis. *Atlantic* 254 (1984): 141–44.

Law and Markets in United States History: Different Modes of Bargaining against Interests, by J. W. Hurst. *Research Journal of the American Bar Society* 38 (1985): 113–44.

Outgrowing Democracy: A History of the United States in the Twentieth Century, by John Lukacs. *Salmagundi* 67 (1985): 198–205.

The Rise of the Counter-Establishment: From Conservative Ideology to Political Power, by Sidney Blumenthal. *New Republic*, 15 Dec. 1986.

Tombee: Portrait of a Cotton Planter, by Theodore Rosengarten. *New York Times Book Review*, 20 July 1986.

Masters and Statesmen: The Political Culture of American Slavery, by Kenneth S. Greenberg. *Journal of Southern History* 53 (1987): 111–12.

Slave Culture: Nationalist Theory and the Foundations of Black America, by Sterling Stuckey. *New Republic*, 12 Oct. 1987.

Unfree Labor: American Slavery and Russian Serfdom, by Peter Kolchin. *Journal of Economic History* 47 (1987): 1079–81.

Proslavery: A History of the Defense of Slavery in America, 1701–1840, by Larry E. Tise. *Georgia Historical Quarterly* 72 (1988): 670–83.

A Turn in the South, by V. S. Naipaul. *New Republic*, 13 Feb. 1989.

The Arrogance of Faith: Christianity and Race in America from the Colonial Era to the Twentieth Century, by Forrest G. Wood. *New Republic*, 13 Aug. 1990.

Carolina Cavalier: The Life and Mind of James Johnston Pettigrew, by Clyde N. Wilson. *Chronicles* 14 (1990): 33–35.

Without Consent or Contract: The Rise and Fall of American Slavery, by Robert William Fogel. *Los Angeles Times Book Review*, 18 Feb. 1990.

A Government of Laws: Political Theory, Religion, and the American Founding, by Ellis Sandoz. *Reviews in American History* 19 (1991): 338–46.

A Guide to Critical Legal Studies, by Mark Kelman. *Yale Journal of Law and the Humanities* 3 (1991): 131–56.

Illiberal Education: The Politics of Race and Sex on Campus, by Dinesh D'Souza. *New Republic*, 15 April 1991.

The Papers of Martin Luther King, Jr., vol. 1, ed. Clayborne Carson et al. *New Republic*, 11 May 1992.

Keeping Faith: Philosophy and Race in America, by Cornel West. *Boston Globe,* 24 Oct. 1993.

Beautiful Losers: Essays on the Failure of American Conservatism, by Samuel T. Francis. *Crisis* 12 (1994): 44–49.

The Age of Extremes: A History of the World, 1914–1991, by Eric Hobsbawm. *New Republic,* 17 April 1995.

The End of the Nation-State, by Jean-Marie Guéhenno. *Washington Times,* 29 Oct. 1995.

The Martin Luther King, Jr., Plagiarism Story, ed. Theodore Pappas. *Common Knowledge* 4 (1995): 95–99.

The Myth of American Individualism: The Protestant Origins of American Political Thought, by Barry Alan Shain. *First Things* 55 (1995): 45–47.

The Papers of Martin Luther King, Jr., vol. 2, ed. Clayborne Carson et al. *Reviews in American History* 23 (1995): 1–12.

Stalin's Letters to Molotov, 1925–1936, ed. Lars T. Lih, Oleg V. Naumov, and Oleg V. Khlevniuk. *New Republic,* 4 Sept. 1995.

The Sword of Imagination: Memoirs of a Half-Century of Literary Conflict, by Russell Kirk. *New Republic,* 11 Dec. 1995.

The Work of Reconstruction: From Slave to Wage Labor in South Carolina, 1860–1870, by Julie Saville. *Journal of Social History* 29 (1995): 423–26.

At the Limits of Political Philosophy: From "Brilliant Errors" to Things of Uncommon Importance, by James V. Schall. *Washington Times,* 18 Aug. 1996.

A Companion to American Thought, ed. Richard Wightman Fox and James T. Kloppenberg. *Books and Culture: A Christian Review* 2 (1996): 19–20.

Jesse: The Life and Pilgrimage of Jesse Jackson, by Marshall Frady. *New Republic,* 15 July 1996.

A Requiem for Karl Marx, by Frank E. Manuel. *National Review* 48 (1996): 65–67.

Richard M. Weaver, 1910–1963: A Life of the Mind, by Fred Douglas Young. *New Republic,* 17 June 1996.

Slouching to Gomorrah: Modern Liberalism and American Decline, by Robert Bork. *Washington Post,* 20 Oct. 1996.

The Unknown Lenin: From the Secret Archive, by Richard Pipes. *New Republic,* 14 Oct. 1996.

Redeeming the Time, by Russell Kirk. *University Bookman* 37 (1997): 3–8.

Them Dark Days: Slavery in the American Rice Swamps, by William Dusinberre. *African American Review* 32 (1998): 159–61.

Africana: The Encyclopedia of the African American Experience, ed. Kwame Anthony Appiah and Henry Louis Gates Jr. *Wall Street Journal,* 29 Oct. 1999.

Contributors

DOUGLAS AMBROSE teaches early American and southern history at Hamilton College in Clinton, New York, where in 1996 he received the Class of 1963 Excellence in Teaching Award. He is author of *Henry Hughes and Proslavery Thought in the Old South* (1996) and "Of Stations and Relations: Proslavery Christianity in Early National Virginia," in *Religion and the Antebellum Debate over Slavery,* ed. John R. McKivigan and Mitchell Snay (1998).

PETER A. COCLANIS is George and Alice Welsh Professor and Chairman of the Department of History at the University of North Carolina, Chapel Hill. He received his Ph.D. from Columbia University in 1984 and is the author, most notably, of *The Shadow of a Dream: Economic Life and Death in the South Carolina Low Country, 1670–1920* (1989), which won the Allan Nevins Prize of the Society of American Historians. He has published broadly in economic and business history and is currently at work on a book on the world rice market between 1700 and 1930.

DAVID BRION DAVIS, Sterling Professor History at Yale University, is completing a trilogy on the history of slavery. Volume 1, *The Problem of Slavery in Western Culture* (1966), won the Pulitzer Prize; volume 2, *The Problem of Slavery in the Age of Revolution, 1770–1823* (1975), won the Bancroft Prize in American history. His many other publications include *Slavery and Human Progress* (1984) and *Reflections on American Equality and Foreign Liberations* (1990).

STANLEY L. ENGERMAN is John H. Munro Professor of Economics and Professor of History at the University of Rochester. His numerous publications on slavery and economic history include *Time on the Cross: The Economics of American Negro Slavery* (1974), coauthored with Robert W. Fogel, which won the Bancroft Prize in American history. He has coedited (with Eugene Genovese) *Race and Slavery in the Western Hemisphere: Quantitative*

Studies (1975); (with Manuel Moreno Fraginals and Frank Moya Pons) *Between Slavery and Free Labor: The Spanish Speaking Caribbean in the Nineteenth Century* (1985); (with Barbara Solow) *British Capitalism and Caribbean Slavery: The Legacy of Eric Williams* (1987); (with Joseph Inikori) *The Atlantic Slave Trade: Effects on Economics, Societies, and Peoples in Africa, the Americas, and Europe* (1992); (with Robert Paquette) *The Lesser Antilles in the Age of European Expansion* (1996); and (with Seymour Drescher) *A Historical Guide to World Slavery* (1998).

DREW GILPIN FAUST is Walter H. Annenberg Professor of History at the University of Pennsylvania. She is the author of *James Henry Hammond and the Old South: A Design for Mastery* (1982), which won the Charles S. Sydnor Award of the Southern Historical Association, the Jules and Frances Landry Award, and the Society for Historians of the Early American Republic Book Prize. Her *Mothers of Invention: Women of the Slaveholding South in the American Civil War* (1996) won the Francis Parkman Prize of the Society of American Historians and the Avery O. Craven Award of the Organization of American Historians. Among her many other publications are *The Ideology of Slavery: Proslavery Thought in the Antebellum South, 1830–1860* (1981) and *The Creation of Confederate Nationalism: Ideology and Identity in the Civil War South* (1960).

LOUIS FERLEGER is Professor of History at Boston University. He is coauthor (with Jay Mandle) of *No Pain, No Gain: Taxes, Productivity, and Economic Growth* (1992) and *A New Mandate: Democratic Choices for a Prosperous Economy* (1994) and (with Lucy Horwitz) of *Statistics for Social Change* (1980; 4th printing, 1998). He is the editor of *Agriculture and National Development: Views on the Nineteenth Century* (1990).

ROBERT W. FOGEL is Charles R. Walgreen Distinguished Service Professor of American Institutions at the University of Chicago. He is coauthor (with Stanley L. Engerman) of *Time on the Cross: The Economics of American Negro Slavery* (1974), which won the Bancroft Prize in American history. His many other books include *Railroads and American Economic Growth: Essays in Econometric History* (1964) and *Without Consent or Contract: The Rise and Fall of American Slavery* (1989). In 1993 he was awarded the Nobel Prize in economic science.

THAVOLIA GLYMPH is Assistant Professor of History at Pennsylvania State University. She has served as editor for the Freedmen and Southern

Society Project at the University of Maryland, which produced the multi-volume *Freedom: A Documentary History of Emancipation, 1961–1867.* She is also coeditor (with John Kushma) of *Essays on the Postbellum Southern Economy* (1985) and the author of *The Substance of Power and the Meaning of Freedom: Southern Women, Slave and Free,* forthcoming.

MARK G. MALVASI, Associate Professor of History at Randolph-Macon College, is the author of *The Unregenerate South: The Agrarian Thought of John Crowe Ransom, Allen Tate, and Donald Davidson* (1997). He has published extensively in journals of scholarship and opinion and has recently had essays included in *Steps toward Restoration: The Consequences of Richard Weaver's Ideas* (1999) and *Defender of Southern Conservatism: M. E. Bradford and His Achievements* (1999). He is currently at work on a study of southern conservative thought since the Second World War and on a novel about his Italian-American family. He completed his Ph.D. in 1991 at the University of Rochester under the direction of Eugene Genovese.

ROBERT L. PAQUETTE is Publius Virgilius Rogers Professor of American History at Hamilton College. His *Sugar Is Made with Blood: The Conspiracy of La Escalera and the Conflict between Empires over Slavery in Cuba* (1988) won the Elsa Goveia Prize of the Association of Caribbean Historians. He has coedited with Stanley Engerman *The Lesser Antilles in the Age of European Expansion* (1996). He received his Ph.D. in 1982 at the University of Rochester under the direction of Eugene Genovese.

RICHARD H. STECKEL is Professor of Economics and Anthropology at the Ohio State University and a research associate at the National Bureau of Economic Research. He is coeditor (with Roderick Floud) of *Health and Welfare during Industrialization* (1997) and the author of dozens of essays on fertility, mortality, migration, and other issues of historical demography.

CLYDE N. WILSON, Professor of History at the University of South Carolina, has written extensively on southern history and politics for *Chronicles: A Magazine of American Culture.* For more than a quarter century, he has served as editor of *The Papers of John C. Calhoun,* which began in 1959 and has reached twenty-five volumes to date. He is also author of *The Most Promising Young Man of the South: James Johnston Pettigrew and His Men at Gettysburg* (1998) and the editor of *A Defender of Southern Conservatism: M. E. Bradford and His Achievements* (1999).

Index